Eyewitness Bloody Sunday is a definitive account of one of the greatest tragedies of the Northern Ireland troubles underlining the enormity and profundity of the events of that day. In reading these detailed statements one is made aware of the shock, the disbelief, the distress which the crowd felt when the shooting started and their great sense of helplessness as the death toll increased.

In producing this book, Don Mullan has done an invaluable service to the people of Derry and the Bloody Sunday relatives who have been tireless in pursuit of truth and justice for their loved ones.

JOHN HUME MP
1998 Nobel Peace Prize Winner

Don Mullan's book, *Eyewitness Bloody Sunday – The Truth*, stands as one of those very few publications which have succeeded in making a real difference to the people it writes about. There can be no doubt that its revelations and new evidence contributed significantly to the British Government's belated decision to hold a public inquiry.

Bloody Sunday was one of those watershed moments in Anglo-Irish history. Don Mullan has produced an account of that, which is essential reading for anyone who truly wants an understanding of that terrible event and its place in Irish life.

GERRY ADAMS MP

Don Mullan's *Eyewitness Bloody Sunday* breathed new life into a subject which was part of our collective memory. Yes, I marched each year from Creggan to a rally in the Bogside, but until I read his book I did not even begin to understand the profound effect these events had really had on this community. *Eyewitness Bloody Sunday* inspired me on another journey to develop an exhibition and another book, *Hidden Truths*. Mullan's book has been a major milestone, not only for the case of those murdered on Bloody Sunday, but in helping those of us not present to truly understand the horror of that day.

TRISHA ZIFF
Editor, *Hidden Truths Bloody Sunday 1972* (USA, 1998)
Curator, Hidden Truths Exhibition

DON MULLAN is the author of the acclaimed bestsellers *Eyewitness Bloody Sunday*, which played a crucial role in British Prime Minister Tony Blair's decision to establish a new Bloody Sunday inquiry in 1998, and *The Dublin & Monaghan Bombings*. Don is a native of Derry and was educated at St Joseph's Secondary School, Creggan; the Development Studies Department, Holy Ghost College, Kimmage, Dublin; and Iona College, New York. At fifteen years of age he witnessed the Bloody Sunday massacre while attending his first Northern Ireland Civil Rights march. His involvement with the Northern Ireland Civil Rights movement led him to work on civil and human rights issues around the world. In 1980, aged twenty-four, he became Director of AFrI (Action From Ireland), a Dublin-based justice, peace and human rights organisation. In 1983-1984 he worked as a volunteer in Recife, Brazil. In 1994 he attended the inauguration of President Nelson Mandela, as a guest of Archbishop Tutu. He worked with Concern Worldwide for almost two years, beginning in July 1994, during which time he visited Rwanda and Zaïre. He now works as a freelance journalist, writer and broadcaster. His most recent book, *A Gift of Roses: Memories of the Visit to Ireland of St Thérèse*, was published in 2001.

Since *Eyewitness Bloody Sunday* was first published in 1997, there have been many developments. These are dealt with by Don Mullan in a new afterword on page 221.

Eyewitness Bloody Sunday

Eyewitness
Bloody
Sunday

Don Mullan
and John Scally

MERLIN
PUBLISHING

First published in 1997 by Wolfhound Press Ltd.
Reprinted in 1997, U.S. edition 1997.
Second edition 1998. Reprinted in 2000.
Third edition 2002.

This fourth edition published in 2002 by
Merlin Publishing
16 Upper Pembroke Street
Dublin 2
Ireland
www.merlin-publishing.com

The publishers wish to acknowledge that certain material in this book is Crown copyright
and is reproduced with the permission of the Controller of Her Majesty's Stationery Office.
The material concerned is as follows:

HO 129/50
HO 219/64 Memorandum, W. J. Smith, 10 March 1972
HO 219/58 (27915): SA 56/57/60 and 61
HO 219/64 (27915) Memorandum, 'Provisional List of Important Points Still to be
Covered in Drafting the Report'.

ISBN 1-903582-16-4

CIP
A catalogue record for this book is available from the British Library.

10 9 8 7 6 5 4 3 2 1

Typeset by Pierce Design, Dublin
Printed by MPG Books Limited, Cornwall.

Royalties from this book will be donated to the Fund of the Bloody Sunday Justice
Campaign, who can be contacted at 1 Westend Park, Derry BT48 9JF;
Tel: (01504) 268 846.

The publishers have made every reasonable effort to contact the copyright holders of
photographs reproduced in this book. If any involuntary infringement of copyright has
occurred, sincere apologies are offered and the owner of such copyright is requested to
contact the publisher.

To Rossa

and

to Todd Allen

and

to Leonard Peltier whose suffering of a marathon miscarriage of justice adds salt to the historical wounds of Native America.

As with Bloody Sunday there can be no real reconciliation when Truth and Justice are subverted in the interests of a political and institutional cover-up.

ACKNOWLEDGMENTS

There are many people to be thanked for their support and advice in the creation of this book. First and foremost are the families of those killed on Bloody Sunday, for their agreement to let me have access to the eyewitness accounts published in this volume. I would especially like to thank Mary Donaghy, Geraldine Doherty, Kay Duddy, Ita McKinney, John O'Kane, Linda Roddy, Tony Doherty, Gerry Duddy, John Kelly and Micky McKinney, of the Bloody Sunday Justice Campaign. Thanks are due to all of the eyewitnesses who gave permission for their statements to be published. Even after 25 years, that decision took courage. Appreciation is offered to Madden & Finucane Solicitors for making the eyewitness statements available and, in particular, special thanks are due to Patricia Coyle for her advice and support. Sharon Teggart, her secretary, was always courteous and helpful. Thanks are also due to the Bloody Sunday Justice Campaign, the Pat Finucane Centre and the Bloody Sunday Trust. Colm Barton and Máirtín Ó Cathain's help is greatly appreciated. Special thanks are due to my good friend Marcus Fearon for the endless hours he spent helping to put all of the statements on database. Thanks to Tony O'Byrne and Barry Pimlott, computer geniuses. Deirdre O'Doherty, Joe Murray and AFrI, Richard Moore and Marty Creggan, for generous help with photocopying. I also wish to acknowledge Seamus McKinney, Sean McLoughlin and Eamon McDermott for their support. Thanks to Desmond J. Doherty, Michael Mansfield, QC, Greg McCartney, Arthur Harvey, QC, Richard Harvey, QC, Lord Anthony Gifford, QC, Paddy McDermott and John Coyle; Martin Finucane, Ciaran and Fearghal Shiels of Madden & Finucane Solicitors. For sound professional advice the following are acknowledged: Robert Ballagh; Pat Crehan; Gerry McColgan; Michael McGuinness; John Pilger; Garret Sheehan; E H D; Sr Kathleen Deignan; John G. Driscoll, CFC; Harry Dunkak, CFC; Dr Michael Hovey; Br Gerry Boland and Br Quinn of Iona College, New York. Liz Curtis and Dr Christine Kinealy, as always were a source of encouragement and technical help. Thanks are due to Assemblyman Joseph Crowley (Queens), Cheryl Harrington, Mr Frank Bolz, and to Robert J. Breglio for his expert advice and opinion on ballistic and forensic aspects to this book. Special thanks to Mary Kierney and Dr Michael Quigley. The assistance of photographers Kit DeFever, New York; Gilles Peress, New York; Colman Doyle, Wicklow; Hugh Gallagher, Derry; and the *Derry Journal*, was invaluable. I am particularly grateful to amateur photographer Robert White whose courageous photography close to the Rossville Street barricade captured the horror of Bloody Sunday as it unfolded. Thanks are also due to Paul and Robert Mahon for their time and interest. The Order of Malta and the Inter-national Law Department of the British Red Cross are thanked for their information and help. Very special thanks are due to Dr Raymond McClean, his wife Sheila and son Sean for their patience and professional support. Their encouragement was vital. Seamus Cashman and the entire staff of Wolfhound Press, in particular Emer Ryan, are gratefully acknowledged for their commitment to seeing this book brought to fruition. Liam Carson is thanked for his work on publicity. I am especially indebted to two important friends who helped me understand the meaning of Bloody Sunday in its wider international context: Wendy Murphy (Canada) and Gary White Deer (Oklahoma, Choctaw). Thanks are also due to P. Anderson who made me determined to express and claim my Irishness proudly. I am especially grateful to Rev. Terence McCaughey, Trinity College, and Jane Winter, British Irish Rights Watch, for their Foreword and Preface to this book. Terence McCaughey is part of the great Presbyterian tradition of Ireland. Jane Winter is one of the many English and British people who have been important friends to Ireland. I am especially indebted to my colleagues Paul Greengrass and Mark Redhead, director and producer of the film *Bloody Sunday,* who have worked at all times with integrity and fairmindedness on this project. I must also thank Lucy Dykes, Pippa Cross and Bill Shephard of Granada Film for their support. Jim Sheridan and I first spoke of a film about Bloody Sunday in November 1996 on a flight to New York. It has been a privilege to work with Jim and his many colleagues at Hell's Kitchen production company. I must also thank my editor for this edition, Aideen Quigley, whose eye for detail is amazing, and also Selga Medenieks, Chenile Keogh, Aoife Barrett, Julie Dobson, Susan Jefferies and Deirdre Tuchy at Merlin Publishing. Thanks also to Lynn at Pierce Design. John Scally, assistant editor, was a pleasure to work with. From the moment I spoke to him about this book he was deeply committed to helping in its creation. Finally, my families in Derry and Dublin cannot be forgotten for living with my quiet absorption in this work. My mother Sarah was always welcoming and kind when I returned home to my beloved Derry. In Dublin, my wife Margaret and children Therese, Carl and Emma were always sensitive, encouraging and immensely supportive.

CONTENTS

FOREWORD TO THE THIRD EDITION

It was April 1999. I was sitting in an Irish café in Kilburn drinking Italian espresso. Across the street Ahmed the crazy Moroccan was laying mangoes out on his stall outside my local Indian restaurant. Two French students were at the table next to me watching in wonder as Real Madrid swept everything before them in the Champions League. The sun was shining. Britney was soaring up the charts with her American jailbait pop. Tony Blair was running away in the polls and a nasty, vengeful, xenophobic Tory Party were going to be buried again at the next election. It was a good day to be alive in my home city of London.

I remember feeling I was watching a new country being born that morning — a cosmopolitan Britain, a Britain proud of its diversity, its tolerance, its eccentricity, its history. And then I picked up a book that my colleague, the producer Mark Redhead, had been asking me to read for weeks. It was called *Eyewitness Bloody Sunday*.

I read it in a single sitting. It's an extraordinary book — first-hand accounts woven with commentary that tell the story of a Derry Civil Rights march on a crisp winter's morning in January 1972. As I read, I could see the families in their Sunday best gathering in Bishop's Field after lunch. I could feel the hope that swelled the singing of 'We Shall Overcome' as they walked down the hill through the Bogside towards Derry City centre, where the British Army stood waiting. An irresistible force was about to meet an immovable object — a perfect metaphor, if metaphor were needed, for the beginning of the 'Troubles'.

And so it all began to go wrong. The march split; a riot broke out in front of the army positions, stones, bricks and bottles rained down; a water cannon hosed the crowd, more stones, then army rubber bullets, and meanwhile the Paras waited in side streets desperate for the order to go in. Derry, like all of Northern Ireland, was a powderkeg waiting to explode.

And then, at seven minutes past four, it did. As I turned the pages of Don's book I could see the whole scene in my mind's eye — pigs

revving and accelerating into the Bogside, Paras de-bussing into a fleeing crowd. Running, shouting, fighting, screaming. The thump of rubber bullets. And then suddenly — some thought almost immediately
— the awesome percussive sound of British Army SLRs firing live
rounds. And firing. And firing. And firing. And people scrabbling for
cover and running for their lives. And people dying. By the time I finished *Eyewitness Bloody Sunday* I felt as if I myself was crouching in
terror amidst the dust and rubble of the Rossville Street barricade as
the rounds echoed around that godforsaken landscape. And I knew
then I wanted to make a film about Bloody Sunday.

This was a story from another Britain. Not the vibrant Britain outside my café window but the long-forgotten Britain of the grey, dismal,
distant 1970s. A Britain at war with a community of its own citizens
but refusing to admit it. A Britain determined to crush dissent, rather
than listen to it. This was the Britain we preferred not to look at, pre-
tended did not exist. A fearful, insular, class-ridden Britain. The
Britain I grew up in.

I was seventeen when Bloody Sunday happened — old enough to
know that what happened had been shocking; young enough not to
understand that it was a fateful turning point, the moment when the
Civil Rights Movement was destroyed, when hope was driven from the
political stage and the struggle in Northern Ireland became one
between men with guns. Ever since that day, the Troubles have cast a
dark shadow across the lives of every one of us.

Bloody Sunday had a particular significance for me. I first went to
Derry in 1980 as a young *World in Action* reporter to cover the IRA
hunger strikes. I began to delve into the life of Raymond McCartney, a
young man from Derry then in the process of starving himself to death
inside the Maze/Long Kesh Prison, having been sentenced to twenty-
five years for the shooting of a Special Branch Officer and a local busi-
nessman. I travelled around Derry trying to trace what had led him to
join the Provos. I met his friends, his family, his victims, his enemies.
He and I began to correspond — furtive, smuggled handwritten notes
from inside the Maze, which I still possess. He wrote about his history,
his beliefs, his hopes and motivations. And in his first letter he wrote
simply this: 'It all began for me on Bloody Sunday.'

Later I had a brief meeting with him inside a cell in H Block 3.
It was an encounter I will never forget. Here at last, after weeks of

waiting, was the hunger-striker Raymond McCartney in the flesh. He was my age; we had watched the same football teams, listened to the same music, laughed at the same TV. Yet he had killed for a cause and now was willing to die for it — slowly, agonisingly, on a grey hospital bed. He was gaunt, bearded, emaciated — like a medieval religious zealot. He told me he was a soldier, not a criminal.

And I knew then that the difference between us was simply this — I had grown up in the prosperous south-east of England and had come of age when the biggest choice was whether or not to use condoms. And he? He had grown up in Derry in the middle of a political crisis that had begun long before he was born. And while I can never approve of or sympathise with the methods of the IRA, I do know this: that you cannot — if you are British — possibly understand the Troubles unless you visit Derry and feel the lasting bitterness engendered by the events of Bloody Sunday.

My colleague and producer Mark Redhead, with whom I had just made *The Murder of Stephen Lawrence*, a film about the shocking race murder of a young black teenager in South London, had always wanted to tackle Bloody Sunday. He felt the most constructive thing one could do, as a British filmmaker, was to explore the subject, try to make sense of its painful legacy, and hence promote reconciliation. When we read Don's book we knew we had found our collaborator.

Don is a Derry man born and bred. Little wonder then that he grew up to be a writer whose passion is ensuring forgotten voices are heard. His dictum is that of Nelson Algren, Chicago's great neglected poet of the American underbelly. The role of the writer, said Algren, was to be on the side of the underdog. And that is what Don has always been. He has campaigned tirelessly for many causes throughout Ireland and the world — but none with more conviction than for the families of the dead and wounded of Bloody Sunday.

Since 1972 Bloody Sunday has been largely a forgotten subject in the world beyond Ireland. An Inquiry chaired by Lord Chief Justice Widgery mounted in the months after the tragedy quickly concluded that the army had been fired upon by the IRA as they entered the Bogside and that several of the dead had been involved in handling weapons. It was a grotesque injustice, but its findings still stand today.

Many writers have challenged Widgery — most notably Eamon McCann, Nell McCafferty, Raymond McClean, the *Sunday Times*

Insight team, and Peter Taylor in his brilliant BBC documentary *Remember Bloody Sunday*. But mostly the families themselves, alone and often ignored, have had to pursue their courageous three-decade-long campaign to reverse Lord Widgery's findings. In 1997, when Don wrote *Eyewitness Bloody Sunday*, they found a priceless ally.

Don was fifteen years old on Bloody Sunday. He marched. He threw stones. He was standing just two feet away from seventeen-year-old Michael Kelly on the Rossville Street barricade when Michael was shot dead. But unlike so many of the young men of Derry, Don did not join the Provos. The Church beckoned. Then campaigning in the Third World. He married. Settled in Dublin. Bloody Sunday became a distant memory.

And then a chance remark on a return visit to Derry rekindled a memory of a statement he'd signed twenty-three years earlier about what he'd witnessed on Bloody Sunday. He went to the community centre in the Bogside to inquire if his statement still existed. It was still there, along with hundreds of civilian statements taken by Civil Rights activists in the days following the shootings. They were lying in a plastic bag in a filing cabinet, unanalysed since Lord Widgery refused to accept them as evidence in 1972. Don painstakingly read every statement, and used them to piece together his account of what happened that day. The forgotten voices of Bloody Sunday became the basis of this extraordinary book and the source of its immense power.

Publication of *Eyewitness Bloody Sunday* had a profound impact on public opinion in Ireland. It helped reawaken public interest in Bloody Sunday and gave new impetus to the campaign by the families of the dead and wounded for a reinvestigation of the case. Finally the Irish government began to lobby the British government and a chain of events was set in motion that would ultimately lead to Tony Blair establishing a new Tribunal of Inquiry to investigate the events of Bloody Sunday, chaired by Lord Saville.

The Saville Inquiry hearings were about to open when Mark and I first met Don in the summer of 1999. We asked him if he would join with us in making a film to mark the thirtieth anniversary of Bloody Sunday, which would attempt uniquely to bring together the people of Derry and former British soldiers with experience of serving in the conflict in Northern Ireland, to tell the story. It would be a film that would utilise the best talents from all over these islands, a film about war designed to promote peace and reconciliation — a kind of *Battle of Algiers* for our times. Don was immediately enthusiastic and agreed to co-produce the film. Together we travelled to Derry to seek the views of the families of those who had been shot.

We met them in a moving and emotional evening at the Trinity Hotel and Mark and I explained that we were British filmmakers and that from where we stood Bloody Sunday was just as much a British tragedy as an Irish one — because the results of what happened in Derry that day had been felt in British cities ever since. Although we were not seeking their permission, we needed their support as without it the project was meaningless. I told them that our film wouldn't change the world. No film ever can. But I had been waiting for this opportunity ever since I had first visited Derry in 1980. I wanted to put my brick in the wall of peace.

They agreed, doubtless influenced by the tremendous trust they had in Don.

We felt from the start that it was important to make the foundations of the production span Derry, Dublin and London. Pippa Cross, the head of Granada Film, and the celebrated Irish director Jim Sheridan had a long-standing relationship since working together on *My Left Foot* and *The Field*, so *Bloody Sunday* was established as a British/Irish co-production between Granada Film and Jim's production company, Hell's Kitchen. Jim and his long-standing professional partner, Arthur Lappin, joined as executive producers, along with Rod Stoneman from the Irish Film Board, Paul Trijbits of the UK Film Council, and Tristan Whalley from Portman Film.

But how to tell it — where should we begin? Early January 1972 when the march was conceived? With the introduction of Internment in the summer of 1971? The start of the Civil Rights Movement in 1968? Partition in 1921? The Seige of Derry? Tracing the roots of Bloody Sunday was an endless journey into the mists of history. Eventually, after weeks of discussion, we decided to tell the story in one day — one day that stood for any day because it seemed to us that Bloody Sunday symbolised the terrible dance of death that Britain and Ireland have been engaged in since at least the time of Cromwell.

Having narrowed the film down to the almost classical timeframe of a single day, we then had to decide which stories to tell of the nearly 20,000 civilian marchers and 3,000 British troops in Derry on that day.

Again, after weeks if not months of agonising, we decided to focus on four main characters, two from each side of the conflict, each of whom was trying to ensure the day passed off peacefully.

First we chose Gerard Donaghy, a seventeen-year-old boy from the Bogside, played in the film by Declan Duddy, a nephew of Jackie Duddy, who was the first to die on Bloody Sunday. Gerard Donaghy was one of the last to die, shot down as he tried to escape from Glenfada Park. According to Lord Widgery, he was found dying minutes after the shootings in a car at an army roadblock with IRA nail bombs in his pockets. Here was the 'proof' the British Army needed: a member of the so-called 'Derry Young Hooligans' with lethal weapons on his person.

The truth was very different, of course. In fact Gerard Donaghy, like many boys of his age, was at a crossroads in his life. He had been active in the defence of Free Derry; he hated the British Army presence and weeks before had been released from prison after serving six months for stone throwing. The Provos beckoned. But he was in love with a Protestant girl and was looking to stay out of trouble and marry her. His was the classic conflict of loyalties. Sadly, we will never know which way Gerard would have gone. He was shot before he got to make his choice. And afterwards the nail bombs were planted on his body.

On the other side of the conflict that day was a young Para, Soldier 027, who witnessed Bloody Sunday as a member of the anti-tank platoon. Soldier 027, played by former British soldier Mike Edwards, was the youngest member of his platoon, probably of his company, and had served continuously in Northern Ireland for almost a year — a year of exhausting, stressful, brutalising combat, driven only by fear and adrenaline.

Soldier 027 saw at close quarters most of the shootings on Rossville Street and in Glenfada Park — and almost certainly came face to face with young Gerard Donaghy as he was killed. But later that night, the young soldier lied to army investigators about what he had seen, in order to protect his platoon. It was to be twenty-five years before he finally decided to tell the truth. In 1999 he entered the British government witness protection programme and has now provided the Saville Inquiry with a detailed account of what he now says occurred on the day (see Appendix 7).

Our third character was Brigadier Patrick MacLellan (played by

Nicholas Farrell), Commander of 8 Brigade and the man tasked to stop the Civil Rights march by his superior, the Commander Land Forces Northern Ireland, General Robert Ford (played by Tim Pigott-Smith). MacLellan had reservations about the plan and tried his best to ensure minimum force was used. But he was undone by more aggressive voices — notably Ford and the officer in charge of 1 Para, Colonel Wilford — and shortly after 4 p.m. he gave the fateful order to send in the Paras.

Finally, our fourth character was Ivan Cooper MP, one of the key figures responsible for organising the march. Cooper was an unlikely Civil Rights leader. He was not a Catholic from the Bogside or a university-educated radical. He was the Protestant manager of a shirt factory, whose own father had been in the loyalist paramilitary UVF. Yet it was Cooper who emerged as one of the leading figures of the Derry Civil Rights Movement in 1968, along with John Hume, Bernadette Devlin and Eamon McCann. It was Cooper who led the march down the hill that day in January 1972, Cooper who struggled at the barriers to avert violence, and Cooper who watched helplessly as those he had called out to march were shot in front of him. The guilt remains with him to this day.

As soon as we settled on the character of Cooper, Mark, Don and I were clear it had to be played by Jimmy Nesbitt. Jimmy comes from a Protestant background near Coleraine in County Derry, not far from where Cooper grew up. For him, making the film became a very personal exploration of his own background and the conflict, and the result is one of the great performances of Irish Troubles film history. In my view Jimmy's portrayal of Ivan Cooper stands comparison with Liam Neeson in *Michael Collins* and Daniel Day Lewis in *In the Name of the Father*.

Supporting these four stories, and every bit as important, was the fact that we used the film as an opportunity to bring together the people of Derry and the people of Ballymun — who came out in their thousands to support our filming — and former members of the British Army. They agreed, with great courage, to travel to Dublin to re-enact the events of the day and to use their personal experiences to tell the truth about what happened.

I remember standing next to Don one cold winter's day in March 2001 on our film set version of Rossville Street in Dublin's Ballymun area, as we prepared to send our Paras into the Bogside. Would it work or would the scene disintegrate into meaningless chaos? We watched as the British Army pigs revved up and accelerated into the scattering crowd. Bloody Sunday was occurring again in front of our very eyes. It was violent, harrowing, gut-wrenchingly real. And yet, in its realism, incredibly moving. This was a script that everyone knew. And all played their parts to perfection.

When it was over, I embraced Don, as did Mark. I knew we had done our best. We had told the truth — or at least the truth as this group of individuals saw it. The long journey that began for Mark and myself when we read *Eyewitness Bloody Sunday* was nearly at an end.

Whether or not our film works, of course, remains to be seen. But in a sense that is not really the important issue. What counts is that the people of Derry in their thousands, the people of Ballymun in their thousands, former members of the British Army who served in Northern Ireland, and actors from all over Ireland and the UK joined together to relive the event. The experiences we shared while making the film will stay with us forever. Together we learnt many things, of which the most important was this: that we all inhabit these beautiful islands scattered on the north-western edge of Europe, and that we hold so much more in common than that which divides us. We should all hope that in the future we can celebrate our diversity rather than fight over it, as we have done in the past.

So read *Eyewitness Bloody Sunday*. It is written by a man I am proud to call my friend, and it stands as a reminder to all of us of what happens when we lose sight of what we share in common, and the pain and suffering that innocent families endure as a result. It is one of the handful of great and enduring books to emerge from the Troubles — one of the many memorials that will stand long after these thirty years are consigned to the history books.

Paul Greengrass
Director, *Bloody Sunday*
London, 20 December 2001

FOREWORD

Among other documents published in this volume (some for the first time) is a minute recording details of a visit paid by Lord Widgery, Lord Chief Justice of England, to the then Prime Minister in Downing Street. The visit took place two days after what was in Ireland already coming to be called 'Bloody Sunday'. Lord Widgery had agreed to chair a Tribunal of Inquiry into the events in Derry on that day. In his briefing, the Prime Minister counselled Lord Widgery and the Lord Chancellor, who had accompanied him, to be careful to remember that in Northern Ireland they were fighting 'not only a military but a propaganda war'. The material published in this book raises serious questions as to how exactly Lord Widgery took that warning to heart and as to how he acted upon it.

The greater part of the book is taken up with eye-witnesses' accounts of what they saw that day. More than 500 such accounts were collected by the Northern Ireland Civil Rights Association (NICRA) and the National Council for Civil Liberties (NCCL). Evidence adduced here makes it clear that Lord Widgery did not see any of these until 9 March 1972. Even then, having looked at the fifteen of them which were actually brought to his attention, he in effect dismissed them all, conceding however that in his report he would be prepared to say that 'the Tribunal had taken note of all the statements, on the basis that they had all been inspected by Counsel for the Tribunal or by Treasury Solicitors' officers'. Although he apparently went on to say that 'in the last resort' he was in fact prepared to read them all himself, he was assured that this was 'not necessary'. There is no evidence that he ever did read them all.

The value of the eyewitness statements published here lies in the fact that they give us accounts of the events of Bloody Sunday as they appeared to a large number of those who were there. In some ways their accounts tally with the official version of events as it appears in the final text of the Tribunal's report. But, in other significant ways, the account they give (clearly without any collusion) differs from the 'official' version as it appears in Widgery but, at the same time, tallies with the version of events as still re-told and

XXII EYEWITNESS BLOODY SUNDAY

believed on the streets of Derry. This applies most importantly with reference to the oft-repeated allegation that from early on there was gunfire at targeted and verifiably unarmed persons from the vicinity of the walls of the city. The post-mortem examinations are, in fact, consistent with this — finding, as they do, that in three cases the victims were shot from the front as they faced away or were running away from the oncoming paratroopers.

The report of the Tribunal of Inquiry is the official account of how people lost their lives in Derry on Sunday, 30 January 1972, of who was to blame and of who could not, in the Tribunal's view, reasonably be blamed at all. The eyewitness accounts published here give another account. They lay responsibility where Lord Widgery was reluctant to place it. The publication of them seriously calls into question his good faith and calls others to account who have not previously been called to account at all.

Their publication, however, should not be seen simply as a demand for revenge, but rather as a call (even now after twenty-five years) for those responsible to bear the consequences of their actions, or at least to acknowledge publicly their involvement.

Whenever persons responsible for serious violations are neither punished nor disciplined and the impression gains credence that they are being shielded, then doubt is cast upon the democratic ideals of the state. A refusal on the part of the state to investigate and discipline serves to create ambiguity where there should be clarity, and actually encourages disrespect for the law — even tempting people to take the law into their own hands, as so many have in fact done. Furthermore, the obscuring of the truth at the highest level, or denial of what has happened, renders reconciliation virtually impossible, because it seriously limits the possibility of real communication between people *as between fellow-citizens*. Dr Alex Boraine, deputy chairperson of the Truth and Reconciliation Commission in South Africa has put it this way — albeit with reference to a very different situation:

> *The lack of official verification of former events leaves room for doubts and scepticism about the stories told.*

He points out that it leaves both the survivors and the dead in a kind of historical 'no-man's land'. A continuing uneasy co-existence of the two stories — one official and the other not — actually inhibits the possibility of our working effectively for a *common* just society. As a commentator from El Salvador has put it in a meditation on the situation in his country:

> Unless a society exposes itself to the truth it can harbour no possibility of reconciliation, reunification and trust. For a peace settlement to be solid and durable it must be based on truth.

Don Mullan has done us all a service by enabling those who want to do so, and can bear to do so, to hear these voices which have been silent for twenty-five years. Those who made their statements in 1972 offer us an opportunity to see the situation whole and entire and to act firmly, justly and compassionately as a result. To the families of those who died they hold out the possibility of a more profound peace of mind than most of them have enjoyed for a quarter of a century.

A Chilean writer, committed to a similar project in his country, concludes the matter this way. He says:

> Although the truth cannot really dispense justice, it does put an end to many a continued injustice. It does not bring the dead back to life, but it brings them out from silence.

This book promises to do just that.

Terence McCaughey
Minister of the Presbyterian Church
and Senior Lecturer at Trinity College Dublin
November 1996

PREFACE

Bloody Sunday is named after the events that occurred on Sunday, 30 January 1972, when thirteen people were killed by British soldiers and fourteen others were injured. The dead were: Gerard Donaghy, 17; James Wray, 22; Gerard McKinney, 35; William McKinney, 26; John Young, 17; William Nash, 19; Michael McDaid, 20; Michael Kelly, 17; Kevin McElhinney, 17; Patrick Doherty, 31; Jack Duddy, 17; Hugh Gilmore, 17; and Bernard McGuigan, 41. Those injured were: John Johnston, Damien Donaghy, Michael Bridge, Michael Quinn, Patrick O'Donnell, Patrick McDaid, Alexander Nash, Margaret Deery, Michael Bradley, Patrick Campbell, Joseph Mahon, Joseph Friel, Daniel McGowan and Daniel Gillespie. John Johnston died prematurely of a brain tumour, not long after Bloody Sunday; his family is convinced that the trauma of Bloody Sunday contributed to his untimely death.

The victims were taking part in an illegal demonstration against internment without trial. A crack battalion of the British Army, the 1st Battalion Parachute Regiment (the Paras), reputed to be the toughest regiment in the army, was deployed to mount an arrest operation within the Bogside area of the city of Derry, which had been a nationalist 'no-go area' for British troops for the previous two years. The Paras opened fire on the demonstrators, a small number of whom had previously been engaged in low-level rioting, such as stoning soldiers. Accounts differ as to whether the soldiers were fired upon before opening fire or whether they fired without provocation, but it is undisputed that army statements issued after the incident, claiming that the deceased were gunmen and bombers, were untrue. There is no evidence that any of the deceased was engaged in attacking soldiers at the time of his death; on the contrary, most of them were fleeing from the soldiers. No soldier was prosecuted for any of the killings.

The British government ordered an immediate judicial inquiry into the incident, undertaken by the Lord Chief Justice, Lord Widgery. His report, published in April 1972, less than three months after the event, has been criticised and discredited in a number of important respects. Important fresh evidence that has come to light since the Widgery report has shed new light on the tragic events of Bloody Sunday. So far, pleas from the relatives of the deceased for a new inquiry to establish the true facts and to exonerate properly the reputations of the deceased have been denied by the British government.

This book gives a voice to some of the people who were present on Bloody Sunday. In the immediate aftermath, The Northern Ireland Civil Rights Association (NICRA) interviewed several hundred eyewitnesses and submitted their accounts to Widgery, who paid them scant regard. These statements are vital historical documents. They are the starting point for anyone who wants to know the truth about Bloody Sunday. The purpose of this preface is to explain the context in which the statements came to be made, so that those who are not already familiar with the events they describe can understand their significance.

The Political Background to Bloody Sunday

Northern Ireland has been in the grip of a savage sectarian conflict, euphemistically described as 'the Troubles', which has its origins in the British invasion and subjugation of Ireland in Tudor times and the partition of Ireland in 1921, but which has intensified since 1968, claiming over 3,400 lives in the past twenty-seven years.[1] The conflict exists between nationalists, who want to see a united Ireland and who are predominantly Catholic by religion, and unionists, who want Northern Ireland to remain a part of the United Kingdom and who are predominantly Protestants. Nationalists who support the use of violence to achieve their ends are known as republicans, and unionists who do so are known as loyalists, although not all those who would describe themselves as republicans or loyalists support political violence. The British Army has been deployed continuously in Northern Ireland since 1969. The British government claims that there has been a public emergency relating to Northern Ireland because of the conflict since 1974;[2] it had not made any such claim at the time of Bloody Sunday.

On 9 August 1971, the unionist government of Northern Ireland (known as the Stormont government), with the support of the

British government, introduced internment without trial. By the end of 1971 around 900 people, virtually all of them nationalists, were imprisoned, in violation of international standards on the right to a fair trial. At the same time that internment was introduced, a six-month ban on public demonstrations was imposed under emergency legislation in force at the time. NICRA, formed in 1967 to combat the widespread political and social discrimination against Catholics in Northern Ireland, which is one of the roots of the conflict, called a demonstration in Derry for Sunday, 30 January 1972, as much in protest against the ban on the right to demonstrate as a protest against internment itself.

The city of Derry[3] is situated on the north-western border of Northern Ireland with the Republic of Ireland. At the time of Bloody Sunday, it had a population of around 55,000, about 33,000 of whom lived in the predominantly Catholic districts of Creggan and the Bogside. The Bogside had been a republican no-go area for about two years, which meant that the Irish Republican Army (IRA), rather than the police or the army, had effective control of the district. The British security forces were obviously dissatisfied with this situation and were looking for an opportunity to carry out the orders of the Commander Land Forces in Northern Ireland, General Ford, issued on 26 October 1971 to Brigadier MacLellan, Commander 8 Infantry Brigade, who had overall command of the troops on Bloody Sunday,

> so far as possible, to recreate the state of law in the Creggan and Bogside as and when he could.[4]

A week before the Bloody Sunday demonstration, a smaller anti-internment demonstration had been held outside the internment camp at Magilligan, not far from Derry. This demonstration had been broken up with extreme violence by about 300 soldiers. NICRA was anxious to avoid a repetition, and placed 'special emphasis on the necessity for a peaceful incident-free day' on 30 January.[5] According to Ivan Cooper, a Member of Parliament at the time and one of the organisers of the march, assurances had been obtained from the IRA that it would withdraw from the area during the demonstration.[6] The IRA confirmed that this was the case to the *Insight* team of reporters who published their own analysis of Bloody Sunday.[7]

On 27 January 1972 the Democratic Unionist Association in Derry, in an act of provocation aimed at both nationalists and the Stormont government, announced that its members intended to hold a public religious rally in the Guildhall Square, the intended termination point of the NICRA march, on Sunday 30 January. The Association's Vice-President, the Rev. James McClelland, was reported as saying,

> The civil rights march is not legal.

Theirs (the DUA's), he said, would be. He continued:

> The authorities will have to keep their word and stop the civil rights march and give us protection.[8]

On 30 January, several newspapers announced that the religious rally had been called off. McClelland was reported as saying on the previous day:

> We were approached by the Government and given assurances that the Civil Rights march would be halted — by force if necessary. We believe wholesale riot and bloodshed could be the result of the Civil Rights activities tomorrow and we would be held responsible if our rally takes place. We have appealed to all loyalists to stay out of the city centre tomorrow.[9]

Thus the demonstration on Bloody Sunday took place against a background of high political tension and in an atmosphere of the apprehension of violence, which would have been as apparent to the security forces as it was to everyone else involved.

The Plan for Policing the Demonstration

According to Lord Widgery's report,[10] on 25 January 1972 General Ford put Brigadier Andrew MacLellan in charge of the operation to contain the march. He prepared an Operation Order[11] that provided for the erection of 26 barriers, designed to cordon Creggan and the Bogside off from the rest of the city, each of which was to be manned by a platoon from the 8 Infantry Brigade and a token police presence. If rioting broke out, water cannon and rubber bullets were to be used if necessary and CS gas as a last resort. 'Hooligans and rioters' were to be arrested by a central arrest force, furnished by the 1st Battalion Parachute Regiment (1 Para).

On 24 January 1972 Chief Superintendent Frank Lagan of the Royal Ulster Constabulary (RUC)[12] told MacLellan that he was of the opinion that the only way to avoid serious violence was to let the march proceed, but that the marchers should be photographed with a view to prosecuting them later for defying the ban on demonstrations and/or for rioting. MacLellan agreed to recommend this approach to General Ford. However, on the same day Ford had sent orders to Lieutenant Colonel Derek Wilford, commander of 1 Para, to prepare for service in Derry on 30 January 1972. *Insight* alleged that the plan was approved by the Northern Ireland Committee of the Cabinet[13] because it carried the obvious risk of casualties. Certainly the Prime Minister, Edward Heath, confirmed that the plan was 'known to [government] Ministers'.[14]

The arrest operation was carried out by Support Company of 1 Para, under the command of Major Ted Loden. According to Widgery,[15] Support Company was the only company to fire live ammunition on Bloody Sunday and was thus responsible for all the deaths and injuries that occurred. However, eyewitness statements, some of which are included in this book, suggest that firing also came from the Derry Walls, where another regiment was stationed.

The *Insight* team said that Wilford drew up an operational plan for the arrest operation, which Loden declared unworkable only two hours before the demonstration was due to begin. As a result, 1 Para was deployed through the barricade on Little James' Street, which had the effect of driving the demonstrators down Rossville Street.

Wilford said of his own orders:

> I asked . . . the question which in fact for a long time has . . . worried me. I said, 'What happens if there is shooting?' To which I got really a very . . . sparse reply to the effect that, 'Oh well, we'll deal with that when it comes.' It's my greatest regret that I didn't actually pursue that question and say, 'Right you know what — what do you want us to do if we're shot at?'

Soldiers in Support Company, however, were briefed to expect to be shot at. The Company Sergeant Major said:

> I did expect when we went into the Rossville flats to be fired at.

The Platoon Sergeant said:

> I was just told that there was a possibility that gunmen would be in the area and to keep our eyes out especially for high ground like the Rossville flats — obvious sniper position. [16]

Lord Widgery said of 1 Para's attitude to the use of lethal force:

> In the Parachute Regiment, at any rate in the 1st Battalion, the soldiers are trained to take what may be described as a hard line upon these questions. The events of 30 January and the attitude of individual soldiers whilst giving evidence suggest that when engaging an identified gunman or bomb-thrower they shoot to kill and continue to fire until the target dis-appears or falls. When under attack and returning fire they show no particular concern for the safety of others in the vicinity of the target. They are aware that civilians who do not wish to be associated with violence tend to make themselves scarce at the first alarm and they know that it is the deliberate policy of gunmen to use civilians as cover. Further, when hostile firing is taking place the soldiers of 1 Para will fire on a person who appears to be using a firearm against them without always waiting until they can positively identify the weapon.[17]

Wilford put it more succinctly:

> When we moved on the streets we moved as if we in fact were moving against a well-armed well-trained army.[18]

What Actually Happened?

The march passed off peacefully, as the organisers had intended, until it reached the junction of William Street and Rossville Street, where the lorry at the head of the march turned right up Rossville Street, leading the marchers away from any confrontation with soldiers at the barrier in William Street. However, about 200 marchers, most of them young men, broke away from the march and began throwing stones at the soldiers on the barricade. The soldiers responded with rubber bullets and water cannon, and these rioters were effectively repelled. At this point, 1 Para requested permission to commence its arrest, or 'scoop-up' operation. According to the official Brigade Log, one sub unit was ordered forward at 16:07 hours. Three minutes later, at 16:10, Support Company began firing. Less than thirty minutes later, thirteen civilians were dead and another thirteen lay injured.

The facts set out above are generally agreed to be correct by all concerned. Virtually all other significant matters of fact are disputed and are the subject of conflicting evidence. Even the number of people taking part in the demonstration is contested: Lord Widgery said that there were between 3,000 and 5,000;[19] according to *Insight*, the organisers claimed that there were 30,000; Bernadette Devlin MP, a speaker at the demonstration, said in Parliament that there were at least 15,000.[20]

Who Gave the Orders?

Much controversy surrounds the question of who precisely sanctioned Support Company's opening fire upon the demonstrators. According to Widgery,[21] the order to commence the arrest operation came from MacLellan and was given to Wilford over a secure wireless link, as a result of which it was not recorded in the verbatim record of the ordinary brigade radio network. However, the official Brigade Log does not record the order either, but only a limited authorisation to deploy a sub unit, no mention being made of Support Company. Furthermore, a tape recording of the actual messages relayed over the ordinary radio network was produced in evidence at the Widgery Inquiry, which is at odds with the official log, in that the log records permission for the sub unit to carry out the scoop-up operation, but the tape does not; its absence was explained by the Brigade Major as resulting from the fact that this order was also given over the secure link, but this does not explain why one such order appears in the log but the other does not. However, MacLellan, his Brigade Major, and Wilford all gave Widgery sworn testimony that MacLellan gave the order, and Widgery accepted their evidence. Chief Superintendent Lagan of the RUC, though, told Widgery that he had formed the impression that 1 Para had gone ahead without authority from MacLellan. *Insight*, on the other hand, alleged that, in the heat of the moment, with the original plan in tatters, it was really Loden who was in charge of the troops during the crucial thirty minutes when all the shooting took place, and that MacLellan had no idea what Support Company was doing or even where it was. 1 Para's Company Sergeant Major said that he clearly remembered the order from his company commander as being, 'Move, move, move!'[22] Brian Cashinella, Northern Ireland correspondent for the *Times* in 1972, said that as 1 Para came through the barricade,

> . . . I was standing next to General Robert Ford . . . who was a new

commander, and he was waving his swaggery stick saying, 'Go on the Paras, go and get them, go on, go and get them.' And then all was mayhem.[23]

Who Fired First?

Equal controversy surrounds the question of whether the soldiers opened fire without justification, or whether they came under fire first. Lord Widgery attached very great importance to this issue, to the extent that it overshadowed any consideration of whether the level of lethal force applied by Support Company was justified, either generally or, especially, in each individual case where someone died or was injured. Widgery was faced with a direct conflict of evidence between soldiers who gave evidence at the inquiry, all of whom maintained that Support Company came under fire first and that they continued to experience heavy and sustained fire throughout the thirty crucial minutes, and all the evidence that he heard and statements that were made available to him from eyewitnesses who claimed that the Paras had opened fire without justification and that none of those who were killed or injured was armed or firing upon or throwing bombs at the soldiers.

Widgery made a curious decision, considering his high judicial office and his considerable legal experience, not to go into in any depth the evidence of the thirteen wounded, many of whom he did not interview, despite the fact that they had survived being shot at by the soldiers and were able to give first-hand evidence regarding their behaviour. In any event, he preferred the evidence of the soldiers to those of the eyewitnesses, saying:

> *Those accustomed to listening to witnesses could not fail to be impressed by the demeanour of the soldiers of 1 Para. They gave their evidence with confidence and without hesitation or prevarication and withstood a rigorous cross-examination without contradicting themselves or each other. With one or two exceptions I accept that they were telling the truth as they remembered it.*[24]

It is difficult to square Widgery's attitude to the soldiers' evidence with his finding:

> *None of the deceased or wounded is proved to have been shot whilst handling a firearm or bomb.*[25]

All the soldiers who gave evidence claimed to have fired only in response to a perceived threat from an identifiable person who was either firing at them or threatening them with a nail or petrol bomb, yet Widgery found that:

> *Although a number of soldiers spoke of actually seeing firearms or bombs in the hands of civilians none was recovered by the Army. None of the many photographs shows a civilian holding an object that can with certainty be identified as a firearm or a bomb. No casualties were suffered by the soldiers from firearms or gelignite bombs. In relation to every one of the deceased there were eye witnesses who said that they saw no bomb or firearm in his hands. The clothing of 11 of the deceased when examined for explosives showed no trace of gelignite.[26]*

Where were the Bombs?

Another conflict of evidence which the Widgery Inquiry failed to resolve was the difference between the soldiers' accounts of the bombardment they suffered at the hands of the crowd and the eye-witnesses' insistence (with a very few exceptions) that they saw no gunmen, heard no bombs exploding, and were unaware of any hail of bullets except those fired by the soldiers. The soldiers said that they came under heavy and sustained gunfire, were pelted with nail and petrol bombs, and came under a rain of bottles, some of them acid bombs, yet the only report by any of them of damage was the report by two soldiers who said that acid fell on their trouser legs without burning through to their skin. Not a single soldier was hurt, despite Widgery's finding that:

> *Civilian, as well as Army, evidence made it clear that there was a substantial number of civilians in the area who were armed with firearms. I would not be surprised if in the relevant half hour as many rounds were fired at the troops as were fired by them.[27]*

He went on immediately to explain the soldiers' miraculous lack of injury:

> *The soldiers escaped injury by reason of their superior field-craft and training.*

Where was the IRA?

It seems clear that, despite NICRA's attempts to ensure a peaceful demonstration and to secure the withdrawal of the IRA from the area, there were nonetheless some IRA gunmen around. In 1972, both the Official and the Provisional IRA were operating in Derry. The Officials told *Insight* that they withdrew all their weapons from the Bogside, except those held by the Bogside Official Unit, which were dispersed in several safe dumps. All other weapons were held in two cars patrolling in Creggan. They also decreed that no firing against the army was to be initiated by their men, who were only to open fire defensively. However, they admitted that seven unauthorised shots were fired by Officials during the time in question, and that one authorised defensive shot was fired in William Street by one of their members. According to Insight, the Provisionals said that they had withdrawn all their weapons from the Bogside, except for those members who were also acting as stewards on the march.[28] Both wings of the IRA admitted that they sent for reinforcements from the Creggan when the firing started, but they did not arrive and were not in a position to fire upon the army until after the army had ceased firing, although the IRA did indeed fire upon soldiers then. There is also independent evidence of the presence of gunmen in the crowd. Fr (now Bishop) Daly saw a gunman just after Jack Duddy was killed by army gunfire, and photographer Fulvio Grimaldi took a photograph of this gunman. The *Insight* team also interviewed a witness who said that he saw someone with a carbine fire seven shots at the soldiers from the fifth floor of the Rossville Flats. One of the wounded, Alexander Nash, was hit in the arm by a low-velocity bullet, which may have come from a gunman rather than a soldier. However, all the available evidence suggests that the IRA was not present in force; that those of its members who were present and armed fired very few shots; and they could not have produced the fusillade of firing that the soldiers claimed to have experienced.

Who Killed the Victims?

Another inconsistency in the evidence was the difficulty of marrying up the evidence given by the soldiers as to the shots they had fired with the indisputable evidence of the wounds suffered by the dead and injured. The ammunition check made after the event by the army showed that Support Company had fired 108 rounds of 7.62 mm ammunition from self-loading rifles. Of these rounds, 102 were fired during the crucial thirty minutes. In only two cases out of the thirteen deceased were identifiable bullets recovered from the bodies, so that it is possible to say with certainty that Soldier F shot Michael Kelly and Soldier G shot Gerard Donaghy. In no other case can any soldier's description of his actions be matched exactly to the gunshot wounds suffered by any victim, although Widgery was able to make an educated guess as to which soldier or group of soldiers may have been responsible for some of the killings. Widgery said that he had no way of knowing how many shots each soldier had fired other than by their own account.

1 Para's Company Sergeant Major revealed that one soldier had actually expended two more rounds than he had been issued.[29] Peter Taylor, the reporter, asked the Company Sergeant Major what his reaction had been and what he had said to the soldier.

CSM: *I said, 'What the hell were you doing?' And he said, 'I was firing at the enemy,' he said, 'I was firing at gunmen.'*

PT: *Did you believe him?*

CSM: *I didn't know what to think at the time.*

PT: *Did you believe him?*

CSM: *No. Knowing the soldier as — as I do know him I don't believe he was firing at gunmen.*

PT: *Did you see any gunmen?*

CSM: *No.*

PT: *Did you see any weapons?*

CSM: *No.*

PT: *Did you see any nail bomber?*

CSM: *No.*

Forgotten Factors

Four aspects arise from the known facts about the circumstances in which the deceased died, none of which was commented upon by Widgery. First, nearly all of the deceased were killed by single, aimed shots to the head or trunk. This does not suggest the uncontrolled firing of soldiers who were in a state of panic, but highly disciplined action by soldiers who were trained to shoot to kill. Indeed, Widgery himself concluded:

There was no general breakdown in discipline.[30]

Secondly, all the deceased were men, and nine of them were under the age of 25. This suggests that soldiers were targeting particular members of the crowd, perhaps in conformity with a preconceived picture of who should be targeted in such a situation.

Thirdly, in all the cases, but most notably those of Gerard Donaghy, James Wray, Kevin McElhinney, William McKinney, Jack Duddy, Patrick Doherty and Bernard McGuigan, serious questions arise as to whether the deceased were in fact murdered. Far from considering that question, Widgery seems to have been at pains to put the construction on the evidence which is most favourable to the soldiers, at the expense of the reputation of the deceased.

Fourthly, many of those who died or were injured, as well as many of the eyewitnesses, behaved with extra-ordinary courage in a terrifying situation, trying to rescue the wounded and to protect others from death or injury. For example, Bernard McGuigan, the oldest of the victims, died in the act of going to the assistance of a wounded man in the forecourt of the Rossville Flats. Their bravery has never been officially recognised.

Official Versions of the Events

On 1 February 1972, the Ministry of Defence issued a detailed account of the army's version of events, relayed by the British Information Services, Third Avenue, New York, as follows:

The march in Londonderry on January 30 was held in contravention of the Government's ban on all processions and parades. This ban of course applies to both communities in Northern Ireland.

Of the 13 men killed in the shooting that began after the bulk of the 3,000 marchers had been peacefully dispersed, four were on the security force's wanted list. One man had four nail bombs in his pocket. All were between the ages of 16 and 40.

The shooting started with two high-velocity shots aimed at the troops manning the barriers. No one was hit and the fire was not returned. Four minutes later a further high-velocity shot was aimed at a battalion wire-cutting party. This shot also was not answered.

A few minutes later a member of the machine-gun platoon saw a man about to light a nail bomb. As the man prepared to throw, an order was given to shoot him. He fell and was dragged away.

Throughout the fighting that ensued, the Army fired only at identified targets — at attacking gunmen and bombers. At all times the soldiers obeyed their standing instructions to fire only in self-defence or in defence of others threatened.

The bulk of the marchers dispersed after reaching the barricades, on instructions from March Stewards. A hard core of hooligans remained behind and attacked three of the barriers. When the attacks reached an unacceptable level, the soldiers were ordered to pass through and arrest as many as possible. They were not, however, to conduct a running battle down the street.

As they went through the barriers the soldiers fired rubber bullets to clear the streets in front of them. They made 43 arrests.

The troops then came under indiscriminate firing from apartments and a car park. The following is the army's account of the return fire:

1. *Nail-bomber hit in the thigh.*
2. *Petrol-bomber, apparently killed in the car park.*
3. *A bomber in the flats, apparently killed.*
4. *Gunman with pistol behind barricade, shot and hit.*
5. *Nail-bomber shot and hit.*
6. *Another nail-bomber shot and hit.*
7. *Rubber bullet fired at gunman handling pistol.*
8. *Nail-bomber hit.*
9. *Three nail-bombers, all hit.*
10. *Two gunmen with pistols, one hit, one unhurt.*
11. *One sniper in a toilet window fired on and not hit.*
12. *Gunman with pistol in third floor flat shot and possibly hit.*
13. *Gunman with rifle on ground floor of flats shot and hit.*
14. *Gunman with rifle at barricade killed and body recovered.*

Lord Widgery concluded:

None of the deceased or wounded is proved to have been shot whilst handling a firearm or bomb. Some are wholly acquitted of complicity in such action; but there is a strong suspicion that some others had been firing weapons or handling bombs in the course of the afternoon and that yet others had been closely supporting them.[31]

That account and those conclusions are now wholly discredited. It is now obvious that nail bombs photographed on the body of Gerard Donaghy were planted there after his death, and that traces of firearms residue found on some of the deceased came from contact with soldiers and their vehicles.

Nevertheless, official recognition of the innocence of the victims of Bloody Sunday has been slow and grudging. In a letter addressed to Derry MP John Hume, dated 29 December 1992, Prime Minister John Major said:

> The Government made clear in 1974 that those who were killed on 'Bloody Sunday' should be regarded as innocent of any allegation that they were shot whilst handling firearms or explosives. I hope that the families of those who died will accept that assurance.

This is the closest the families of the dead have ever come to receiving any kind of apology or recognition of the justice of their case.

The Widgery Tribunal

Much detailed criticism has been levelled at Lord Widgery's report.[32] In particular, the report contained many internal inconsistencies; it failed to resolve the conflicting evidence and to give the evidence its due and proper weight; it failed to recognise the complete unreliability of the forensic evidence; it incorrectly applied the law on lethal force; and it failed to reach conclusions that were justified by the facts.

Lord Widgery voluntarily and quite unnecessarily limited his own terms of reference. On 1 February 1972, parliament adopted a resolution:

> That it is expedient that a Tribunal be established for inquiring into a definite matter of urgent public importance, namely the events on Sunday 30th January which led to loss of life in connection with the procession in Londonderry on that day.

This appeared to give Lord Widgery *carte blanche* to investigate anything that seemed relevant. However, at the preliminary hearing on 14 February 1972, he announced that the tribunal would be 'essentially a fact-finding exercise', which would avoid making moral judgments 'so that those who were concerned to form judgments would have a firm basis on which to reach their conclusions'.[33]

Stressing his desire for expedition which the report so graphically reflects, he said:

> I emphasised the narrowness of the confines of the Inquiry, the value of which would largely depend on its being conducted and concluded expeditiously. If considerations not directly relevant to the matters under review were allowed to take up time, the production of the Tribunal's Report would be delayed. The limits of the Inquiry in space were the streets of Londonderry in which the disturbances and the shooting took place; in time, the period beginning with the moment when the march first became involved in violence and ending with the deaths of the deceased and the conclusion of the affair.[34]

On 4 August 1995, a letter was discovered in the Public Record Office in London, headed 'CONFIDENTIAL'. It contained a minute of a meeting between Widgery, the Prime Minister (Edward Heath), and the Lord Chancellor (Lord Hailsham) on 1 February 1972, two days after Bloody Sunday (see Appendix 1). The minute was taken by Robert Armstrong, then Principal Private Secretary to the Prime Minister, who was later to become famous for coining the phrase 'economical with the truth' in the *Spycatcher* trial. These minutes revealed a top-level, confidential discussion between the Lord Chief Justice who was to chair the independent public inquiry and the Prime Minister, concerning the remit of the inquiry and the political context in which it would take place. Heath outlined a number of issues that he 'thought it right to draw to the Lord Chief Justice's attention', including that:

> It had to be remembered that we were in Northern Ireland fighting not only a military war but a propaganda war.[35]

The minute also revealed that Widgery himself proposed that:

> It would help if the Inquiry could be restricted to what actually happened in those few minutes when men were shot and killed; this would enable the Tribunal to confine evidence to eyewitnesses.

It also, of course, precluded any investigation of the planning that led up to the deployment of the Paras against civilian demonstrators.

Partly as a result of the publicity attendant upon this find, pressure was put on the government to release thirteen sets of documents classified in the Public Records Office as 'closed', three of them for thirty years and ten of them for seventy-five years. Twelve of them have recently been released and their impact is still under evaluation, but it is likely that they will shed further light on Bloody Sunday.

Indeed, two of these new documents have already done so. In a memorandum dated 10 March 1972 and signed by W. J. Smith, apparently a civil servant assisting Lord Widgery with the tribunal, it is reported that 700 or so statements have been received from the National Council for Civil Liberties — these were NICRA's eyewitness statements. It suggested that Lord Widgery, far from understanding the enormous voluntary effort that went into amassing the statements, believed that they had deliberately been delivered to him late in the day 'to cause him the maximum embarrassment'. The memorandum went on:

> I enquired whether the LCJ intended to make a public statement about the 700 statements. He said he did not, but agreed that he should deal with the matter in his report. He was quite prepared to say in the report that the Tribunal had taken note of all the statements, on the basis that they had all been inspected by Counsel for the Tribunal or the Treasury Solicitor's officers. Indeed, in the last resort he was prepared to read them all himself, though Mr Stocker [Counsel to the Tribunal] assured him that this was not necessary.[36]

The second document, also an internal memorandum, confirms that Widgery agreed to look at 'relevant statements' selected by staff, of which he was told there were ten. In his report, Widgery referred to the statements in these terms:

> The Northern Ireland Civil Rights Association collected a large number of statements from people in Londonderry said to be willing to give evidence. These statements reached me at an advanced stage in the Inquiry. Insofar as they contained new material, not traversing ground already familiar from evidence given before me, I have made use of them.[37]

Thus the eyewitness statements, collected with such care and recounted with such pain and terror, were never given due or proper consideration by the man bearing the highest judicial office in the land, who clearly regarded their perusal as of no great import and a task to be undertaken in the last resort. This book begins to redress that terrible injustice.

The Verdict of History

There are many questions still to be answered about Bloody Sunday.

Lord Widgery himself encapsulated the United Kingdom government's policy towards the demonstration on Bloody Sunday:

> To allow such a well publicised march to take place without opposition however would bring the law into disrepute and make control of future marches impossible.[38]

Speaking on *Remember Bloody Sunday*, transmitted on 28 January 1992, twenty years later, Colonel Derek Wilford said of the situation immediately after the shootings:

> Quite honestly I owned the Bogside in military terms. I occupied it.

That was, from the point of view of the security forces and the government, a marked improvement on the previous situation, when the Bogside and Creggan had been no-go areas, and many will conclude that it was the object of the exercise.

In another programme shown on the twentieth anniversary, Bishop Daly said:

> What really made Bloody Sunday so obscene was the fact that people afterwards at the highest level of British justice justified it and I think that is the real obscenity.[39]

Major Hubert O'Neill, the Coroner who held the much-delayed inquest on those who died on Bloody Sunday issued a statement on 21 August 1973 in which he said:

> This Sunday became known as Bloody Sunday and bloody it was. It was quite unnecessary. It strikes me that the Army ran amok that day and shot without thinking what they were doing. They were shooting innocent people. These people may have been taking part in a march that was banned but that does not justify the troops coming in and firing live rounds indiscriminately. I would say without hesitation that it was sheer, unadulterated murder. It was murder.[40]

New material is still emerging and awaits analysis, but it is already well beyond dispute that those who died were unarmed and that those who killed them have never been brought to justice. Even more serious is the fact that those who planned the operation that led to their deaths have never been held accountable, and no admission of responsibility has been made or apology offered by the British government.

The statements in this book bring to life vividly the horror and the heroism of Bloody Sunday. They are the implacable voice of history and of truth. They demand an unequivocal answer to all the outstanding questions about the tragic events of Bloody Sunday.

Jane Winter

Director, British Irish RIGHTS WATCH

London, October 1996

---

[1]   At the time of writing an uneasy peace prevails, the loyalist ceasefire holding but the IRA's no longer in place.

[2]   Fourth Report of the Special Rapporteur on States of Emergency, E/CN.4/Sub.2/1991/28/Rev.1, 21.11.1991.

[3]   Officially known as Londonderry.

[4]   *Insight, Times*, 23.4.1972.

[5]   *Irish News*, 28.1.1972.

[6]   *Secret History: Bloody Sunday*, broadcast by Channel 4 television on 22.1.1992.

[7]   *Sunday Times*, 23.4.1972.

[8]   *Irish Press*, 28.1.1972.

[9]   *Sunday Post*, 30.1.1972.

[10] Paragraphs 16–23.

[11] No. 2/72, dated 27.1.1972.

[12] The Northern Ireland police force.

[13] The executive of the British government.

[14] *Hansard*, col. 523, 19.4.1972.

[15] Paragraph 26.

[16] All quotes from the BBC television documentary, Inside Story: Remember Bloody Sunday, broadcast on 28.1.1992.

[17] Paragraph 94.

[18] Remember Bloody Sunday.

[19] Paragraph 24.

[20] Hansard, col. 293, 1.2.1972.

[21] Paragraphs 27–29.

[22] *Remember Bloody Sunday.*

[23] *Secret History.*

[24] Paragraph 97.

[25] Conclusion 10.

[26] Paragraph 65. A twelfth victim's clothing had been laundered by the hospital and could not be tested, and the thirteenth had been photographed, after he died, with nailbombs in his pockets.

[27] Paragraph 95.

[28] It is not suggested that the IRA were officially stewarding the march.

[29] In an interview during the *Remember Bloody Sunday* programme. The soldier was identified as Soldier H.

[30] Conclusion 11.

[31] Conclusion 10.

[32] See, for example, Justice Denied, produced by the International League for the Rights of Man; The Impaired Asset, by Bryan McMahon of University College, Cork, reproduced in Vol. VI No. 3 of Le Domain Humain, Autumn 1974; *The Murder of 13 Civilians by Soldiers of the British Army on 'Bloody Sunday', 30th January 1972*, Submission to the United Nations' Special Rapporteur on Summary and Arbitrary Executions, British Irish RIGHTS WATCH, 1994.

[33] Reported by Widgery himself at paragraph 2.

[34] Paragraph 3.

[35] HO 219/50, item 13, Public Record Office, London.

[36] HO 219/64, Public Record Office, London.

[37] Paragraph 8.

[38] Paragraph 16.

[39] *Secret History: Bloody Sunday*, broadcast by Channel 4 television on 22.1.1992.

[40] *Irish Times*, 22 August 1972.

INTRODUCTION

The objections which have been brought against a standing army, and they are many and weighty, and deserve to prevail, may also at last be brought against a standing government. The standing army is only an arm of the standing government. The government itself, which is only the mode which the people have chosen to execute their will, is equally liable to be abused and perverted before the people can act through it.

Henry David Thoreau, 1849

This introduction has been divided into two sections. The first part deals with the general background to the hundreds of civilian eye-witness statements, recorded in the immediate aftermath of Bloody Sunday. Over 100 of these statements are made available to the general public for the first time, in this book. They have been published to coincide with the twenty-fifth anniversary of Bloody Sunday. Very specifically, they have been published to give civilian eyewitnesses the opportunity, at last, to counteract what they believe was both calculated and deliberate misinformation disseminated throughout the world by the British Information Service in the immediate aftermath of Derry's darkest day.

The huge voluntary effort expended in collecting several hundred eyewitness accounts, was not appreciated by either Lord Widgery or the civil servants assigned to assist the Lord Chief Justice of England at his Tribunal of Inquiry. We now know from documents recently obtained from the Public Records Office, London, that Lord Widgery, on advice from his civil servants, did not afford these eyewitness accounts the respect and consideration they deserved.

The second part of this introduction deals with an extremely important body of evidence contained within these statements,

which Lord Widgery's Tribunal of Inquiry chose, for whatever reason, to ignore. It deals in particular with the role of British soldiers
positioned in the vicinity of the old Derry Walls. It became clear in
the course of reading the statements that soldiers positioned in this
quarter were also very actively engaged in firing live ammunition
into Derry's Bogside on Bloody Sunday. Reading the eyewitness
accounts has led very specifically to the consideration that three of
the Bloody Sunday deceased — William Nash, John Young and
Michael McDaid — may not, in fact, have been killed by soldiers of
1 Para. Medical and ballistic opinions obtained support the possibility of an army sniper operating in the vicinity of the Derry Walls.
Analysis of police and army radio transcripts, the Brigade Log Book
and recently released statements of soldiers who were positioned on
the Walls, lend weight to this growing suspicion.

I General Background

First Civil Rights March

I was a 15-year-old schoolboy when I witnessed Bloody Sunday. It
was, in fact, the first Civil Rights demonstration I had ever taken
part in. As I left my home in the Creggan Estate, that sunny Sunday
afternoon, little did I realise that I would find myself in the vortex
of a military operation which would leave thirteen civilians dead,
fourteen wounded, a community in deep shock and a nation in tur-
moil.

I was at the corner of Glenfada Park and the rubble barricade on
Rossville Street when the 1st Battalion Paratroop Regiment
advanced. I have very clear memories of the Paras fanning out across
the waste ground to the north of the Rossville Flats complex. I can
still vividly recall one Para, about 20 metres away, firing a rubber
bullet which bounced off the barricade. Another took up a firing
position at the corner of the first block of flats diagonally across the
road. Behind him I could see three paratroopers viciously raining the
butts of their rifles down upon a young man they had caught. Then
the unmistakable cracks of high-velocity SLR shooting started.

I distinctly remember a youth clutching his stomach a short distance away, his cry filling the air with despair and disbelief. For a

moment we were stunned. People ran to his aid while others, including myself, sheltered behind the barricade.

Suddenly the air was filled with what seemed like a thunderstorm of bullets. The barricade began to spit dust and it seemed to come from every direction. The wall above me burst. That's how it appeared as bits of mortar and red brick showered around us.

Our nervous systems reacted simultaneously, as though a high-voltage electric shock had been unleashed. Absolute panic ensued as we turned and ran. Doors and alleyways choked as waves of terrified adults and children tried to reach safety. 'Jesus! They're going to kill us!' 'Jesus, let me through!' 'For fuck sake, get out of the way!' 'Ah Jesus, they're after shooting a wee boy!'

I escaped through Glenfada Park but there are several minutes of that afternoon of which I have absolutely no memory. Five young men died at the barricade and four between Glenfada Park and Abbey Park. A further six were wounded in those locations. What I saw is somewhere hidden in my subconscious. All I know is that three-quarters of a mile later, as I ascended the steep steps between Eastway Road and Beechwood Avenue, a woman's voice brought me back to reality. 'What's happening, son?' she asked. 'Missus,' I answered, 'there must be at least six people dead.'

I don't know why I said that, but I did. Her face registered disbelief and I knew that she thought I was exaggerating. I didn't wait to explain or try to convince her. A primeval instinct had taken possession of me and I was, unashamedly, running home to safety.

I had never before experienced collective shock on this scale. The entire west bank of Derry was deeply traumatised by the attack. It must be something akin to the aftermath of an earthquake. I shall never forget the silence that descended upon my native town.

The rest of the evening was spent with my family listening to the radio and watching an old black and white television set for bulletin updates. The pictures of Fr Edward Daly from the Cathedral parish, waving a white bloodstained handkerchief, as he led a group of men carrying the limp body of a teenager, was very distressing. There was something surreal about watching television coverage of a bloodbath I had just escaped, at the bottom of the local hill. This was something that happened in Sharpeville or Soweto, but not in Derry. Certainly not to neighbours and friends.

As midnight approached, we realised that not six but thirteen people had been killed by the British Army, and a further fourteen wounded.

Sleep did not come easy that night. We knew that the angel of death had entered many homes in our estate and throughout Derry. Tomorrow, thirteen homes would have a brown box delivered, containing the packaged remains of loved ones with whom, just twenty-four hours before, they had sat down to their Sunday dinners. We were stunned and grieving.

Ramifications

The ramifications of this afternoon would be felt throughout the islands of Ireland and Britain for decades. The next three days would be not just a time of community mourning, but a national wake. In Dublin the British Embassy would be petrol bombed. In Westminster, Bernadette Devlin would create history and pan-demonium in the House of Commons when she would confront the lies of the British government by slapping the Home Secretary, Reginald Maudling. Our streets were too laden with grief to meet the news of Bernadette's action with loud cheers. But we quietly approved.

The next morning, my best friend, Shaunie McLaughlin, called for me at my home. We made our way back to the Bogside to retrace our steps.

I brought Shaunie to the gable end of Glenfada Park maisonettes on Rossville Street. I pointed to the large chunk torn from the wall by the bullet that had showered us with brick and mortar the previous afternoon. To this day I still point out that bullet hole to the many visitors I bring to my beloved Derry. I have always suspected that this particular bullet was fired from high ground, possibly the British Army gun post on top of the Embassy Court Building on Strand Road.

Shaunie and I stopped for a moment to look at the bloodstains around the barricade. Everywhere the silence was reverential as friends and neighbours stood and stared and tried to make sense of insanity.

From the barricade we looked up at a window on the third floor of the high-rise flats with six web-like bullet holes in it. The shots had been fired by a Para at a young Italian photographer, Fulvio

Grimaldi, who was trying to take pictures of three bodies lying on the barricade.

The scene I shall never forget, however, is that of finding the blue and white Civil Rights banner, carried at the front of the march the previous day, now lying on the ground a few yards from a telephone kiosk. It was soaked in the blood of 41-year-old Barney McGuigan, probably one of the most inoffensive and good-hearted people in Derry at that time.

In the days, weeks and months after the massacre, our entire community found itself gasping in disbelief as lies about the circumstances of Bloody Sunday were disseminated. The collusion in the web of deceit seemed to have no limit.

A quarter of a century later, the impact of that day is still vividly etched in our memories, and people throughout Ireland recall their deep sense of shock and outrage at the news. Several generations from now, when the wounded and witnesses are long gone, Bloody Sunday will still be remembered and its political impact on subsequent years, discussed.

NICRA/NCCL Statements

About two years ago, during a weekend visit to my home in Derry, I had a chance meeting with Tony Doherty, on Rossville Street in the city's famous Bogside. Tony's father, Patrick, was one of the thirteen people shot dead on Bloody Sunday. Tony said that he had come across a statement I had made to the Northern Ireland Civil Rights Association (NICRA) and the National Council for Civil Liberties (NCCL), a couple of days after the massacre in 1972.

I had completely forgotten ever having given such a statement, but Tony's reminder unleashed a flood of memories. I remembered retelling the story of my experience at the rubble barricade to my friend Shaunie and our mutual friend, Murray Gormley. I described how I had witnessed at least one person shot dead and had seen others falling from the hail of bullets that engulfed us.

Both Murray and Shaunie had listened intently. Murray was in his mid-twenties, wiser and more experienced. After I had finished my story, he told me that eyewitness statements were, at that moment, being taken in the Holy Child Primary School, Central Drive, Creggan, and that he felt I should, based on my experience, make a statement. I agreed. They both walked with me through the sad and sombre streets of the Creggan that evening, past the home of Jackie Duddy, and into the serious and industrious atmosphere of a school assembly hall.

A dozen or so desks were arranged across the floor of the hall, with people busily taking statements from all who had come to tell their story. I stood in a line of some twenty or thirty people, waiting to be called forward. Eventually, a young woman, Winifred R. Day, beckoned me to take the vacant seat before her.

Some twenty-three years later, my chance encounter with Tony Doherty made me curious about what I had written on that adolescent evening.

On my next visit to Derry, I made arrangements with the Pat Finucane Centre to see the statement. There was some initial difficulty in locating both my statement and several hundred others amongst a sea of documents related to justice, peace and human rights issues. Eventually a well-worn plastic supermarket bag, containing the statements, was retrieved from the top drawer of an old battered filing cabinet and handed to me.

I sat at a window, overlooking the junction of Westland Street and Laburnum Terrace, along which the anti-internment march had passed on that fateful day in 1972, and there, for several hours I was enthralled in what was to become the seed of this book. Almost all of the statements had an immediacy and a vividness that was compelling. One could sense, even after two decades, the quiet determination of the people of Derry to see justice done — to counteract the propaganda and lies being disseminated, in the immediate aftermath of Bloody Sunday, by the British Army and their government, through the British Information Service.

Reading the statements, I had a growing unease that sometime in the future, someone might find this old bag of photocopied paper and, not realising its historical importance, dump it. At that moment I began to think about having the statements published.

I was back in Derry for the Bloody Sunday lecture in late January 1996, at the Guildhall. After the lecture I discussed with my old schoolfriend, Gerry Duddy (brother of Jackie) and John Kelly (brother of Michael) and Micky McKinney (brother of Willie) the idea of publishing the eyewitness statements for the twenty-fifth anniversary. All agreed that it would be a valuable means of providing the public with an insight into the events of Bloody Sunday.

The Bloody Sunday Families

The next day, 27 January, I met Tony Doherty again, in Pilot's Row Community Centre, following a talk given by Eamon McCann. Tony was both enthusiastic and encouraging about the idea of publishing the statements. I was assured that I would have the support and good wishes of the families of those killed on Bloody Sunday. It was suggested that I contact Patricia Coyle, at Madden & Finucane Solicitors, Belfast, to have a set of statements made available to me.

In spring 1996 I collected a large box of documents from Patricia Coyle. In addition to copies of the eye-witness statements, the box also contained transcripts of army and police radio messages on the afternoon of Bloody Sunday; a copy of Lord Widgery's Tribunal Report; and an unpublished article by *Sunday Times* journalists Sayle and Humphry, dated 3 February 1972.

Original Intentions

My original intention was to publish all the eyewitness accounts. However, as my aim was to give the wider national and international community an important insight into the experience of ordinary Derry citizens on Bloody Sunday, I soon realised that such a publication would be impractical and too expensive to produce. In addition, many of the statements are repetitive, with scores of eyewitnesses describing the same incidents, albeit in their own individual ways.

By now, I had also realised that the copies of statements held at the Pat Finucane Centre were not the only ones available. Other sets were safely deposited in the Public Records Office in both London and Belfast, and with the law firm of Madden & Finucane, the solicitors currently representing the families of those killed on Bloody Sunday. Anyone wishing to read all eyewitness accounts can, therefore, do so.

I next contemplated the possibility of editing all of the statements into a book-size volume. I decided against this for two reasons. First, each statements is a complete historical document in its own right, telling the story of an individual or small group, as witnessed and experienced on that day. Second, if a statement had been edited, the reader might be left suspicious as to what had been left out, as well as what had been left in. Therefore, all civilian eyewitness statements that appear in this book are complete documents in themselves, as given by the named person(s) to NICRA/NCCL, in the hours and days after the massacre. Also included are thirteen statements prepared separately for the Widgery Tribunal of Inquiry. These are indicated by an asterisk in the Index of Eyewitnesses. The only editorial liberty taken was to clear up any misspellings or typing errors, solely for reader comfort.

The next task was to decide which statements to include in the book. To help me do this I asked John Scally to assist me. I considered it important to have someone to work with who had not been present on Bloody Sunday and who would, in as far as possible, remain objective and detached.

It was no easy task. An equally powerful second and third volume could be produced from the hundreds of statements that we were unable to include.

The interested reader is invited to consult all of the NICRA/NCCL statements, which can be viewed at the locations already mentioned. Those not published will, we know, serve only to complement and support those that are.

We are grateful to everyone who gave their written consent to their eyewitness statements being published. We have respected the wishes of those who asked that their accounts not be published. Some, for personal reasons, asked that only their Christian name or initials be published. With the help of the families of those killed on Bloody Sunday, we have endeavoured to locate the authors (or their next of kin) for permission to publish. Where this was not possible, mainly because of relocation and the passage of time, we have not published surnames in full. There were some eyewitnesses who did not give their age or occupation when making their statements.

In the course of reading the statements, John Scally and I decided to present them under chapter headings that attempt to follow the sequence of events, to highlight particular incidents, and to offer relevant insights from specific eyewitnesses such as march stewards, ex-servicemen, paramedics and the wounded. Each chapter also includes a short commentary in which I introduce the main emphasis of that chapter.

Before reading the statements the reader should be aware that each author (especially those in the open) endeavoured to recall incidents that were traumatic and life threatening, and that happened rapidly and as their survival instincts were triggered. In their statements, some authors cover several incidents. For example, as an eyewitness fled from the advancing paratroopers across the car park of Rossville Flats, through the alleyway that led to the forecourt and perhaps to shelter in a house at St Joseph's Place, he or she may have witnessed several incidents in a relatively short period of time. Sometimes the eyewitness may recall these incidents out of sequence and in a way that may appear to be at variance with another eyewitness. There is nothing unusual in this. Seldom, if ever, do two people remember the same incident in exactly the same way.

There is a remarkable consistency, however, concerning the controversial issue of civilian gunfire and bomb throwing. What gunfire there was from the civilian side was very little and certainly did not constitute, as the government and army claimed, 'a fusillade of bombs and bullets'. None of those killed or wounded by the army was seen by any eyewitness to be in possession of a firearm or nail bomb. Indeed, it was to counteract the propaganda and lies of the British Information Service that so many people came forward to give their testimonies. As a consequence, we are left with invaluable primary-source historical documents for one of the watershed events of the so-called 'Troubles'.

The Downing Street Meeting

During the course of working on this book, I believe we have begun to witness the rapid unravelling of the official position on Bloody Sunday.

Full credit must be given to Jane Winter, Director of British Irish Rights Watch, who first discovered the Confidential Downing Street Minutes (Appendix 1) of the meeting between Prime Minister Edward Heath, Lord Chancellor Hailsham and the Lord Chief Justice of England, Lord Widgery. The meeting was held on the evening of 1 February 1972, shortly after the British government announced its intention to hold a Tribunal of Inquiry into the Derry killings.

Lord Widgery, who held the highest judicial office in the United Kingdom, was presented as a man of impeccable integrity and scrupulous impartiality. Given his high-ranking military background we should have known better. Today, the people of Derry would be less innocent and naïve. But even after the killings on Bloody Sunday, there were still people in our community who were prepared to trust the Establishment.

Had we known then the nature and content of that meeting between Lord Widgery and Prime Minister Heath, we would not have been shocked by his subsequent laundering of the truth and his determination to shield and protect military personnel who had participated in the murder of unarmed civilians. From the moment he agreed to accept his government's invitation to head the Tribunal of Inquiry, the civilian community of Derry were, as he referred to them during this meeting, 'the other side'. Furthermore, he seemed to take to heart Prime Minister Heath's extraordinary understanding of the British role in Northern Ireland — that 'we [are] in Northern Ireland fighting not only a military war but a propaganda war'.

Read in the context of the Downing Street meeting and in the light of new and invaluable information that has recently been released by the Public Records Office, London, the *Widgery Report*, published on 18 April 1972, is nothing short of a convoluted propaganda document. History has begun to judge the role of the Lord Chief Justice of England severely. It will continue to do so until the truth of what actually happened in Derry on Bloody Sunday is acknowledged by the government responsible and until the *Widgery Report* is publicly repudiated in its entirety.

The Impact of Bloody Sunday

During a visit to Derry on 27 June 1996 by Prince Charles, Colonel-in-Chief of the Parachute Regiment, the subject of Bloody Sunday was inevitably raised. Councillor Gregory Campbell, a member of Ian Paisley's Democratic Unionist Party, is quoted in the *Derry Journal* (28 June 1996) as describing it as 'a controversial subject which most people would regard as being somewhat distant, if not irrelevant'.

The truth is that Bloody Sunday has cast a long shadow over the past two and a half decades. Before then the IRA had minimal support within the wider nationalist community in the North of Ireland. Thereafter, the floodgates opened, attitudes hardened and the war intensified. Bloody Sunday is not just the day on which thirteen unarmed civilians died in Derry's Bogside, it is also the day when the British Army effectively killed the Northern Ireland Civil Rights Association.

The anger of all Ireland was symbolised in the torching of the British Embassy in Dublin. A few months later, Stormont fell, with Westminster assuming responsibility for the governance of the Province. Thereafter the people of the six counties that constitute 'Northern Ireland' were subjected to a roller coaster of political initiatives, which seemed to rise and fall with the regularity of the seasons.

The publication of the *Widgery Report* the following April had an equally damaging effect. It caused much anger in Derry. It became clear that people's good faith in the British political and legal system had been betrayed. Our education in the politics of collusion was developing fast. As each piece of the jig-saw began to fall into place, a very dangerous alienation from the institutions of so-called Law and Order accelerated rapidly.

Bloody Sunday, Widgery and his political masters created a climate in which violent opposition to the British presence in Ireland once again became more acceptable. The incident and its legal arbitrator helped to create a political vacuum in which military minds (on all sides) held sway. I have no doubt that Bloody Sunday unleashed a wave of violence across the Province, which resulted in the death of many other innocent people.

It is no coincidence that more people died during the following six months (256) than during the previous three years of the 'Troubles' (210). It is no coincidence that more people died during the following eleven months of 1972 than during any other year of the conflict. Between 1 February and 30 December 1972, 445 deaths occurred. Adding these deaths to the toll for the following four years — 1973 (252); 1974 (294); 1975 (257); and 1976 (295) — the total of 1,543 deaths represents 47 per cent of all deaths (3,285) that occurred in the twenty-five years between 1969 and the end of 1993. Republican violence was responsible for 52 per cent of all deaths (801) during that period.[1]

Widgery and the Eyewitness Statements

As Jane Winter's Preface highlights, the attitude of Lord Widgery and his officials towards the huge volume of eyewitness statements presented to the Tribunal of Inquiry is extraordinary.

Given the seriousness of the incident under inquiry, one wonders why the Lord Chief Justice was in such a hurry to reach his conclusions without giving due weight to all available evidence. The importance of these eye-witness accounts and the consequential clues that they contained, warranted more respect and time. If this meant prolonging his Inquiry by a few more days or weeks, so what? In the end, Widgery, under direction from various civil servants, considered the hundreds of civilian statements to be of little relevance and did not read them (see Appendix 2).

Widgery deals with the issue of the eyewitness statements in his final report as follows:

> The Northern Ireland Civil Rights Association collected a large number of statements from people in Londonderry said to be willing to give evidence. These statements reached me at an advanced stage in the Inquiry. In so far as they contained new material, not traversing ground already familiar from evidence given before me, I have made use of them (paragraph 8).

I am a layman and have not been trained in legal science. However, it became very clear to me in reading those statements almost a quarter of a century after the event that they did indeed contain new material. Clues hidden within almost fifty of those statements, supported now by recently released documents from the Public Records Office in London, have led me to the conclusion that three of the thirteen people killed on Bloody Sunday, may not, in fact, have been shot by 1 Para in the vicinity of Rossville Street.

I believe that the statements, allied to the post-mortem examinations, inquest reports and forensic and ballistic opinion, raise serious doubts concerning who actually shot John Young, Michael McDaid and William Nash. I am increasingly of the opinion that these three young men (all of whom fell close to one another at the rubble barricade on Rossville Street) may have been shot by an army sniper operating in the vicinity of the Derry Walls. I shall deal with these important and crucial issues in the second part of this introduction.

Basic justice and humanity demands that the many questions around Bloody Sunday be resolved quickly. In their epilogue to this book, the families of those killed say that neither the dead nor the living can rest easily while the injustice remains. Because of the enormity of the crime committed and the obscenity of people in high places still reluctant to confront the truth, the families are left in a kind of perpetual wake. While they have buried the bodies, they are unable and unwilling to let go because the verdict of Lord Widgery has made it impossible for them to do so.

After twenty-five years, the people of Derry have re-covered sufficiently from the trauma of Bloody Sunday to join, once again, with the families of those who were killed. We are wiser and more experienced now and we have many friends around the world. While the British government and media might like to characterise Bloody Sunday as a narrow Republican propaganda issue, the truth is that it will increasingly rank as a major inter-national human rights question, which must be resolved.

Political Bereavement

The people of Derry and especially the families of those who died on that day, would not wish to minimise the collective suffering of other cities and families who have also experienced the tragedy of political bereavement. Dublin, Belfast, Enniskillen, Birmingham, Guildford and Greysteel, immediately bring to mind shocking images of devastation and grief, which are only part of a long litany of sorrow and shame.

Neither I, nor the families of those who were killed on Bloody Sunday, would wish the painful memories of that day to be used by any individual or group as an excuse or justification for further killings. Too many innocent human beings have already lost their lives. Too many human beings have been injured and maimed. Too many families, on all sides, have had to cope with the eternal emptiness of places in the home which will never again be filled by a loved one.

II The Derry Walls

The nature of this book changed considerably in the course of its preparation. During the process of reading hundreds of eyewitness testimonies, a fact began to emerge which was totally ignored by Lord Widgery in his *Tribunal of Inquiry Report*: the fact that the British Army, in addition to firing live ammunition at ground level in the vicinity of Rossville Street, was also firing live ammunition from the vicinity of the Derry Walls.

Curiously, as I began to encounter this fact, my mind was, at first, doubting the accuracy of the eyewitness statements — perhaps because for almost twenty-five years our attention had been rigidly focused on the brutality and murderous aggression of 1 Para who entered the Bogside. As statement after statement continued to insist that gunfire was coming from the Walls, my mind began to resist the idea that the army might be shooting from this quarter to wound or kill. I was assuming that such gunfire was intended to cut off the main body of demonstrators at Free Derry Corner from those caught in the Para operation around the Rossville Flats.

I could find no mention of army fire from the Derry Walls anywhere in Lord Widgery's *Tribunal Report*. He gave details of 108 rounds expended by 1 Para during their operation, and nothing else.

My concerns deepened during a meeting with the director of British Irish Rights Watch, Jane Winter, on 22 October 1996, at her office in London. I raised the issue of army firing from the Walls, as found in the statements. Jane, probably the most informed international human rights expert on the circumstances surrounding Bloody Sunday, looked at me in surprise and said, 'I never knew that!' I then pulled out several of the statements which appear in Chapter 7 and read extracts from them.

Later that afternoon, at Carlton Television, we raised this point with journalist John Pilger, whose support we were trying to enlist for an anniversary documentary. Also present at the meeting were Kay Duddy (sister of Jackie Duddy), Geraldine Doherty (niece of Gerard Donaghy) and Gerry McColgan, an independent documentary film producer.

As we flew home that evening, I took from my briefcase a copy of Dr Raymond McClean's excellent book *The Road to Bloody Sunday*, and passed it to Gerry. He drew my attention to appendix F, 'post-mortem examinations carried out at Altnagelvin Hospital on 31 January 1972'. Dr McClean had attended these as the medical representative of the Catholic Primate, Cardinal Conway. Gerry had heard me speak about my growing suspicions concerning the role of the army on the Walls. He pointed to Case 2: Michael McDaid, where the trajectory of the bullet that hit him was stated to have been 'From left to right and travelling downward'. Case 3: John Young, again noted the trajectory of the bullet that killed him as 'From the front, travelling backward and downward'.

A New Direction

I had read Dr McClean's post-mortem notes on at least two other occasions. My mind had simply imagined a standing Para, aiming his rifle from shoulder height and firing downwards at people trying to shelter on or near to the ground. Now, however, my thoughts were being directed in a new and previously unexplored direction.

In studying the reports, very quickly a pattern emerged that appeared too consistent to be random. Five of the thirteen people shot dead had wounds with downward trajectories. All five were at, or near, the rubble barricade in Rossville Street, which was partially visible from the Derry Walls. For the first time I began to consider the very real possibility of a shoot-to-kill strategy in operation also on the Walls.

When I arrived home I immediately phoned Dr McClean to discuss my suspicions. His initial reaction was encouraging. As always, though, he was professional, advising that this should be treated initially as a theory and, as such, subjected to rigorous analysis.

Early next morning I phoned Dublin Solicitor Garrett Sheehan, a friend, for a legal opinion. Garrett confirmed my growing belief that if it were possible to get a forensic or ballistic expert to support this theory, then this, coupled with the eyewitness accounts, could very seriously undermine the findings and conclusions of the Widgery Tribunal.

I next found an illustration of the human body in a medical book and placed beside it a pencil, ruler and protractor. I spoke with someone in the engineers' Department at Derry City Council. I needed to ascertain the angle of elevation between Rossville Street and the Derry Walls, allowing for a variation in angles as one moved from left to right. The angle is approximately 9 degrees, rising to 15 degrees, taking into consideration the buildings behind. With this information I returned to the medical book and carefully began to plot the entry and exit wounds in each of the five deceased.

In the case of Hugh Gilmore, the angle of trajectory was not convincing. Furthermore, the Derry Walls were not visible from where he was shot. I noted with interest, however, Lord Widgery's determination to discount any suggestion that he had been shot while running in the direction of Free Derry Corner (paragraph 71).

In the case of Michael Kelly, Widgery was again at pains to discount any suggestions that he had his back to the Paras and was running in the direction of Free Derry. He writes:

> Kelly was shot while standing at the Rossville Street barricade in circumstances similar to those already discussed in the cases of Young, Nash and McDaid. The bullet entered his abdomen from the front which disposes of a suggestion in the evidence that he was running away at the time (paragraph 80).

Dr McClean took my phone call seriously and, four or five days later, we spoke again. During a weekend break in Donegal he had spent hours examining all available evidence and drawing diagrams. He said that he had set out to disprove my theory and had ended up increasingly convinced that there were grounds for my suspicions, especially regarding John Young, William Nash and Michael McDaid.

I looked at Widgery again, specifically in relation to the three deceased whose bodies lay on the barricade. Young, he wrote, 'was one of the three who were shot at the Rossville Street barricade by one of a cluster of 10 to 12 shots' fired from soldiers at Kells Walk (paragraph 75). Lord Widgery again appeared anxious to have us believe that John Young was facing the 'right' way: 'the track of the bullet suggests that he was facing the soldiers at the time.' 'But what soldiers?' I was asking myself.

Widgery goes on to link closely the shooting of McDaid and Nash to that of Young. In the same paragraph he states that Soldiers P, J, U, C, K, L and M, 'fired from the Kells Walk area at men who were using firearms or throwing missiles from the barricade.'

Presumably Lord Widgery is now assuming that those reading his report will have a clear picture of the three deceased facing the Paras down Rossville Street. He asserts 'the three men were shot almost simultaneously (paragraph 78). McDaid's bullet 'struck him in the front in the left cheek', and in the case of William Nash 'the bullet entered his chest from the front'.

Serious Allegations

It is significant, I believe, that Lord Widgery seeks to raise the most serious allegations against Young, Nash and McDaid collectively:

> When [Young's] case is considered in conjunction with those of Nash and McDaid and regard is had to the soldiers' evidence about civilians firing from the barricade, a very strong suspicion is raised that one or more of Young, Nash and McDaid was using a firearm. No weapon was found but there was sufficient opportunity for this to be removed by others (paragraph 76).

The truth is that any who dared to go near these young men — either to retrieve fictional guns or, more importantly, to administer medical and spiritual assistance — were in mortal danger of being shot themselves.

The assertion of firearms at the barricade by Widgery also flew in the face of scores of civilian eyewitness accounts, as well as that of the Assistant Chief Constable of Renfrew and Bute, Mr Robert Campbell, who was an observer on the Derry Walls. All testified that they saw no weapons. Remarkably, according to the *Sunday Times Insight* team, Lieutenant Colonel Derek Wilford of the Paras did not see any either.[2]

Eyewitness

There is one important account which deserves careful study regarding the innocence of the deceased and the crucial issue of shooting from the Derry Walls.

Denis McLaughlin was at the barricade:

> I saw a man dressed in a brown suit and with black hair, running over the loose stones of the barricade towards Free Derry Corner. As I caught sight of him he fell back and rolled over on his mouth and nose on the Free Derry side of the barricade. . . .

McLaughlin's statement details a very traumatic and horrific experience. The three deceased all fell on top of or close to him. His testimony also contains the following statement:

> People over at the Flats were calling out and roaring, 'There's men dead', meaning us. I also heard the voice of someone saying they were shooting from Derry's Walls.

The man whom McLaughlin describes as 'dressed in a brown suit and with black hair' was William Nash. Nash, according to McLaughlin, was facing Free Derry Corner and, at the time, running away from the advancing Paras. When shot, he fell back onto the barricade.

The trajectory line of the bullet was from the front, travelling backward and downward. Since William Nash, according to McLaughlin, was running away from the Paras, he could only have been shot from the front and from above. The angle of the entry and exit wound is steep and would appear to be consistent with having been shot from an elevated position, such as the vicinity of the Derry Walls.

William Nash was dressed in the suit that he had worn to his brother John's wedding the previous day. Hardly the regalia of a 'terrorist'.

Inquest Report

The Inquest Reports detailing the trajectory of the bullets which caused the death of Young, Nash and McDaid, are uncannily similar. Dr John R. Press, who carried out all post-mortem examinations at Altnagelvin Hospital on 31 January 1972, stated the following:

> William Nash: A probe inserted into the wound passed downwards and backwards at an angle of 45 degrees to the horizontal plane and an inclination backwards of 40 degrees but no deviation to right or left.
>
> If he were erect at the time he was shot then the bullet must have come from in front and slightly above him.

William Nash was hit in the right upper chest between the third and fourth ribs, and 4.5 cm to the right of the mid line. The exit wound was below the right twelfth rib at the level of the 2nd lumbar vertebra and 4.5 cm to the right of the mid line (Dr R. McClean).

> *Michael McDaid: A probe inserted into the wound extended down-*
> *wards at about 45 degrees to the horizontal plane, with an inclina-*
> *tion backwards of about 30 degrees and a deviation of about 25*
> *degrees to the right.*
> *If he were erect at the time he was shot then the bullet must have*
> *come from above, to his left and slightly in front of him.*

Michael McDaid was hit on the left cheek. The exit wound was
below the right scapula (Dr R. McClean).

> *John Young: A probe inserted into the wound extended downwards*
> *at an angle of about 45 degrees to the horizontal and backwards at*
> *an angle of about 40 degrees with a slight deviation of about 10 to*
> *15 degrees to the right.*
> *If he were erect at the time he was shot then the bullet must have*
> *come from above and slightly in front of him.*

John Young was hit at the inner angle of the left eye. The exit wound
was below the left scapula at the level of the seventh rib (Dr R.
McClean).

I may be completely wrong but, as a lay person, it seems to me
highly unlikely that a cluster of ten to twelve bullets, fired from any
one of seven soldiers (as Lord Widgery would have us believe), all
of varying heights, in varying firing positions and all at ground level,
could have produced such remarkably similar 45-degree downward
trajectories.

I refer the reader to Appendix 3 for the medical opinion of Dr
Raymond McClean.

A Can of Worms

During a visit to the United States in November 1996, I had the
opportunity to meet Mr Robert J. Breglio, an independent ballistics
consultant, who had spent over twenty-five years working as a
detective in the New York City Police Department's ballistic squad.
I was referred to Mr Breglio through the good offices of
Assemblyman Joseph Crowley (Queens), and Mr Frank Bolz, New
York City's chief hostage negotiator. Bolz recommended Breglio
because of his reputation and also because he did not have a strong
Irish background.

I sat with Mr Breglio for several hours, during which he examined all the documents I could carry. At one point he looked at me

across the table and said, 'You realise you are opening up a can of worms?'

'Mr Breglio,' I replied, 'Bloody Sunday is a can of worms!'

Breglio proffered the opinion that William Nash, Michael McDaid and John Young were likely hit by a single marksman, using a telescopic lens. He was anxious, however, to emphasise that this could be considered only an opinion.

Before parting, Mr Breglio dictated the following statement, which he signed:

> On 23 November 1996, at the Unicorn Diner, Staten Island, I had a conversation with Don Mullan regarding the incident known as Bloody Sunday, which occurred on 30 January 1972, in Derry City, Ireland.
>
> After examination of photographs and statements and inquest reports regarding this incident, in my opinion the angles of trajectory of bullet wounds of three deceased named: William Nash, John Young and Michael McDaid, originated from an area in the vicinity of the Derry Walls and from a height that would inflict wounds of this angle trajectory.

Taking the Staten Island Ferry back to Manhattan that evening, the eyewitness testimony of Michael McCallion, written on the evening of Bloody Sunday, haunted me as I looked across at the floodlit statue of Lady Liberty:

> I have witnessed this as God is my judge and I say it was cold-blooded murder. . . . It was deliberate murder and this I will swear on a stack of bibles as high as the Statue of Liberty and may God be my judge on this. It is the gospel truth.

On 21 August 1973, Major Hubert O'Neill, the Bloody Sunday Inquest Coroner, stunned the gallery with a conclusion which echoed that of Michael McCallion:

> I would say without hesitation that it was sheer, unadulterated murder. It was murder.

The Army and the Walls

On 23 October 1996 I had written to Patricia Coyle, Madden & Finucane Solicitors, expressing my growing suspicion concerning the role of the British Army operating on the Derry Walls. Before leaving for the US on 8 November, I called Patricia, who indicated that the questions I was raising were certainly worth asking. She informed me that Madden & Finucane had just recently received from the Public Records Office, London, statements made by both the Paras and other regiments in the immediate aftermath of Bloody Sunday. She said that there were statements from soldiers on the Derry Walls which would substantiate what I was saying. She also encouraged me to read the transcripts of the police and army radio messages again.

The radio transcripts were revealing: not only were the soldiers on the walls clearly very active, but they were also claiming hits. For example, the following message was radioed by the army just before 4.11 p.m.:

Army: *Hello Zero and 90 Alpha and 76 this is 54 Alpha we have just had four shots fired at our call sign Correct 21 on the wall. Two high velocity rounds were returned, over.*

HQ: *Zero out.*

Relevant messages from both army and police radio transcripts, together with a section from the log book of the headquarters of the 8th Infantry Brigade, detailing their activities on Bloody Sunday, are reproduced in Appendix 6.

A reading of the full radio transcripts of police and army messages is also revealing on another crucial point. Nowhere in the transcripts is there any report of nail-bomb or petrol-bomb explosions.

It should be noted that in addition to these radio messages, which the army and police knew would be monitored and recorded, they had also established a secret means of passing information. For example, the following message was relayed while 1 Para was still actively engaged in the Bogside:

Army: *65, we have been telling you on other means, the secure means, in fact we have just given you a sit. [situation] rep. [report] of exactly what we are doing, over.*

HQ: *Zero Roger (page 28).*

So what exactly was 1 Para doing? Are there any recordings or transcripts of the 'secure means'? I would suggest that 'what exactly' the Paras were doing is described quite vividly in the over 100 civilian eyewitness statements contained in this book.

Testimony of Soldiers on the Walls

On 26 November 1996, I received copies of recently disclosed statements from four soldiers positioned on Derry's Walls: Soldier 227; Soldier 030; Soldier 012 and Soldier 156.

Soldier 227 stated:

> I am a lieutenant serving with 22 Lt AD Regiment RA in Londonderry. I have been here since November 1971. . . .

2. On 30 January at about 12.30 I commenced duty in command of Charlie OP on the city wall between the Royal Bastion and the platform. I was armed with an SLR with 10 rounds of ammunition. I had a radio and my duty was to report on my regimental note anything of significance. Apart from observation two men were engaged in sniping duties and were to engage any targets e.g. men armed with weapons and likely to use them.

3. From the OP we could see through the opening between blocks 2 and 3 of the Rossville Flats, over the waste ground as far as the junction of William Street and Rossville Street. We could see the courtyard between block 2 and Joseph Place including the telephone box at the end of block 1. Across the road we could see the far side of the barricade and the courtyard of Glenfada Park through the opening.

4. I heard the paratroops were coming, over the radio, and saw the arrest operation start on the waste ground. I heard at this time two distinct bursts of automatic fire, in my opinion from a Thompson SMG. The sound appeared to come from the area of Glenfada Park. I then heard an explosion on the William Street side of Rossville Flats which sounded like a nail bomb. I then heard three deliberate shots from an SLR.

5. At the sound of the shots a crowd of about 100 [200] at the barricade turned and ran towards Free Derry Corner. I saw two bodies left on the far side of the barricade. I did not see any of those at the barricade armed. If they had been carrying weapons I think I would have seen them. . . .

Soldier 227's statements continues for another ten paragraphs. However, there are a number of important pieces of information revealed in the lines above.

He confirms that the army on the walls had sight of the far side of the rubble barricade, which ran across Rossville Street from Glenfada. He states that he heard two distinct bursts of machine-gun fire, which appeared to come from the area of Glenfada Park. Soldier 227 then claims to have heard what sounded like a nail-bomb explosion. As the radio operator of Charlie OP, he did not report this. He then states that he heard 'three *deliberate* [emphasis added] shots from an SLR'. After these shots the crowd turned and ran towards Free Derry Corner. He could see two bodies left on the far side of the barricade. He states very clearly that he did not see any of those at the barricade armed: 'If they had been carrying weapons I think I would have seen them.' At no point in his statement does Soldier 227 make any reference to his position coming under fire or of fire being returned (which the radio transcripts record). In paragraph 10, Soldier 227 reveals that he was monitoring events through a telescopic rifle sight.

Soldier 030 was a gunner in the 22nd Lt AD Rgt Royal Artillery, positioned at the platform on the City Wall, five yards from a soldier named as 001. His statement is interesting in that he claims to have seen a youth with 'dark well kept hair', wearing a brown jacket and faded blue jeans, firing a pistol in the gap between blocks 2 and 3 of Rossville Flats. According to Soldier 030, the youth was 75 yards away.

3. . . . *I could not shoot him as there was a crowd of about 10 to 15 people gathered round him.*

He then claims to have heard a burst of 'low-velocity automatic fire which to my mind came from a Thompson SMG'. The direction and location of this firing was pointed out to him by Soldier 001 as '. . . a high wooden fence on the far left-hand corner of Glenfada Park in the block nearest Columbcille Court which has trees in the centre of a carpark'. He then heard more automatic fire from this direction and saw muzzle flashes coming from the top of the fence.

I started to aim my SLR at this position. Just at that moment a soldier came into my view. He stopped and knelt down. . . . He aimed his SLR in the direction where I had seen the muzzle flashes from the top of the fence and fired 3 rounds. I could not see behind the fence to tell whether anyone had been hit.

At no point in his statement does Soldier 030 make any reference to his position on the Derry Walls coming under attack. Nor, interestingly, as recorded in the radio transcripts, does he admit to army fire from the Walls. He is most anxious, however, to establish that it was the low-velocity shots (i.e. civilian gunfire) that first caused the crowd to panic:

8. *I would like to add that it was after the first low-velocity fire I have described above that the crowd in the Rossville Flats area seemed to panic and started to disperse everywhere.*

Soldier 012 was a gunner with 22nd Lt AD Regiment Royal Artillery. He was positioned to the left of Charlie OP and to the right of Walker's Monument, with binoculars. His statement is interesting in that he too makes no reference to army positions on the Walls coming under attack, nor to the army firing from that quarter.

Soldier 012 claims to have seen a large group of youths at about 4.15 p.m. running from Free Derry Corner towards the barricade on Rossville Street:

> *When they reached the barricade I could [see] that one of the youths was holding a pistol. There is no doubt in [my] mind. Then I heard a burst of low-velocity automatic fire which sounded to me like a Thompson coming from the direction of Columbcille Court or Glenfada Park. Immediately after this the youths who were at the barricade turned and ran back down Rossville Street towards Free Derry Corner but ran off up side streets in all directions. I did not see the youth with the pistol again. At the same time I heard two high velocity shots from the area of Columbcille Court and Glenfada Park and I looked in the direction of Free Derry Corner; the people at the meeting were lying flat on the ground. I also heard several loud shots from an SLR coming from further up Rossville Street towards William Street. . . .*

In this paragraph, Soldier 012 attempts to establish the presence of three gunmen in the general vicinity of Glenfada and the barricade. He does not say whether or not the youth he claims to have seen at the barricade, holding a pistol, fired it or not. However, it is only after the other two gunmen fired that he heard 'several loud shots from an SLR coming from further up Rossville Street towards William Street'. His purpose, of course, is to establish that it was only after being fired upon that the army returned fire. Again, I was at the precise location where he claims to have heard shooting. I am very clear that the shooting was coming towards my position and not from it.

The statement of Soldier 156 is most interesting.

1. *I am a private soldier attached to 22 Lt AD Rgt Royal Artillery and on the 30 January 1972 I was a member of a 2 man patrol situated on the Londonderry City Wall at the Double Bastions by Roaring Meg. Our task was to keep observation on the civil rights procession. . . . I would say the size of the march was about 20,000. . . .*

2. *At about 4.15 I was observing Rossville Street as there was noise coming from that direction and then I heard 2 bullets strike the City Wall below me and since on previous occasions (but not on the 30 January) shots had been fired from the direction of St Columb's Wells which is directly in front of where I was, I presumed this was where the shots had come from. At about 4.25 a crowd had gathered at Free Derry Corner but there were a lot of people moving down Rossville Street and a lot more waiting at the flats. I then heard the sound of automatic fire which sounded like a Thompson SMG come from the direction of Rossville Flats and at the same time I saw two soldiers who were in Rossville Street run to cover behind a wall at the south end of Glenfada Park. All those people who were in Fahan Street either fell flat on the ground or ran to cover. At that particular time I did not hear any fire being returned by the soldiers. A few seconds later I heard baton rounds and CS gas being fired from the direction of Rossville Flats and I could only see the face of Block 2 of the flats and the south side of the other two blocks so I could not see what was happening.*

3. *About 10 minutes later a further two shots were fired at my location and although I could not say for certain where these shots had come from I believe them to have come from the direction of St Columb's Wells. The shots went overhead. An army sniper who was situated on my left about 15 yards away in the attic of a derelict house outside the City Walls returned three shots but I did not see where his shots had gone and there was no return fire. A few minutes afterwards I heard some more machine gun fire and single mixed velocity shots being fired from the Rossville Flats direction but my view of where the fire was coming from was obscured and I was too far away to identify who it was who was firing or where exactly the shots had come from.*

This testimony is particularly interesting. To begin with, timings are askew. The Paras had begun their advance just before 4.10 p.m. By 4.25 p.m., their operation was half over.

To suggest that his position was fired upon at 4.15 p.m. from, presumably, St Columb's Wells, while at the same time the crowd continued to gather for the Civil Rights meeting at Free Derry Corner is fantasy.

It is clear from the eyewitness testimonies that up to the point of the Para incursions, the crowd at Free Derry Corner was relaxed. If gunmen had been operating in the vicinity of St Columb's Wells, which was literally around the corner, the mood of the crowd would have been very different. Indeed, ten minutes later there wouldn't have been a crowd at Free Derry Corner.

Once again, Soldier 156 confirms that shooting was coming from the vicinity of the Walls. Most revealing of all is the fact that the army had snipers operating in the attic of derelict buildings just outside the old City Walls.

Very probably, this included derelict buildings in a street called Nailor's Row, which was built adjacent to the Walls. It once ran from the Double Bastion to the far end of the Royal Bastion, just below the impressive 90-foot high Doric column of Governor Walker. The houses on Nailor's Row, also had a commanding view of the Bogside. In fact, Nailor's Row can be seen in one of the photographs (first page in the second picture section of this book), high above the barricade through which an ambulance is passing. In the foreground of the picture is quite possibly the Saracen which had already collected the bodies of William Nash, Michael McDaid and John Young.

Typically, 156 heard civilian gunfire first, before there was any suggestion of the army replying. Indeed, he would have us believe that the Paras responded to a Thompson submachine gun by firing rubber bullets and CS gas. It should be noted that, once the Paras began their incursion into the Rossville Street area, at no stage did they fire CS gas.

The army sniper operating in the attic of one of the derelict houses fired, according to 156, three shots, although he could not see where the shots had gone. Might these have been the three 'deliberate' shots heard by Soldier 227?

The Framing of John Young, William Nash and Michael McDaid

There is an unsolved mystery about the killings of John Young, William Nash and Michael McDaid — who killed them and from where?

There is also something curious and unsettling about their removals from the Rossville Street barricade.

All three lay dead and dying on the barricade for fifteen to twenty minutes. No one — absolutely no one, including parents, pastors and paramedics — was allowed to go near them. Alexander Nash, for example, on seeing the fallen body of his son, William, did what any father would do, and ran to his aid. He was shot and lay wounded during that interminable period.

At the Coroners Inquest he stated the following:

> I went into Glenfada Park and I heard shooting. I turned back to Rossville Street and as I turned I saw three bodies at a wee barricade across Rossville Street. I identified one of the bodies as that of my son, William Noel Nash. I ran across and put my hand up to stop the shooting so that I could lift my son out of the way. I could see that he was dead. As I was trying to stop the shooting bullets were striking the barricade and I received two bullet wounds. I saw the army put the three bodies in a Saracen and I was left to go to the hospital by ambulance.

At approximately 4.30 p.m. a Saracen armoured vehicle slowly advanced towards the barricade and all three bodies were manhandled by Paras and dumped 'like refuse' into the Saracen.

There were at least four other bodies within sight of the Paras who collected Young, Nash and McDaid from the barricade. While collecting their bodies the Paras would have had sight of Paddy Doherty, Bernard McGuigan and Hugh Gilmore in the forecourt of the Rossville Flats, and Jim Wray and others in Glenfada. They all lay within a 30-yard radius. All of these, as well as Alexander Nash who was beside the bodies at the barricade, were ignored. Why?

The bodies of John Young, Michael McDaid and William Nash were not taken to Altnagelvin Hospital by the British Army until after 6 p.m. Fr John Irwin, who had managed through persistence to give the Last Rites to the three bodies in the Saracen, saw them later delivered to the hospital mortuary at 6.15 p.m. There are questions concerning whether or not young McDaid was actually dead when thrown into the Saracen. There are questions as to why the army took so long to bring these bodies to the hospital and what they were doing with them in the meantime.

The forensic evidence used against Young, Nash and McDaid was very positive. There probably wasn't a hair on their head which wasn't contaminated. It certainly proved that they were in very close proximity to people using guns — the Paras.

For almost a quarter of a century many in Derry have been nursing an anger over the way these innocent young men, and others, were coldly and very deliberately framed. The possibility of their heads and chests being framed in the telescopic sight of a marksman's weapon, high up or near the Walls, had never crossed our minds.

Against the Deceased

If, even after the presentation of the above facts, the reader still has doubts concerning the honesty and integrity of Lord Widgery's role in the Bloody Sunday cover-up, there is yet another piece to the jigsaw.

In another memorandum, recently released by the Public Records Office in London, alarm is being expressed regarding doubts raised at the Tribunal on the forensic evidence relating, in particular, to the young men behind the barricade. Headed 'Provisional List of Important Points Still to be Covered in Drafting the Report', paragraph 4 in the memorandum reads:

4. *Forensic Evidence*

> *Mr McSparran succeeded in throwing doubt on the significance of the paraffin swab tests. But surely it should be said that it is a remarkable coincidence that the soldiers say that they fired at gunmen behind the barricade and that the swab tests on all the people behind the barricade were positive. Dr Martin's scrupulous fairness under cross-examination had the effect of giving a large slice of the benefit of the doubt to the deceased.*

Most damning of all is the hand-written note on the memorandum, detailing the Lord Chief Justice's response to the issues raised in this paragraph:

LCJ's Response

4. *LCJ will pile up the case against the deceased . . . but will conclude that he cannot find with certainty that any one of 13 was a gunman.*

The Unanswered Questions

As a 15-year-old schoolboy I witnessed Bloody Sunday. I know that those killed were unarmed. I know that they were innocent. I know that they were murdered.

The soldiers responsible have never been brought to justice. In the days and weeks that followed, my young mind was conscious of powerful forces colluding to cover up what I know was military homicide.

The role played by Lord Widgery and other sectors of the Establishment created a very dangerous alienation from the institutions of government and law. In the aftermath of Bloody Sunday, Republican violence was, indeed, responsible for terrible acts. But to blame Republican violence in isolation is dishonest. Where a democratically elected government shows itself to be an active and willing participant in a violent crime against its citizens (and subsequently involves its judiciary in a cover-up), the government cannot escape responsibility for the consequences of its actions.

There are still too many unresolved questions related to Bloody Sunday, which involve the British military, the British government and a former Lord Chief Justice of England.

The following questions still demand answers:

- Why did Lord Widgery choose to ignore the role of the British Army on the City Walls?

- Why did he choose to ignore the clear evidence in civilian eyewitness statements, military statements, police and army radio transcripts, and the Brigade HQ Log Book, that the army, including snipers, were also active in this quarter — even claiming hits?

- Why did he confine himself to accounting for only the 108 rounds that 1 Para claim they fired?

- How many rounds were fired by military personnel on the Derry Walls?

- At what were they shooting and where did their rounds go?
- Is it possible that 1 Para were not the only military killers on Bloody Sunday?
- Specifically, who shot William Nash, John Young and Michael McDaid?

These questions should not allow us to lose sight of the role of the 1st Battalion Parachute Regiment on Bloody Sunday. While this introduction has questioned the circumstances around the homicide of John Young, William Nash and Michael McDaid, no such questions arise concerning the deaths of Jackie Duddy, Paddy Doherty, Bernard McGuigan, Hugh Gilmore, Kevin McElhinney, Michael Kelly, Jim Wray, Gerard McKinney, William McKinney and Gerard Donaghy. All were shot dead by soldiers under the command of Lt. Col. Derek Wilford. Major Hubert O'Neill, the Bloody Sunday coroner, described the soldiers' actions as 'unadulterated murder', and so it was. Nor should we overlook the wounding of thirteen people, including the mother of thirteen children, Mrs Peggy Deery, and 59-year-old John Johnston who died the following June.

Equally, questions must be asked of the RUC and other police observers on the Walls as to why they did not insist on having the issue of army gunfire from the Derry Walls considered in the context of the overall scheme of events.

Was it because they, and Lord Widgery, knew that what happened in Derry's Bogside, on Sunday, 30 January 1972, was part of a wider political and military operation? Was it because political and military decisions had been made in advance to teach the nationalist community within this rebellious 'no-go area', on the edge of the Kingdom, a lesson? Was it hoped that by extension, the wider nationalist community throughout the colony would also get the message?

The people of Derry have always known that Bloody Sunday was more than a 'scoop-up operation' by 1 Para which went wrong. We have always suspected that it was planned and premeditated and that Lord Widgery was employed to do some legal cosmetics on the ugly face of hard-core political and military decisions. The decision to reward Lt. Col. Derek Wilford, the commander of 1 Para on Bloody Sunday, with an OBE later that year not only threw salt on the wounds, but confirmed our suspicions that we were dealing with very sinister and powerful forces.

Conclusion

The eyewitness stories you will read in this book will likely stir deep emotions of anger and revulsion, and so they should. Bloody Sunday, for the people of Derry, was both traumatic and quite unbelievable. It was a day when the British military, especially the 1st Battalion Parachute Regiment, showed callous inhumanity towards a civilian gathering, irrespective of its legal status.

If this book has any contribution to make towards rescuing the squandered opportunity for peace and new beginnings, which the 1994 ceasefires offered, let it be this. Bloody Sunday teaches us that no side in the current conflict can pretend that it has not been responsible for terrible deeds. There is no high moral ground. All sides have blood on their hands.

The political violence of the past quarter of a century, rooted as it is in the unresolved issues of colonialism in Ireland, has inflicted deep wounds and hurt which somehow must be healed. Despite this, and because of it, we must, for our children's sake, enter into un-conditional dialogue with one another.

Ireland now stands at a crossroads of despair and hope. Politicians on all sides have a critical responsibility. On the road of despair, they can lead us towards the darkening clouds of more Bloody Sundays. On the road of hope they can lead us towards a new dawn, where neighbours, having honestly confronted the hurts of many centuries, are committed to building new friendships based on mutual respect and understanding. One road is a cul-de-sac, the other an open highway to a new future. Dialogue is the key.

On 30 January 1972 an Irish Civil Rights Movement, committed to non-violent change, was effectively killed along with thirteen innocent civilians. The irony of this event occurring on the twenty-fourth anniversary of the assassination of Mahatma Gandhi has never escaped me. As the bullets struck Gandhi on 30 January 1948, his last words, 'Oh God!' were a prayer of both despair and hope.

The families of those killed and wounded in Derry's Bloody Sunday have had to nurse a great hurt and confront powerful forces throughout the past quarter of a century. As part of the healing process that must begin, it is time that this enormous wrong be put right. One day it will be. We have no doubt about that. In the words of Mahatma Gandhi:

Yes, but we have something more important than guns. We have truth and justice — and time — on our side.

Don Mullan
10 December 1996
Human Rights Day

---

[1]   Malcolm Sutton, *An Index of Deaths from the Conflict in Ireland 1969–1993*, Beyond the Pale Publications, 1994.

[2]   *Insight, Sunday Times*, 23.4.1972

1: 'A Carnival Atmosphere'

Early Impressions of the Day

It was a beautiful day. There was early morning sunshine and the air was cold and crisp. Perfect conditions to guarantee a big turnout for the anti-internment march that afternoon.

People in Creggan, Bogside and Brandywell went, as always, to Mass. Afterwards, a few of the men went for their usual Sunday morning dander, bought the paper and returned home for dinner. Sunday dinner in Derry in those days consisted almost always of roast beef, green peas and spuds.

There was an air of expectation around. Dinnertime conversation that day was mainly about the afternoon anti-internment march. If nothing else, the day was fine and it would be a walk in the fresh air.

Everyone knew that the march had been banned. Everyone knew the plan — march as far as the edge of Free Derry where the army would inevitably halt it, register a protest and then return to the traditional meeting place at Free Derry Corner.

Everyone knew too that a deal had been brokered between the Northern Ireland Civil Rights Association and the IRA. For the duration of the march the IRA was to withdraw all units to the Creggan, thus greatly reducing the danger of any serious incidents which might threaten the safety and lives of the marchers.

Against this background, as demonstrators began to arrive at the Bishop's Field in the Creggan, a sense of relief and elation contributed to an almost carnival atmosphere. In spite of being late in starting, thousands of good-humoured men, women and children set off on a march which was to end, two hours later, in widescale bloodshed.

* * * * * * * * * * * *

Fr Andrew Dolan
PRIEST, AGED 24

A very peaceful march — a carnival atmosphere even when assembling and going up Westway — no rowdy element present. March progressed to William Street. A number of people were in front of the lorry. They moved on to the army barricade. Lorry moved right with people on board at Rossville Street. It stopped about 20 yards along that street. There seemed to have been a discussion at the army barricade between the front liners and the military personnel. A couple of stones were thrown but these were soon stopped by fellow marchers. I then felt the effects of CS gas. The crowd moved backwards and then halted and reassembled. Water cannon was used on the front line whose activities I am not sure of. I moved up Rossville Street as far as the flats and chatted with fellow marchers standing about. The effect of the gas was increasing. At this stage the march appeared to be a non-event. Everything seemed disorganised. Like many more I was about to leave the area. The people on the lorry were at Free Derry Corner and then called on people to reassemble there. Ivan Cooper was invited to the platform. Miss Devlin was now about to address the meeting. At this stage I had passed the lorry and was at the barricade nearest to Free Derry Corner. Miss Devlin had her first sentence said when a sharp burst of gunfire rang out from the William Street direction. This was then followed by continual rake of gunfire as if hell were let loose and at this stage it also seemed to be coming from the walls. I can vouch for the fact that no gunfire had come at any stage from the FDC area of the Bogside. I cleared the barricade and ran up the Lecky Road with others. I could still hear the click and ring of heavy gunfire around me. At the Holy Well Bar I was told to be careful as there was gunfire coming from Long Tower Street. This confirmed my suspicion that there was gunfire reaching the Lecky Road from this area. I left the area via the Christian Brothers' grounds.

* * * * * * * * * * * *

Patrick Friel
RETIRED RESTAURANT OWNER, AGED 59

On Sunday morning coming from 12 o'clock Mass in St Eugene's Cathedral with Mr King and Mr Maginess, I was passing three army vehicles. On passing the third vehicle I heard a voice 'You'll get it today you bastards'. We said to each other 'Did you hear what he said?' We replied that's right, that's what he said. Mr King, I think said 'That doesn't sound too good for today.' I went in the direction of the Guildhall and I had to pass the army preparing a barricade in William Street. I heard the smashing of glass. When I looked the army were over McCools newsagent and confectionery breaking out the top windows. I left Willie — close to the bus and returned back home.

I had my dinner and went to the march. At the end of the march at Bradley's corner the army had been firing gas. I decided to return home. On my way up I noticed Mr and Mrs McLaughlin badly affected by the gas, and my own sister. I came up to the flat and put some water on my face. Drying my face I went to the back bedroom window which looks out over the courtyard. From there I could see straight into William Street. The first Saracen passed by at Quinn's fish shop, then a second and a third.

The first had turned into Rossville Street and made straight towards the flats. There were three more behind. These last three turned quickly to the left onto the waste ground. There were 1,000 people on the waste ground. The tanks were about 15 yards apart. They ran straight through the crowd. The first Saracen, I saw it strike an elderly man. This man seemed to be moving in a daze. He went through the air for about three or four feet. One army soldier jumped from the back of the Saracen and ran towards the man. He had his rifle in a position where he was going to bash the man with it when a youth or young man jumped on the soldier to prevent him from striking the man lying on the ground. A second young man went to assist as well. At this point I left the bedroom window and made my way to the landing at the front of the flat. I heard my sister calling 'Jesus, Jesus, Pat, they have shot a young boy.' I ran through the corridor onto the Rossville Street side of the flats and saw Fr Daly making his way towards the boy. He was in a crouched position during this.

On reaching the Rossville Street side I heard a Mrs Cunningham call 'There's a man dead in my bedroom. He was only looking out of the window.' I made my way from pillar to pillar till I got to the lady's front door and dived down the stairs. The man was lying on the floor, his face covered in blood. I looked at the man's head to see if it was a bullet wound. I couldn't see what looked like one. I then felt around his body to see if there was any blood around his body. There was none.

I went back up to the top of the landing and called from the front door 'Someone get help. There is a man badly injured.' I went back to where the man was and tried to control him the best I could.

Later a young Knight of Malta came up and we got a pillow and put it under the man's head, got some bandages and cotton wool and dried the blood from round the man's face. At that point I left and went into the front room where Mrs Cunningham seemed to be in hysterics, shaking in convulsions. We got the blanket from the bed and put it around the woman. While putting the blanket round the woman I glanced out of the front window looking into Rossville Street. I saw the army with a lot of young boys and a lady behind them. The army was pushing the lady in the back with a gun and kicking her along to make her move faster. I then turned my attentions towards Mrs Cunningham again and there was another woman with her. I went back into the bedroom and the red-cross boy was still working with the man on the floor. The man looked at me and said 'Pat' and that was the relief of knowing he was alive.

There was another man and two or three women came. One of them was his wife. The red-cross boy asked me to come upstairs with him. When we got to the door the army was still in the courtyard and I heard the crashing of glass. It sounded close. I told the red-cross man to put his red cross in front of him. He opened the door a second time and I made my way back to my own flat. This is a true and accurate account of the events. I don't mind its publication.

* * * * * * * * * * * *

Alan Finnis
Chemical Operator, aged 26

I didn't take part in the Civil Rights march on Sunday but I decided to come with my wife to the Guildhall to listen to the speakers at the Civil Rights meeting at Guildhall — if the meeting took place.

When I got to Wellworth's I noticed a large number of people, mostly men, standing on the footpath in front of Wellworth's. I knew that the crowd was a Protestant one because many of them were wearing red tartan scarves.

The army and police then made this crowd back up towards the Guildhall as far as the Rainbow Café. The army and police then blocked the road with land rovers at the pedestrian crossing at the Rainbow Café.

I should add at this stage that about 80 per cent of the Protestant crowd were adults rather than teenagers.

I then moved over towards the Creggan bus stop beneath the Walls and stood there for a while. At this time we noticed a crowd of between twenty and thirty people coming over Foyle Street carrying a blue flag and a placard. This group were walking on the footpath on the City Hotel side of Foyle Street.

At the front of Guildhall steps they moved out into the middle of the road. The other larger crowd at the Rainbow Café barricade then came across on the road to join the group that had emerged from Foyle Street. Only one policeman, who was on traffic duty at Guildhall Street, saw the event that I have mentioned, as the other police were at the barricade at the Rainbow Café and could not see the crowd coming from Foyle Street.

A few minutes after the two crowds joined together in Guildhall Square I left the area with the crowd still standing in the square.

As to time of events, I arrived at Wellworth's between 3.45 and 4 p.m.

After leaving Guildhall Square I went down the Quay, out Lower Clarendon Street and back up Strand Road as far as Great James' Street. The time now was about 4.20 p.m. When I was standing looking up Gt. James' Street, I saw about twenty soldiers in full riot gear running from Sackville Street into the army post in Victoria Market. Immediately two large lorries full of paratroopers came up

Strand Road and stopped outside Victoria Market behind a water cannon which was refilling from a hydrant. About 20 to 30 Paras, not in riot gear, jumped from the two lorries and stood around the lorries for a few minutes until two Saracens came up Strand Road, slowed down and went in Sackville Street. Some of the Paras straightaway followed the Saracens up Sackville Street. The Saracen doors were closed. Two more Saracens then came up at a very fast speed and went up Gt. James' Street and across Little James Street towards William Street. I now lost sight of the four Saracens. A couple of minutes after the Saracens disappeared from my view I heard shooting.

I would like to point out at this stage that I noticed that the Paras who jumped from the lorries carried rifles and had no batons in their hands. When the shooting started my wife and I went down Strand Road and home.

I should mention that when I arrived at Wellworth's between 3.45 and 4 p.m. I noticed a paratrooper being lifted up on top of a landrover and he was then given a camera by other soldiers. The landrover proceeded up William Street very slowly with the para-trooper standing upright on top of the landrover and holding the camera in his hands. The landrover passed from my view.

This is a true statement of what happened.

* * * * * * * * * * * * *

Liam M.
AGED 51

On Sunday, 30 January 1972, I took part in the NICRA march from the Bishop's Field to the Guildhall. It was the largest and quietest march I ever took part in, there was no shouting or jeering. We were stopped at the bottom of William Street. One thing sticks out in my mind and that was on the top of the GPO sorting office were four or five soldiers lying on top of the roof. They had no riot (gas) guns but they had their SLRs. I got the feeling that they (the B.A.) were going to use them. Anyway the march was stopped and we milled around for some time until a speaker called the people to the area known as

Free Derry Corner. I went with the thousands of others to the FDC. A lot of people were still coming over when we saw the pigs (armoured cars) driving into the people, who ran everywhere, at the same time the soldiers were firing gas and rubber bullets and then above this I heard the crack of SLRs and the bullets whizzed above and about the platform, everyone fell down on the ground. I ran towards some houses, but soon had to get away from there as (I cannot be sure) I thought some were firing from the directions of the Walls overlooking FDC. I have been in many marches since 5 October 1968 and I have been in riot areas since then. I, like many of my fellow citizens of the Six Counties, can tell the difference between nail bombs and Thompsons. I know when petrol bombs have exploded. But I can say without fear that there were no nail or petrol bombs or shots fired from the flats or any place at the B.A. They and they alone were the first ones that opened up with their rifles and whatever else they had to throw at the marchers. There were no provocation from the marchers to cause this bloody slaughter.

2: 'Keep the Peace'

Civil Rights Instructions to March Stewards

The Northern Ireland Civil Rights Association (NICRA) knew that paratroopers were to be deployed in Derry on the day of their march. The previous week the same regiment had attacked an anti-internment demonstration on the beaches at Magilligan Internment Camp, some fourteen miles from Derry City.

Good stewarding was always a concern for occasions like this. But NICRA was especially determined to minimise the risk of violence on this walk. On Friday, 28 January 1972, NICRA placed a notice in both the Derry Journal *and* The Irish News, *announcing a meeting of stewards at 8 o'clock that evening, in advance of the Sunday march. Stewards were to receive final instruction on plans and tactics for the demonstration. The notice stated: 'Special emphasis will be placed on the absolute necessity for a peaceful incident-free day on Sunday.'*

Political opposition to the march was mounting. To begin with, the no-go areas were a national and international embarrassment to the British government and a source of deep resentment to unionists. The fact that parts of the United Kingdom were effectively under the control of the IRA was not helping military egos either.

The Unionist Prime Minister at Stormont, Brian Faulker, announced on Tuesday, 25 January: 'individuals and organisations which . . . attempt to break the ban . . . will be dealt with firmly by the security forces.'

Against this background, the Civil Rights Association was both concerned and determined to minimise the risk of any violence at its demonstration.

About one hour after leaving the Bishop's Field in the Creggan Estate, the march, now comprising an estimated 20,000 people, reached the army barricade near the bottom of William Street. This was always meant to be a symbolic gesture of defiance and at no stage was there any question of the demonstration attempting to force its way through to Guildhall Square, less than 100 yards away. Army and police intelligence would have been well aware of this fact.

Insults were hurled across the barricade. In the short stand-off that followed, the stewards were working hard to control the aggression and resentment, of the young especially. The main body of the march was by now making its way up Rossville Street behind the lorry that was to be the platform for the speakers at Free Derry Corner.

The stewards were successful insofar as only a very minor riot, by Bogside standards, ensued. Insults were exchanged, followed by stones, planks of wood and scraps of metal. The army replied with rubber bullets, tear gas, smoke canisters and a water cannon, spraying coloured dye.

Suffering from the effects of both gas and a cold, uncomfortable drenching, most of the demonstrators in William Street retreated and began to make their way along Chamberlain Street and Rossville Street to Free Derry Corner. A steward with a megaphone was encouraging a group of stone-throwing youths attacking soldiers at Sackville Street to proceed to the meeting, soon to be under way. Many obeyed his instructions.

The mini-riot was already dying a natural death.

* * * * * * * * * * * *

Anthony M.
ANTENNA RIGGER, FORMER LANCE CORPORAL, UDR, AGED 34

I was a steward in the protest march which began on Sunday, 30 January, from Bishop's Field. The march proceeded in orderly fashion until we were stopped by the army in William Street. I decided to go to the meeting at Free Derry Corner. I cut down Chamberlain Street and Eden Street to Rossville Street where I met two friends. I left in the company of one of these to a house in Kells Walk in which we asked permission to use the toilet. On leaving the house we heard two shots which seemed to be coming from the other side of William Street somewhere in the vicinity of a Methodist church. There was a lot of shouting taking place and people in St Columb's Court [Columbcille Court] who were outside the door of Mrs Shiel's house shouted to a nearby camera crew to come and film two men who had just been wounded in the leg by shots from the other side of William Street. After that, we cleared the balcony we were standing on of young girls who were crouching to take cover, and put them in safer cover. As the firing had ceased we stayed talking in Rossville Street. At that time the army was not in Rossville Street. We decided to walk down towards the platform. Suddenly a crowd of youths came running into Rossville Street, throwing stones back towards William Street. The crowd began to run and we ran with them. A lot of CS gas was then being fired into Rossville Street. I decided to cross the road towards the flats, intending to go into the flats to take cover from the gas, by now very thick. I had just reached the first barricade which is half-way down the length of the flats on Rossville Street when the crowd started running in panic. I started to scramble over the barricade. At that time I grabbed a hysterical woman and assisted her away from the direction of the army, who were now coming in force from the direction of William Street. As I got her to the end of the flats, I commenced to take her across the open space between the flats and the platform at Free Derry Corner. When I was half-way across the open ground, I heard shots coming from behind me. I flung the woman to the ground and put myself between her and the direction I thought the shots were coming from. As we lay there under fire I noticed pebbles were being kicked up five or ten feet in front of me. The shots could only have come from the British Army. When there was a lull in the shooting, I picked the lady up and commenced to run her across to Abbey Park for safer cover. As she got to cover, more shots rang out and I had to dive once more for cover, lying in front of a small wall. I then assisted two other ladies into the cover of Abbey Park, in which I myself then took cover. I moved down a small back passage behind the first row of houses nearest to Rossville Street. At the end of the passage I met another friend, Arthur Palmer, Dunree Gardens. We stayed there for what seemed like twenty minutes observing a body which was lying at the end of the flats on the opposite side of the road. By this time, the intense firing had died down, and from the Glenfada side of the Bog Road, men were shouting for us to come over and help get the wounded to the cover of the houses. Along with other men who were taking cover, I commenced to walk across the width of the Bog Road with our hands in the air and waving white rags which we had used as a protection against gas. On commencing to cross, we were not fired on, and we reached the other side safely. We went to where the bodies were lying. There were four bodies. On reaching the nearest body, we lifted it and began to carry it to the cover of houses, but gunfire was directed upon us. We had to lower the body to the ground and squatted for cover. I could tell that these shots were low-velocity because they did not make the same noise as a high-velocity bullet on striking the wall. I am certain that we were fired on by the army because by then they were the only ones who were in command of the rear of Glenfada Park. We put the wounded man into the nearest open door and then put him on the living-room floor. I then left the house to look for more wounded. There was at this stage only one wounded man left lying on the ground and he was being given mouth-to-mouth resuscitation. Upon finding that this man could not be moved, and there being no more wounded to bring in, I commenced to look for a priest. I crossed back over to Abbey Park, where I met Mr Michael Canavan and asked him why there were no doctors available. I stayed around until all the wounded were safely away and then I left for home.

* * * * * * * * * * * *

John J. McDevitt
ELECTRICIAN, AGED 50

On Sunday, 30 January 1972, I was a steward at the Civil Rights march. The following is a true account of events as I saw them happen.

When the marchers reached the junction of William Street and Rossville Street the march proper turned up Rossville Street.

A number of people continued to walk on towards the military

road block at the old City picture house. They commenced to throw
stones at the troops who replied with rubber bullets and CS gas. As
stewards we were trying to get those stoning the troops to go up
Rossville Street towards Free Derry Corner where a meeting was
being held.

I was standing at the taxi office in William Street when I heard a
shot, it seemed to come from the direction of the Post Office sorting
office. I ran in the direction of the sorting office and I saw a wisp of
blue smoke ascending from the roof of the sorting office. I could see
noone on top of the roof. Just then I heard a woman say, 'Someone
had been shot' in the vicinity of Stevenson's bakery. Before I had left
the area I saw British soldiers in the sorting office yard. There were
also soldiers with rifles at a window above a newspaper shop at the
city cinema. The number of people throwing stones at the army was
now very small as most of them were driven away by CS gas. I
decided to move in the direction of the meeting at Free Derry
Corner and had just gone a few yards up Rossville Street when I
heard vehicles coming from William Street. They were travelling at
great speed, I ran towards the new houses on my right and as the
vehicles drew slightly past me they stopped. Doors flew open and a
machine gun was fired from the open door. A number of soldiers
jumped from the back and were firing rifles from the hip apparently
at no one in particular. I saw a man fall and a soldier went to him
and turned his body over with his boot, he raised the rifle as if to
shoot the man again but whether he did or not I cannot say as I had
to run for cover behind a wall when I heard the firing getting worse.
There was definitely nothing more than stones being fired at the
army, no nail bombs or petrol bombs whatsoever. This is all I actually saw at this time. But when the soldiers had left it was clear to
me that the situation was a lot worse than I had ever imagined.

I am willing that this statement may be used for publication or
for purposes that the NICRA approve of.

* * * * * * * * * * * *

Michael Bridge
Unemployed Labourer, aged 25

1. I am aged 25 years and am a labourer at present unemployed. I was a steward of the CRA march on 30 January 1972. I was asked to take an armband coming down Southway. The march was orderly till it reached the William Street barricade. There was some stoning and rubber bullets were fired. A water cannon sprayed us with purple dye and CS gas was used. All this time with the other stewards I was trying to control the crowd.

2. The platform lorry went down Rossville Street announcing a meeting at Free Derry Corner. I was affected by gas. I went down the alley into the waste ground. I was sick there. Then I went back into William Street. At the corner of Chamberlain Street I was hit with a rubber bullet. I went and sat down in Chamberlain Street for perhaps 10 minutes or so. People started shouting that the Saracens were coming. Everybody ran over Chamberlain Street. I went to Eden Place. I went down Eden Place and looked into the open ground. I saw the first soldiers there. They were jumping out of the back of a Saracen. The Saracen was parked at the rear of the houses in Chamberlain Street with the rear facing towards Eden Place. The two soldiers who jumped out began firing in the direction of William Street and Eden Place. Beyond, I remember that soldiers were attacking civilians on the open ground.

3. I turned to get back up Eden Place. A soldier appeared behind me, round the corner of Eden Place. He fired a shot. An old man fell down, but he got up again and I am certain he was shot. I was making my way up Chamberlain Street towards the Rossville Flats when someone came running towards me shouting that someone had been shot in the car park at the Flats. I made my way into the car park and noticed a body lying fairly near the end of the low wall. As I approached the body I cannot remember hearing any shooting. I got within a few yards of the body. I turned and started shouting towards the soldiers. At this point I was aware of shooting very close to me. I was hit in the leg.

4. While I was standing in the car park, just before I was shot, I noticed a Saracen parked in the waste ground between the rear of the houses in Chamberlain Street and the High Flats in Rossville Street. I also noticed a soldier in a kneeling position with his rifle

aimed into the car park at the corner of the Rossville Street flats. There was another soldier standing a few feet from the rear wall of one of the houses in Chamberlain Street. He had his rifle on his shoulder in an aiming position. I noticed that he did not have a riot visor down over his face. There was no camouflage paint on his face.

5. I was taken to 33 Chamberlain Street and given first aid and subsequently to the Altnagelvin Hospital.

3: First Shots

Damien Donaghy and John Johnston (14th victim) Wounded

Soldiers in sniping positions had been observed by many of the demonstrators on rooftops to the left of William Street as they made their way towards Rossville Street and the city centre. Some were spotted lurking in the shadows of derelict buildings. A few stones might well have been flung in their direction.

Incredulity and shock stunned demonstrators in William Street at 3.55 p.m. when, for no apparent reason, army snipers opened up, wounding my schoolfriend, 15-year-old Damien Donaghy, and 59-year-old John Johnston. The casualties were carried to nearby houses. These were the first shots fired on what was soon to become Bloody Sunday. Donaghy was shot in the thigh. Several people ran to his aid, amongst them John Johnston. At least two more high-velocity shots rang out, hitting Johnston in the leg and shoulder. John Johnston died on 16 June 1972, as a direct result of his wounds. He was the fourteenth victim of Bloody Sunday. Paratroopers claimed that they had been firing at nail bombers. Neither was ever interviewed by the RUC about their alleged nail-bombing activities. Both of their statements for the Widgery Tribunal of Inquiry follow.

The vast majority of the crowd had no idea of the shooting. I was caught in the crush near the army barricade further down the street and did not hear the firing.

Army and police intelligence were well aware of the agreement brokered by NICRA with the IRA. They knew that armed IRA units were, at that moment, entrenched within the near empty streets of the Creggan. It is now believed by many that these opening shots by the

British Army were aimed at drawing the IRA units down into the Bogside.

How the IRA were to learn of these shootings is not clear. It will become obvious as one reads the eyewitness statements that telephones in 1972 were a very rare luxury in the Bogside. The Creggan Estate would have been no different.

As it happens, the expected IRA reaction did not materialise as seemingly anticipated by British military strategists. General confusion reigned.

When the Paras moved into Rossville Street twenty minutes later, the fusillade of bombs and bullets they later claimed they encountered simply did not occur.

* * * * * * * * * * * * *

Damien Donaghy
SCHOOLBOY, AGED 15

I was coming down William Street on Sunday, 30 January 1972, at about 4.00 p.m. I noticed a cloud of CS gas around the junction of William Street and Rossville Street. As I reached the 'Nook Bar' in William Street I looked over to my left and I saw three soldiers lying on a ledge at the rear of the Great James' Street Presbyterian Church. I also noticed two soldiers inside the former premises of Abbey Taxis in William Street. The soldiers on the ledge had their rifles aimed towards the direction of Columbcille Court. I went round the corner of the 'Nook Bar' and into the waste ground beside it. I was walking towards Columbcille Court then. I heard the sound of a rubber bullet being fired and I saw it bounce off the wall on my right and I then ran to pick it up. As I was bending down to pick it up I heard a shot ring out and I felt a twinge in my right hip. I fell to the ground and I saw the blood coming from a hole in my trousers just above my right knee. I then realised that I was shot. Some men came and I shouted to them that I was shot. Just as these men were coming to pick me up I heard two more shots and they were not rubber bullet shots. Some men then picked me up and carried me to a house in

Columbcille Court and I was eventually taken to hospital in Fr George Carolan's car.

At no stage did I have a gun or a nail bomb in my possession.

* * * * * * * * * * * *

Billy M.
WINDOW CLEANER, AGED 16

I was present in William Street on 30 January. There were two or three youths and some men stoning troops in derelict houses on the GPO side of William Street. Two soldiers were on a low roof, four or five soldiers were climbing inside the derelict building to a vantage point, and a number were on the ground floor. From this building the soldiers fired a number of rubber bullets at these youths in William Street. After the volley of rubber bullets a shot was fired by the soldiers either on the roof or in the building. This shot was fired across the street to where Duffy's Bookmakers shop used to stand. This shot hit Damien Donaghy in the leg. The crowd ran forward to rescue him and another shot rang out. This shot hit Mr Johnston in the leg. Mr Johnston was a distance of about 15 yards away from where Damien Donaghy had been shot. The crowd took the wounded out of the line of fire and they were attended by the Knights of Malta. This incident happened a good twenty minutes before the paratroopers advanced across Rossville Street. After the two wounded had been attended photographers took photographs of the soldiers on the roof and in the building who had fired these shots.

This is my statement and it is correct.

* * * * * * * * * * * *

John Johnston
AGED 59

On 30 January 1972 I was walking down William Street with the intention of calling on a man in Glenfada Park. Because of CS gas I went through waste ground south of the old bakery. I saw soldiers, in firing position, in a burnt-out house almost opposite to this waste ground and north of William Street. As I was crossing this waste ground I turned and looked at the soldiers. I heard a crack of a shot. I was hit in the right leg near the hip and then another shot hit me in the left shoulder. At first I thought I was hit by rubber bullets. Another shot, which I believe was a ricochet, grazed my hand but I have no idea when this happened. Just before I was hit I saw a boy fall near the corner of the waste ground and William Street. I was taken to a house of people named Shiels in Columbcille Court. The boy was already there lying wounded on a couch. I was attended, I believe, by Doctor Maclean and the Knights of Malta. Also I was attended by Fr Carolan who drove me to Altnagelvin Hospital.

I did not have a weapon of any kind nor did anybody else including the wounded boy, as far as I could see. I cannot see any reason for the troops to assume that any offensive action was being taken against them by a civilian.

I heard no other shooting and I heard no nail bombs or anything similar.

4: 'The Saracens are Coming'

The Paras Enter the Bogside

I had passed the rubble barricade which crossed Rossville Street between Glenfada Park and the High Flats, and I was casually making my way towards the meeting, due to get underway at Free Derry Corner. The rioting behind me at William Street and Sackville Street had begun to peter out.

Suddenly, shouts and screams drew my attention towards the mouth of Rossville Street. The army was advancing while a few hundred stragglers were beating a hasty retreat. It looked like a routine snatch squad and, together with other youths and adults, I prepared to deal with it in the usual way.

As I reached the rubble barricade at Glenfada Park, I picked up a few stones. By now, however, I was becoming concerned. The armoured cars were coming at an unusual speed. I saw three paratroopers beating a youth on waste ground behind the High Flats. Foot soldiers fanned out in a wave of aggression.

The suddenness of the incursion had caught many people by surprise. Men, women and children ran helter-skelter, desperately trying to escape. Then the shooting began.

* * * * * * * * * * * *

Heather M.
TEACHER, AGED 27

I am English, I am a Protestant.

I was on the march on Sunday, 30 January 1972. When the crowd came to the barricade the soldiers started to fire CS gas and rubber bullets. I ran to Chamberlain Street and from there to the waste ground just before the High Flats. The Saracens came in, two of them, the first one swung into the waste ground and deliberately hit an elderly man. At this stage we were a few yards behind the Saracens because they had pulled in so fast in front of us. One of the Saracens was in Rossville Street and one was on the waste ground on the other side of the road. A soldier appeared running between the Saracens. He was wearing no riot gear or flak jacket. He was carrying a rifle slung down by his right hip which he was firing repeatedly and totally at random. At one point I was within *two* yards of him. He looked frightened which may account for him not noticing us. He ran straight on past us and we dashed on past the garages at the side of the High Flats.

There was a lull in the shooting so we ran across the road to the houses opposite the Flats. There was a renewal of shooting and we dived into a nearby garden. I looked over the wall of the garden and saw several groups of soldiers, some of whom had dropped on one knee and were firing into the alleyway beside Glenfada Park. Others were firing in our direction from the barricade in Rossville Street. In another lull we managed to get away down an alleyway between the terraces of houses and from there got to safety.

This is my statement and it is correct and it can be used in evidence.

* * * * * * * * * * * *

Isabella Duffy
PUBLICAN, AGED 63

On 30 January I was coming out of my brother's flat in Garvan Place, Rossville Street and looked up to the waste ground off Rossville Street. I saw Saracens (three in all) coming into Rossville Street and across the waste ground. They stopped near the northern corner of Rossville flats. Soldiers jumped out. A boy was running away from them and a soldier went down on his knee and fired his rifle and the boy pitched forward. There was a large amount of blood around him. I then saw three soldiers beating a man with batons. This occurred against a wall near where the boy was shot and I saw a soldier shoot a rubber bullet into the man's face. I shouted at the soldiers and one of them fired at me.

* * * * * * * * * * * *

Tony D.
Chemical Operator, aged 25

I was in William Street and CS gas was fired at the crowd. I moved up to my aunt's house at Kells Walk and went into the living room. Whilst in the house I heard that a young boy and man had been shot in William Street. I was in the house about ten minutes when four Saracens and two lorries came into Rossville Street. They were travelling very fast. Behind that came two other Saracens which parked in front of the house. Two soldiers came down Rossville Street with a man in a black suit — half walking and half dragged, receiving blows from the muzzle of the soldier's gun and from the butt of the other soldier's gun. When they got behind one of the Saracens, I saw him struck on the body and fall. Whilst on the ground, I saw him kicked by two other soldiers. They lifted him and threw him bodily into the Saracen. One of the same soldiers struck him on the face with the fist and with the edge of the soldier's helmet.

I saw another young boy arrested on the waste ground facing the house. He was only struck once with the butt of a rifle. They sat him inside the Saracen.

I noticed a fellow with blue denim jacket and jeans standing on the waste ground facing me. He was empty handed and he looked confused as if he did not know where to run. One paratrooper close to the flats gave a signal to another one to arrest him. The paratrooper went towards him but didn't touch him. The young boy seemed to be pleading with him. The paratrooper who had given the signal ran back behind the boy and hit him on the back of the head with the butt of his rifle. The other paratrooper moved towards the boy and grabbed him and as he marched him to the Saracen kept hitting him with the muzzle of the gun. When he was behind the Saracen he was kicked towards William Street where another soldier was waiting. He made a run at the boy and pulled him bodily to the ground with such force that he fell himself. On rising, he hit the young lad a ferocious kick on the backside and he stumbled towards William Street.

After that, I heard gunfire and we all hit the floor. When we got off the floor again I glanced out the window and I saw a soldier in a kneeling position, firing straight up Rossville Street towards the barricade. He seemed to have fired a full magazine before he arose and ran back into William Street. I stayed away from the window after that.

I did not hear any nail bombs or petrol bombs. I noticed a camera man filming from below the Saracens in Rossville Street (about Eden Place).

This is a true statement of what happened to me on 30 January 1972. I grant permission for this statement to be used in any investigation.

* * * * * * * * * * * *

Agnes Hume
SUPERVISOR, SHIRT FACTORY, AGED 27

I live on the eighth floor of the flats, Rossville Street. I am perfectly sure that there were no gunmen on the roof of the flats. Had there been gunmen there they would have been in the line of vision of the soldiers stationed on Derry Walls.

From the veranda outside my door I watched the crowd filter down William Street. I then moved to the veranda facing Chamberlain Street. Most of the crowd had assembled in Chamberlain Street. I saw water being sprayed on the crowd and I heard rubber bullets and gas canisters being fired at the crowd. At this point the crowd started to move back towards Free Derry Corner. All of a sudden about six Saracens came along at very high speed driving helter-skelter. Two of the Saracens came into the actual courtyard of the Flats. One Saracen knocked a man to the ground and a soldier jumped out. He kept the man on the ground by battering him with the butt of his rifle and another soldier shot at this man from very close range. Then the soldiers seemed to go berserk and were shooting everywhere. Women and children were running for cover, screaming. There was a car parked in the square. I think the soldiers must have thought that there was someone in this car for they began to fire at it. After a lull in the shooting the owner of the car got into it with two girls and a young man. As she was moving her car from its parking position soldiers called to her to halt, and called for the three passengers to get out. All three were in the back of the car. The fellow got out first holding his hands up in the air. I was unable to hear what the man said, but the soldier called to him to bring out the two girls in front of him. He did this and the soldier called to the driver of the car to bring the car up in line with them in Chamberlain Street. The soldiers searched the car then. My impression was that they thought there was a body in the car or else they wanted to remove their own bullets as evidence against them.

* * * * * * * * * * * * *

Shane O'Doherty
STUDENT, AGED 17

I was on the front line of the march at William Street. I advised our group to get the hell out of the way. CS gas was thrown beside the marchers. We tried to move but were caught in the gas. A woman was trampled underfoot and we dragged her to the Knights of Malta. We found ourselves facing the army who were firing rubber bullets point blank at us. We choked our way to Rossville Street. Part of the march was in action at Sackville Street. Gas forced this section back toward us. We heard about a meeting at Free Derry Corner. We moved towards Free Derry Corner.

We reached the first barricade opposite the High Flats when word came that the army were moving up. I was caught in a stream of people who were attempting to squeeze through a two-foot wide space. I was pushed aside and fell over a wall. I was separated from the rest of the group. I helped two people who were carrying a woman to safety. When I got hold of her the shooting started. We ran towards an archway at the top of the car park. We deposited the woman in a backyard. I ran back to try and find my friends. I couldn't make it. I reached one corner and saw my friend Eamonn McAteer, beside L. Bradley. They were bent over a dying person. Shots were being directed at me. I made for an archway five yards away. Before I reached the archway I heard shots. I saw two bodies lying close to the archway. They had evidently been shot while trying to reach safety. I would have been shot if I'd tried to help these people. I went back to see the priest and the group of my friends. I found them trapped. Fire was being directed from the Chamberlain Street direction and also from a corner in the car park. The shots all converged in a type of 'V' formation trapping the group at the point of the 'V'.

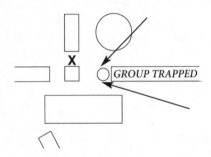

Three people made a break from point X to the High Flats and were shot on the barricade. Two were dead — one seemed alive. One beckoned for Fr Bradley but the shooting was so intense that Fr Bradley could not make it and he gave the last rites from where he stood. The CS gas and the proximity of the paratroopers forced me to leave the area. I took cover close by and lay there for a few hours.

Later on I met Fr Hugh McAteer. We searched for his two brothers, one of whom had been with me. When we found out that more than ten people were killed we decided to go to Altnagelvin Hospital to render any aid we could, and also to check the identity of those shot dead. I saw many families arrive. Each one hoped that the awful rumours they had heard about their relatives were untrue. Each of them was terribly disappointed. I witnessed awful scenes of grief and argument between a man and [a member of staff]*. The man insisted

---

* [We have omitted the name — Ed.]

that he had heard [the member of staff] saying that 'they' (the dead bodies) shouldn't have been on the streets.

When there was nothing more to do we returned to 26 Beechwood Avenue to subsequently learn that two members of the McAteer family had been arrested and charged with riotous behaviour and one of using abusive language. I had accompanied one of the charged, Eamonn McAteer, from the moment we joined the march, almost up until he was arrested. We hadn't taken part in any violence whatsoever. I know that no shots were fired, that no petrol bombs or nail bombs were used and that the army fired indiscriminately at the innocent people.

5: 'Stand Your Ground'

Free Derry Corner

At Free Derry Corner thousands were now standing, waiting patiently for the meeting to get underway. A dozen or so youths had clambered onto the platform lorry and, encouraged by Bernadette Devlin,* were keeping spirits high with their chat and banter.

The British Labour Peer, Lord Fenner Brockway, who had been invited by NICRA to address the meeting, was introduced by Devlin. It was now approaching 4.15 p.m. The crowd responded to his wave with warm and appreciative applause. Bernadette was about to speak again when the sudden and unexpected crisis down at the bottom of Rossville Street drew the attention of the crowd. The distant screams sent waves of unease throughout the crowd. Some began to panic.

Devlin had a clear view of what was happening. 'Stand your ground,' she encouraged the crowd. 'We outnumber the army fifteen to one,' an eyewitness heard her say. Less than two and a half years earlier, Bernadette Devlin had led the defence of this area against the RUC in the Battle of the Bogside. She was greatly loved and respected by many in Derry. In an instant, the crowd responded and stood steadfast. Then, quite unbelievably, a storm of high-velocity shots rang out and Bernadette's words suddenly seemed youthfully naïve.

* * * * * * * * * * * *

---

* Bernadette Devlin (McAliskey) came to prominence in early 1969 when she participated in a students' People's Democracy march from Belfast to Derry. On 17 April 1969 she was elected to Westminster as MP for Mid-Ulster. Aged 21, she was the youngest woman ever elected to Westminster and the youngest MP for half a century.

Margaret H.
Factory Worker, aged 16

Myself and a friend went over to the meeting at Free Derry Corner. We sat on the lorry singing and clapping. Bernadette lifted the mike and said that the army was coming in, but to stay our ground because we outnumbered them 15/1, and they couldn't put so many people into jail.

But my friend was afraid and we decided to go. As we went off walking from Free Derry Corner, fire was opened up at the crowd at the corner and shots hit the gable. I am sure these shots came from Derry's Walls.

* * * * * * * * * * * * *

Pauline M.
Play Group Supervisor, aged 26

My husband and I started with the march at Creggan which proceeded peacefully until we reached the alleyway beside Quinn's fish shop. At that moment the troops started firing tear gas (at close range). Everyone turned but we were blocked. Panic ensued and the army took advantage of this to use red dye from water cannon. At that moment Bernadette Devlin appeared and told everyone not to panic. We were forced down the alleyway. Now we were at waste ground and I was violently sick. It took me about twenty to twenty-five minutes to recover.

Then the Saracens were driven in along Rossville Street at an awful speed, towards the crowds which turned and ran. At that time rubber bullets were fired. We ran all the way to the High Flats. A man came round with a megaphone and told us to go to Free Derry Corner for the meeting.

We got to Free Derry Corner. The speakers were assembled on the platform and Miss Devlin said something to the effect 'We will now have our meeting here peacefully if the British Army will allow us.'

The army then opened fire with live ammunition into the crowd to our consternation, without any provocation, as if under direct command of the C.O.

My husband pushed me to the ground and lay over me. A young lad of about twelve lay on top of my head. The army continued to fire at the crowd on the ground. About twenty to thirty rounds were fired — then a lull (short).

We crawled to St Columb's Wells still under fire, and saw bodies on the ground at the barricade in front of Glenfada Park (directly in front of flats). All this time the army were firing at random towards the crowd. We ran from St Columb's Wells and found army firing from the Walls. We continued running to Stanley's Walk, and by this time the army had ceased fire.

At this point we were told that there were two dead and a boy shot through the cheek.

We decided to return home as quickly as possible.

I am an English Protestant living in Derry and was appalled by the brutality used indiscriminately by the British Army so wish to voice my protest.

* * * * * * * * * * * *

Neil McMonagle
SCHOOLBOY, AGED 12

I, Neil McMonagle, was present at the Civil Rights march on Sunday, 30 January. I was near the front of the march when it arrived at the army barricade at the bottom of William Street. A police man was speaking over a loudhailer and said to 'disperse or we shall use CS gas'. Before the policeman spoke to the crowd a few rubber bullets were fired at the crowd, and a water cannon sprayed a coloured dye. Soldiers opened up the army barricade and came through and I ran over Chamberlain and up to waste ground at Eden Place. I went up Rossville Street towards the small barricade in front of the High Flats. I looked round and I saw Saracens coming up Rossville Street. I ran over the barricade and got in the door of Rossville Flats. I went upstairs to the second flight of stairs. I looked out a window and I saw a man lying beside the small barricade. I went downstairs again and went out onto Rossville Street and got down behind a small stone pillar near the barricade. I saw two men lying on the Lecky Road side of the barricade and a man in between them. He appeared to be crying because he had his hands over his eyes. The other two men at each side of him appeared to be shot because I saw a pool of blood beside their mouths. The man, whose name I think was Harkin, crawled over to the flats and I saw a Malta girl run from the other side of the street towards the man. There was shooting as she ran over to the men. The bullets bounced round the girl. I went back into Rossville Flats again and saw a man lying inside the flats door at the lifts. A priest was with him, the man was Harkin and a couple of other people were also there. The man was covered up to about his mouth by a white sheet. The man's face was all busted open. I heard the other people call the man Barney or Bernie. The men broke down a door at the back of the flats to get out, but soldiers were outside in the court of the flats. The men and I went out one by one and I ran over to Free Derry Corner. Bernadette Devlin was up on a lorry and she said 'There are fifteen men to every soldier.' Just as she said that the soldiers fired shots from Derry Walls. I crept round the corner and crawled over the barricade to the Bogside Inn. I went to Meenan Square and went into Mr Harkin's house.

6: The Killing Zones

Rossville Flats Car Park
— Jackie Duddy Shot

Panic and terror reigned as the Paras advanced. A young woman, 18-year-old Alana Burke, and 53-year-old Patrick Campbell were run down by two Saracen armoured personnel carriers (APCs), which swung left into the Rossville Flats car park. A fourth APC stopped well short of the rubble barricade further up Rossville Street. Still others were chasing demonstrators up Chamberlain Street. They were supported by a Whippet armoured car with mounted machine gun. These were hotly followed by a three-tonner, packed with Paras and foot soldiers. As the vehicles stopped, soldiers immediately dismounted.

A few rubber bullets were fired. This helped to create the impression that the Paras were genuinely in the Bogside on an arrest operation. More than a few heads were cracked with rifle butts.

Then the unbelievable happened. The unmistakable sharp cracks of SLR high-velocity rounds echoed all around. Panic ensued as people fled in terror. And a few minutes later, the Paras could claim that they 'owned' the Bogside, as the dead lay on the ground and the wounded tried to reach safety. Those wounded by Para bullets in this zone were: Margaret Deery, Michael Bridge, Michael Bradley and Patrick McDaid.

The scene from the Rossville Flats car park, which has become the icon of Bloody Sunday, is that of young 17-year-old Jackie Duddy being carried away by four men, led by the cowering figure of Fr Edward Daly holding aloft a bloodstained handkerchief. Jackie Duddy was shot from behind as he too tried to escape the advancing Paras. Lord Widgery concluded that he was hit by a bullet meant for someone else. Fr Daly, who saw him fall, stayed by his side as life ebbed from him. As he administered the Last Rites to the dying youth, and called for medical help, bullets bit at the ground around him and hissed past his head. Jackie Duddy was a well-known and promising young boxer. His ambition was to box for Ireland in a forthcoming Olympics. Three days later, his Olympic dreams were buried, high up on the hill of Creggan, a quarter of a mile from his home.

* * * * * * * * * * * *

Mary Friel
HOUSEWIFE, AGED 36

I was in the doorway of Rossville Flats. There were two young fellas and another woman. The three Saracens pulled up alongside the doorway. The minute they stepped out, they opened up at the fleeing crowd. The young fella McDaid and the two other young fellas were running across the car park. The paratroopers called at them to halt. They did so and they were arrested and put into the Saracen. They threw gas in on top of them. The three of them jumped out. They put McDaid up against the wall beside Chamberlain Street. He had his hands on his head and they shot him. I went berserk and a fella carried me up to the second floor of the flats and was taken in. It was an execution.

This is an accurate statement of what I saw.

* * * * * * * * * * * *

William McChrystal
STOREMAN, AGED 42

I was in Chamberlain Street behind a crowd of youths who were throwing stones. I looked across the waste ground and saw a Saracen tearing across Rossville Street. I was running back towards the flats when I heard a rifle report from the William Street direction and a bullet chipped the wall above my head. Someone shouted at reporters who were running with us 'That's not a rubber bullet —

report that you ——-!' As I came into the courtyard of the flats I saw Fr Daly kneel over the body of a fallen youth. There was another man with him assisting. I ran to their aid — and as I was kneeling with them at the spot, the army fired over our heads. The bullets hit the back wall of the courtyard. When I arrived at the youth's side there was no evidence of any weapon, gun, nail-bomb, or stone.

We carried the youth up either High Street or Harvey Street to Waterloo Street. We spread out the coats and Mrs McCloskey spread an eiderdown which we laid him on. He was dead by this time. His name was Jackie Duddy.

* * * * * * * * * * * * *

Patrick H.
MACHINE SETTER, AGED 42

I was in the parade and had got as far as 'Macari's' when the parade was stopped. When they shot the first lot of gas, I cut across a lane into what was previously Pilots' Row. I made my way to my mother's home in Garvan Place (High Flats). When I got in, I was looking out the window into William Street for a few minutes. There was stone throwing still going on in William Street, but the main body of the crowd had moved towards Free Derry Corner. Three or four Saracens came flying up Rossville Street and one drove into the car park at the rear of the Flats, into the crowd. They could have mowed down several of the crowd, but luckily only hit one boy whom I couldn't identify, but he was taken into the first house in Chamberlain Street. He was aged about 18 years. About five or six soldiers came out of this Saracen and started to attack people with their gun butts. Two soldiers caught hold of one man aged about 50 years. I don't know his name but he was a bin man with the Corporation. They beat him about the head with their rifles. They took him around by what was Eden Place.

Four or five other soldiers then took up positions along the back wall of Chamberlain Street and started shooting with automatic weapons. They had no rubber bullet guns or any other weapons.

They seemed to aim most of their fire in the direction of the opening between the intersection of the Flats in line with the telephone kiosk. They were shooting at a fleeing crowd going in the direction of Free Derry Corner. I noticed then there was a young boy bleeding in the car park in the rear of Rossville Street Flats. He didn't appear to have anything in his hands. I then saw a man coming to his aid and Fr Daly administering the Last Rites. Each time these four or five soldiers emptied the magazines of their guns, four or five others replaced them and continued firing. This went on for about ten minutes. During this time there was no question of any nail bombs or petrol bombs being thrown. My brother-in-law, Patrick O'Reilly, was a witness with me to the above statement and will be willing to verify. At the time of this shooting, I noticed a civilian standing alongside the soldiers. He appeared to be carrying a camera. It was obvious at the time that the soldiers were not being fired at as they were standing in upright position and didn't try to find cover.

* * * * * * * * * * * *

Elizabeth J.
Housewife, aged 40

I was standing at Con Bradley's Public House at the junction of Rossville Street and William Street, when the tear gas seemed to come at us from all directions. Men who were there were calling 'This way, this way', and I found myself at a wall at the back of Con Bradley's which was in waste ground. I was sick and vomiting from the effect of the tear gas and I noticed that many around me were also sick. I then found myself staggering across this waste ground and the next thing I knew, I was caught up in a crowd of screaming, hysterical people, a panic of both men and women. The panic and fear communicated itself to me and I ran. At this point I found myself at a door at the back of the High Flats, which men tried to kick in, in order to get us shelter, but failed. I looked over my shoulder and saw a soldier and a Saracen. At this point, I had a complete blackout. When I became conscious again, I was in the direction of Abbey Street when I heard the sound of high-velocity bullets on walls. This was the first sound of gunfire which I had heard. I did not hear the sound of nail bombs.

This is my statement and it is correct. Permission granted to use this statement in any investigation.

* * * * * * * * * * * * *

Anna McLaughlin
UNEMPLOYED, AGED 16

Rosemary Fisher
SCHOOLGIRL, AGED 13

We took part in the Civil Rights march from Creggan Estate to William Street on Sunday, 30 January 1972. We were near the front of the march. We halted at a point mid-way between Rossville Street Junction and the army barricade in William Street.

At that moment the army began to use rubber bullets and CS gas. We stayed where we were until the army charged out from behind their barricade upon which we ran into Harvey Street. When the soldiers retreated behind their barricade we came back out into William Street. This happened three times.

When the army came out for the fourth time from behind their barricade we again ran into Harvey Street. From here we saw the youth, Jack Duddy, fall to the ground as he was running up Rossville Street. We discovered later that he had been shot dead. We could see soldiers, positioned at the entrance to the laneway leading into the Bogside firing into the crowd who were running up Rossville Street in the direction of the Free Derry Corner.

We made our way to the top of Harvey Street where we observed Fr Daly and four other men carrying Jack Duddy. They laid him on the ground in Waterloo Street and Fr Daly administered the Last Rites to him. We knelt beside the body and said the Rosary.

Afterwards we saw soldiers arresting three youths in Rossville Street and frog-marching them to the Saracen armoured cars stationed in the laneway off Rossville Street.

After this we saw Fr Carolan escorting a wounded man towards

Magazine Street. He was halted by the soldiers at the barricade leading into Magazine Street. At first they seemed to refuse to allow him
through. He was anxious to take the wounded man to Altnagelvin
Hospital. A group of women complained angrily to the troops to let
him through and after some time they allowed him to pass.

We made our way to Waterloo Street and from there we looked
down into Harvey Street. At the far end we saw the soldiers arresting and escorting about twenty men and women in the direction of
Victoria Barracks police station.

We made our way from Waterloo Street to Rossville Street, and
we observed a body lying on the footpath outside the shops in
Rossville Street. it was covered with a blanket and the shoes were
beside the feet. A crowd had gathered round the body. At this
moment the soldiers stationed at the Rossville Flats opened fire on
the crowd. Most of the people fell flat on the ground. We ran into
Barrs (?) shop and while we were there we heard more firing.

Fr Mulvey entered the shop and rang up the Officer Commanding
the paratroopers. Fr Mulvey asked the officer to pull the troops out
of Rossville Street and William Street because they were firing indiscriminately and causing panic. Fr Mulvey did not seem satisfied with
the reply he received and banged down the phone.

We left the shop, walked to Free Derry Corner and made our way
over the Foyle Road, and home.

This is my true statement and I give my consent to it being published or used in any enquiry private or public.

* * * * * * * * * * * *

John Mitchel McLaughlin
REFRIGERATION ENGINEER, AGED 26

I took part in the parade up until we reached and were stopped at
the barricade. We argued with the soldiers and ended up by throwing stones until they brought in the water tank. After a time the
crowd dispersed but we continued stone throwing. After about half
and hour there were only a handful of stone throwers left and it was

at this time the Saracens, at least three of them, and one or two ferret cars, came across Little James' Street into the Bogside. We didn't want to be cut off so we decided to vacate the area and moved straight back along Chamberlain Street towards the multi-storied flats and went towards the car park. As we were crossing the Harvey Street/Eden Place junction we were fired upon by a paratrooper kneeling at the corner at Quinn's Lane. A foreign photographer was the only person left at the William Street end of Chamberlain Street and we shouted for him to come towards us as we saw the soldiers take up position where Hunter's Bakery used to be. He stepped out with both hands in the air, facing the soldier who had shot at us, and this soldier shot at him also. This bullet lifted a chunk out of the masonry surrounding the window of the end house in Harvey Street (this can be seen and the photographer involved photographed it). This was the first real evidence we had that they were using lead bullets. I have, through experience, become familiar with the sounds of nail bombs and I can state without any question or doubt that none had been thrown.

We made our way to the car park and all the time I was assisting a man who had been injured in the leg by a rubber bullet. On arriving there the first thing I saw was a young lad, of not more than 18, lying on his back with people running towards him. He appeared to have been shot in the face as it was covered with blood. I can positively and absolutely say that he had no weapon of any nature on his person as I was among the first to reach him.

As I was running towards this boy I saw Mickey Bridge standing in the middle of the square shouting to the people who were at the gable wall to come over towards him as the paratroopers were taking up position in the waste ground, covering the square. Mickey was shot in the leg by one of these three soldiers. I afterwards recollected that he was waving a white cloth, probably what he had been using to protect himself against the gas.

It was obvious that the aforementioned boy was seriously injured and one of the men asked me to get a priest saying that the nearest phone was at the shop beside the kiosk. At this time no priests were in evidence. When I reached this shop it was closed. Firing was still in progress. A man shouted that a lad had been hit and I helped to pull him in towards the kiosk. He had been shot in the right side, just under the ribs. A first aid man arrived and was able to treat this boy so I continued to try to secure a priest.

I made my way along the maisonettes. I stopped at a house where the door was ajar and in which my friend had taken refuge. As I was talking to him the army opened fire again. I had to dive to the ground as the fire was directed towards these maisonettes. When I got to the corner at St Columb's Wells, I met another friend who was directing people across the open space on Fahan Street. Many panic-stricken people were cowering in the alley at the back of the maisonettes and he and I brought them across.

I made my way across Free Derry Corner to Glenfada Park and while I was approaching it I saw a group of about twenty people with their hands in the air, waving white cloths, approaching the soldiers. At first I thought that this group had been arrested but then I saw two bodies in the open and realised that they were trying to reach them, when the troops opened fire on them. They all fell to the ground for cover but I did not see anyone hit. I went around at least six houses in this area to try and contact my family to see if they were safe and in all these houses I found injured people.

* * * * * * * * * * * *

Rossville Flats Forecourt — Patrick Doherty, Bernard McGuigan and Hugh Gilmore Shot

As the streets cleared, 31-year-old Patrick Doherty found himself isolated and trapped in open ground between the middle block of High Flats and Joseph Place. French photographer Gilles Peress photographed Doherty as he tried to crawl to safety. He was clearly unarmed. Then his body jerked and his cries were in vain. Rescuers who tried to reach him had to retreat. Patrick Doherty lay bleeding to death for a full twenty minutes before paramedics could treat him. He left behind a wife and six young children.

Barney McGuigan, sheltering with a small cluster of people close to a telephone box, heard his cries. McGuigan could not abide the anguished cries any more. Clutching a white handkerchief, he slowly moved towards Paddy Doherty. A few paces out, a bullet, fired from Glenfada Park, spun him around, exposing a massive exit wound at his right eye. Blood poured from his head like an open tap. A young woman at the phone box went hysterical and was silenced with a punch for fear that her screams would draw army fire to that location.

A few moments earlier the same young woman, Geraldine Richmond, had run with the wounded Hugh Gilmore from the barricade where he was shot, as far as the corner of the High Flats. As Gilmore collapsed, she knelt by his side and prayed into his ear. She was helped by Sean McDermott and student nurse Francis Mellon. A few seconds later she was dragged from the dying Gilmore to the shelter of the telephone box. Bullets continued to chip the concrete pavement around the body. Two others were wounded in this area, Daniel McGowan and Patrick Campbell.

* * * * * * * * * * * *

Geraldine Richmond
MACHINIST, AGED 18

I was in the march on Sunday, 30 January. I was at the corner of Rossville Street. I turned back towards Free Derry Corner. The boy Gilman [sic], was walking along the side of the flats at Rossville Street beside me. All of a sudden there was a lot of shooting. There had been no shooting before this. This shooting came from the army because when I turned round there was a soldier on one knee. The boy Gilman stumbled. I went over to him. Some men were already by his side. I prayed into his ear. I helped to carry him to where the telephone box was. A man took off his coat and put it under his head. The shooting continued all the time. The First Aid people came then with some other men. The man McGuigan was there at this time. Another man was lying at Fahan Street steps. I could hear him squealing but nobody could get to him because of the shooting. Mr McGuigan said he was going to try to reach him because he didn't want him to die alone. He took two steps forward and was then shot in the head. The other young boy was now dead. Mr McGuigan seemed to have been shot from the Walls. Myself and some others crawled over to Mr McGuigan to see if we could do anything but he was dead. After this my nerves went and I was taken away in an ambulance. The ambulance was stopped. That is all I remember. The young boy Gilman had nothing in his hands. Neither had Mr McGuigan, he only went to help someone else.

This is my statement and it is correct.

* * * * * * * * * * * *

Sean McDermott
APPRENTICE MECHANIC, AGED 18

On Sunday, 30 January 1972, I witnessed the shooting of Hugh Gilmore, Garvan Place, Derry, and Bernard McGuigan, Iniscairn Crescent, Creggan Estate.

I was standing on the pavement outside the High Flats in Rossville Street. I saw a boy walking alone across waste ground on the William Street side of the flats. A soldier appeared on the corner of the flats on the side nearest William Street. The soldier caught hold of the youth and beat him mercilessly with a riot stick or baton. At this moment Hugh Gilmore emerged from the main door of the High Flats on Rossville Street. He moved past towards the mound of rubble which formed a barricade across Rossville Street. He got on top of the barricade and someone shouted 'They are shooting live ammunition.' When I heard this I crouched and looked round and Hugh Gilmore jumped up clutching the bottom of his stomach shouting 'I'm hit, I'm hit.' I thought he had been hit by a rubber bullet so a friend of mine, Francis Mellon, and myself got hold of him and assisted him around the corner of the flats on the side nearest Free Derry Corner. As we got round the corner he collapsed. A few people gathered round to assist us.

At that moment Hugh Gilmore collapsed. My friend (whom I have already mentioned above) is a student nurse, he opened Hugh's jerkin and bared his body. There was a narrow hole on the left side of his body and an exit on the right side from which his innards protruded. My mate pulled off his pullover and used it to try and stop the blood flowing from him. As he placed the pullover into the wound, blood and matter came from the narrow wound. My mate began to give Hugh Gilmore the 'kiss of life' but blood started to come from the injured man's mouth. There were some Knights of Malta people there and a girl. With the sight of the injured man the girl went hysterical and the Knights of Malta had to take her away. All this time the bullets were flying. I looked around then and saw Bernard McGuigan (who was helping us) further out in the Square (towards St Joseph's Place). I saw him put his hands in the air as a gesture of peace and a bullet hit him in the right eye. I think the soldiers were over in Glenfada Park. He fell to the ground, blood pumping out of his head. I and my friend ran behind the wall beside the phone box near the shops and took cover there. Bernard McGuigan was at this time lying dead about two yards in front of us. He was wearing a dark blue anorak, dark trousers and was a bit bald in front.

While there I looked across the road and saw a soldier chase five young boys, behind a wall. I lost sight of the boys but I saw the soldier raise his gun and fire at the boys who were not more than five yards away from him. I don't know if any of them were hit. I stayed there for an unknown length of time until people waving white handkerchiefs came from the direction of the shops. At the top of the row of shops there was a man lying dead. I (and my friends) went up to a first-floor flat to some people we knew. After ten minutes we came down again. At this time the people were gathering the bodies and putting them into ambulances. People were standing about talking and the army opened up again. Some of the people ran into a nearby shop, others threw themselves on the ground. There were a couple of single shots after that and then the shooting stopped. I went to a flat and stayed there until about 19.10.

* * * * * * * * * * * *

Donna Friel
TECH. STUDENT, AGED 16

I was making my way up to Free Derry Corner. I stopped and spoke to a few friends at 'Jacky's Shop' at the bottom of Eden Place. We hadn't spoken long when the crowd started running past us. We thought it was the gas so we stayed there talking. As people ran past they said the army was coming in. I ran onto the waste ground that leads to the courtyard of the flats. I was running along the courtyard toward the small wall running parallel to the shop side of the flats. I fell and as I fell I noticed a priest behind me and a boy behind him. I kept on running and dived over the small wall. The troops were firing at this time. I made my way up past the back of the shops and ran into the back stairs. After a few minutes I got through the crowd onto the landing. At this time people were lying, running, crouching etc. all over the courtyard. I noticed one of the Paras a few feet away from the middle Saracen which was a few feet away from the end of Chamberlain Street. He was thumping his magazine trying to get it to work. At this time I was pulled in the doorway and all the people were falling on top of me. I got down the stairs and to a back window that looks out on the courtyard.

I saw Fr Daly over a boy trying to give him the last rites and a youngish man standing in front of him trying to protect them. He had his arms outstretched. He then seemed to stumble and fall.

I then ran to the front window which gives you a clear view of the Free Derry area. I stuck my head out the window and I noticed a group of men crouched at the edge of the Joseph Place flats at the end of the bakery trying to make their way to the back of Joseph Place flats. As the group ran on forward an elderly man was shot in the leg and fell. The shot came from the Glenfada direction. Two of the men crawled back to get him and two ran forward. One of the men got behind at his feet and the other at his head. They were crouched down and started to push him in. The other two men came back and helped the man at the wounded man's head pull him in. The two young men then went on, the one at the feet seemed to have fainted. After a few minutes he began to come round. From where I was I asked was he all right. He said he was. He then asked me to tell him when he could crawl away to safety and what direction to.

The man who had stayed was trying repeatedly to grab him and pull him in but he couldn't. I now know the man trying to pull him in was called Welch and the man on the ground was Doherty. As the man raised on his left knee as if to crawl a shot came from Glenfada Park area and got him in the hip or back. The man Welch still couldn't get him in, and it seemed like an hour before the red cross was able to come to help him. They turned him on his back. He breathed once or twice and then died.

This man died getting somebody else who was injured away. He definitely had no gun, nail bombs or petrol bombs.

* * * * * * * * * * * * *

Gerry McBride
BUTCHER, AGED 27

On 30 January I went over Chamberlain Street and into the square behind the flats. I looked around the corner towards Rossville Street and there was a Saracen in the square. There was a soldier at the end of the flats. When I looked the soldier had a hold of a person. He was hitting him with something. There were some people lying there on the ground. As I stepped around the corner, there was a girl crawling so I grabbed her and tried to lift her. She was shouting that her leg was broken. I called a couple of fellows back to give me a hand. When they lifted her, I could see there was a hole right through her leg. I helped to carry her into the first house in Chamberlain Street. After that I rushed over to a body that was lying in the market. As I was kneeling down a Mickey Bridge ran out and the soldier fired and shot him in the leg. He had nothing in his hand. He was able to reach aid and he asked for someone to put a tourniquet on his leg so we helped him into the first house in Chamberlain Street. When I came out of the house, there was a Saracen coming over Chamberlain Street. I could not get back across the market as the army were shooting. No civilians were near them. Eventually I got across and I came out above Doherty's bakery at the Rossville Flats. There was a fellow lying there, shot. No one could reach him as they were afraid of getting shot by the army. A man who looked like a foreigner and who had a camera around his neck waved a white hankie. There was a man crawling out from the houses facing Glenfada Park and he shouted 'Get down, they are shooting from the Walls', but we still ran out. When I got out I whispered an act of contrition in his ear. He was still alive. Two other men and myself tried to give him as much aid as possible. When I looked at his side there was a hole there but no blood. We all stayed with him until he died. I went down the street and saw Mr McGuigan lying dead and below him there was another body at the corner of the flats. A youth was kneeling over him crying. A Civil Rights banner covered his face. The youth said it was his mate. I searched Patsy Doherty for identification. I found two rubber bullets. While I was passing Mr McGuigan I saw a man searching him. He had no weapons on him. All he found was a brown envelope with his name and address on it. After the bodies were removed I left the area.

* * * * * * * * * * * *

Charles McLaughlin
DuPont Employee

I was at the march. At the corner (junction) of William Street/Rossville Street I was gassed. I then proceeded to my home in the flats. I heard shooting and looked out the back window. I saw Fr Daly giving the last rites to a man; he was kneeling beside him. There was a number of persons surrounding the person on the ground. A youth jumped to his feet and ran a few yards from this group of people. He spread his arms out wide and he shouted in the direction of the troops at the corner of Rossville Street Flats. I heard him say, 'Shoot me too'. He said it a second time and with that a shot rang out hitting him on the left leg. Another two youths then ran from the group. They went on each side of him, each catching him by an arm. They took him in the direction of a group of people sitting in the corner of the children's playground.

I then went to my living room in the front of the house. I looked out the window. I saw a man lying on his stomach. He was lying parallel with the front of the flats. He was facing Fahan Street. He started to crawl on his stomach heading for the alley behind Joseph Place. He was trailing his left leg. I shouted to him not to go across or they would shoot him. He kept moving and I shouted again, 'For God's sake don't go across or they will shoot you.' At that stage they shot at him. The bullet passed over him because I saw chippings fly off the wall where the bullet struck. They fired a second shot at him. The bullet struck him high up on the right hand side of his body. He put his hand to his side and said in a loud voice, 'They shot me again.' His head fell to the ground.

When a number of men carried him to the ambulance past my window, it was then I recognised him as a workmate named Paddy Doherty.

This is what I saw on 30 January 1972.

* * * * * * * * * * * *

Columba M.
BUSINESSMAN, AGED 30

This is my statement and it is correct.

Shortly before the meeting at Free Derry Corner began I was standing in Rossville Street near the entrance to Glenfada Park. Up to that time I had heard neither nail bombs nor gelignite bombs. I moved into the car park behind Kells Walk to look for a friend. High-velocity shooting interspersed with automatic fire started from the William Street end of Rossville Street.

I moved in the direction of the first house in Glenfada Park, collected my wife on the way and went into the house of Mrs Mackey, a friend of my wife and myself. My wife and I entered the front room which faces the multi-storey flats' entrance. On looking out the window I saw a number of people, of some seven to ten, sheltering in the corner beside the telephone kiosk. There was a body lying on the ground with two people trying to attend to him. Two people were sheltering behind a tree and a lamppost. I ducked down beneath the window-sill, realising that the shooting was coming from the William Street end of Rossville Street. A few seconds later there was a lull in the shooting — I looked out the window and saw *three* bodies. Two were in the vicinity of the telephone kiosk. One of these, the nearer of the two, was a young person hit in the region of the chest. The second person was an elderly man with receding hair lying on his back with his head facing towards Derry Walls. The third person was lying on his stomach opposite Harley's Fish and Chip Shop in the centre of an open space. His head was facing towards Derry Walls. None of these three people moved and I could see a would-be rescuer crawling towards the third body. When he reached the body, the person lying moved his head as if in response to some question. The rescuer then tried to drag the body away. During this period sporadic shooting was continuing. To me this was quite clearly high-velocity gunfire. The injured man jerked and the rescuer retreated. I moved under cover again beneath the window-sill. I waited there till the shooting died down. When I next looked up, about thirty seconds later, people were starting to move towards the bodies, waving white handkerchiefs and holding their hands in the air. I went outside at this point. I could see paratroopers lining Rossville Street, at the William Street end of the flats, sheltering behind Saracen armoured cars and one ferret car with guns at the ready pointing up Rossville Street. A number were kneeling in a firing position. I looked across to where the bodies were lying and I could see a priest hurrying towards the bodies, waving a white handkerchief. A nurse crossed the street from beside me to examine the bodies. People had moved out to examine the bodies again waving white handkerchiefs and with their hands in the air. I re-entered the house and from the living-room window I could see people attending to the bodies and a number of priests rushing from one body to the next. Some time later, approximately ten minutes, two ambulances came along. One stopped at the entrance to the flats. The other one entered the car park behind Kells Walk. A number of bodies, I would estimate five, were being carried, helped or on stretchers to the ambulance outside the flats. The ambulance drove off after a short time, leaving one body, that of an elderly man, on the ground. I then decided to take my wife home. We left the house in Glenfada Park in company with my brother-in-law, Seamus McCloskey, and made our way towards Westland Street where I had my van parked. On the way I heard that three other people, at least, had been shot dead. A number of people were asking for the use of cars to take people to hospital. I went home at this point with my wife and brother-in-law, Seamus McCloskey.

This statement can be corroborated by other people in the house at Glenfada Park. These included my wife, Noreen, my brother-in-law, Michael McCloskey and the householder, Mrs Mackey.

I made this statement on 2 February 1972 and it is correct in every detail.

* * * * * * * * * * * *

Peter McLaughlin
STUDENT, AGED 17

I was in a flat on the second floor overlooking St Joseph's Street Flats when I heard gunfire. I looked out the window and saw a group of four people, one apparently shot in the leg, trying to make for cover behind St Joseph's Flats.

An injured person, I saw a few minutes later, crawl towards St Joseph's Flats from somewhere around the fish shop. He was approx. half way from the 'Flats' to St Joseph's Flats when shots (two) were fired by a marksman (army) who was beside a Saracen in the entrance to Rossville Flats. The first shot missed and hit a wall behind the injured man; the second shot hit him in the side.

I saw his clothes burst open and a small amount of blood burst out; this was the only apparent shed of blood. The shot man lifted his head and shouted, 'Ah! Christ, they shot me again.'

He dragged himself forward a small distance and dropped his head, then lay motionless.

One of his friends crawled out from behind St Joseph's Street Flats waving a handkerchief. He tried to pull the shot man by the arm and found he couldn't pull him that way. He then turned him over and tried to pull him by the collar of his coat; the soldiers fired four shots at the person trying to give help but missed. He crawled back undercover to St Joseph's Flats.

The shot man then lay out in the open for approx. fifteen minutes before any other help could be given.

Michael McCallion
LABOURER, AGED 45

I was on the march today, Sunday, 30 January. I went down William Street with the march as far as the middle of William Street. Standing beside me was Fr Daly. The British Army started to throw rubber bullets, CS gas and dye. The people went into hysterics and stared running. I started to shout, 'Do not run, do not get into a fuss because you may stampede and kill someone'. Fr Daly and I turned a corner and there was a shot. Fr Daly pushed me out of the road and he may have been grazed on the hand.

As I inhaled a lot of gas and I am a sufferer with bronchitis, I made my way to a friend's in Columbcille Court. I was there for about twenty minutes and then I went to two friends across the way, two ladies who were on their own. The two women were looking out of the window and I looked out. One of them was signalling to a fellow at the top of Glenfada Park to keep down as there were three British soldiers below him. He turned and went behind the corner of the flats. He was there for about twenty minutes. During this time I was looking out the window and I saw four bodies lying on the ground. There was a boy, who I thought was getting respiration. There were three men of the Knights of Malta who came out looking for an ambulance and the soldiers let them pass all right. Then a fellow came out with a white flag, no sooner had he done this when the middle one of three British soldiers pulled the trigger and shot him in the head. I have witnessed this as God is my judge and I say it was cold blooded murder. I have found out who this man was and he was never politically minded. It was Barney McGuigan and he is dead. It was deliberate murder and this I will swear on a stack of bibles as high as the Statue of Liberty and may God be my judge on this. It is the gospel truth.

This is my statement on what I saw in Derry on Sunday 30 January and is to the best of my knowledge a true account of what happened. I agree that this statement may be published.

* * * * * * * * * * * *

The Rubble Barricade
— Kevin McElhinney, Michael Kelly, John
Young, William Nash, Michael McDaid Shot

Five young men died at or near the barricade which crossed Rossville Street, from near the entrance to Glenfada Park to a few metres below the main entrance to the Rossville Flats. They were: Kevin McElhinney, aged 17; Michael Kelly, aged 17; John Young, aged 17; William Nash, aged 19; and Michael McDaid, aged 20.

Kevin McElhinney was shot in the backside as he tried to crawl to the safety of the Rossville Flats doorway. The bullet travelled through his body, causing massive internal damage, and exited around the lower left ribs. He was pulled by civilian rescuers into the doorway and was carried to the second level of the Flats. There he died.

Michael Kelly lived just two streets away from me in the Creggan. I had occasionally played football against him during various street derbies. He fell just a few feet from me by the barricade, although in the shock and panic of the moment I did not recognise him.

John Young, William Nash and Michael McDaid fell almost on top of one another. In my Introduction I have dealt with the circumstances of their shooting and the serious questions that remain concerning who actually shot them.

There was one other shooting at the Rubble Barricade at Rossville Street which must be recorded. Alexander Nash, father of William, saw the slain body of his son lying limp across the barricade. He ran to his son's aid and was shot. Civilian eyewitnesses have no doubt that he was shot by the army. The army, however, claimed that he was shot from the entrance to the Rossville Flats by a revolver poked around the door and fired aimlessly.

* * * * * * * * * * * *

James S.
GANGERMAN ON BUILDING SITE, AGED 41

I and a few friends were near the City Picture house. There was some stone throwing at the soldiers. Then there was an outburst from the

water cannon. Two seconds after that we felt the gas. Then I wanted
to go to the toilet so I used behind some flats. Then there was a mad
rush of Saracens and soldiers behind them. Everyone ran for shelter
and I followed with the crowd. There was at least thirty people in the
flat I was in, men, women and children. We looked out of the window and saw two people shot by the soldiers; men in uniform. One
of the shot people moved. Two girls in the flat shouted 'Don't move,
don't move, the bastard will kill you.' One chap collapsed in the flat,
shouting 'That's my brother dead out there.' I went to the front door.
The soldiers were shooting up at the flats. No one was occupying
chairs. Everyone was on the floor. I looked out of the window and
saw the soldiers taking fifteen to twenty prisoners, kicking the last
couple along the road. I was petrified and didn't know when I would
get home, when it would end. We stopped in the flat for about an
hour until the soldiers dispersed.

My marriage is a mixed marriage. My children are Londoners. It's
twenty-one years since I've lived in Derry.

* * * * * * * * * * * * *

Patrick Joseph Fox
FITTER'S MATE, AGED 38

The Saracens were coming up Rossville Street and I ran into the
High Flats. (I had lived there for three years so I know my way about
them.) I didn't go upstairs and stayed near the Rossville front door
— and then I heard a lot of shooting (SLRs). People were trying to
bust in the back door, and squealing their heads off for someone to
open it so I tried to open it for them but couldn't. A few of them
managed to bust in one of the panels so I enlarged the break so that
anyone outside could squeeze in. The fourth person in was a plump
girl — I pulled her in feet first — and then I looked out to see if anybody else was outside the door that I could help in. I saw Fr Daly on
his knees in the car park beside someone on the ground. There was
lots of firing and someone — a long-haired fellow — ran over
towards the corner on my left with hands outstretched and shouting, 'Don't shoot Fr Daly — shoot me!' — and the soldier standing

at the corner shot him in the leg — and the fellow ran — as if nerves were taking him on.

I ducked back into the hallway and was trying to quieten a few women — some were hysterical. I told them they'd be safer if they went higher up the flats. Then another man and I noticed that there were three or four young lads outside the front door of the flats. They were lying on their bellies on the pavement — the shooting was very strong just now. The other man with me started to talk through the side of the door (door jam) to these four lads outside, telling them it was safer inside in the hallway. They started to move round the side of the door to come in. We got them in safely but the fourth lad was just coming round the end of the door when he let a scream and I told the other man that the young fellow was hit. He kept coming all the same and we dragged him in. I saw the blood spurting from the bullet wounds in his side (the bullet had come right through the door — and took a piece of wood with it which hit me on the leg). I started up the stairs on hands and knees and my first stop was Garvan place. I asked the people there if any of them knew how to give first aid. Nobody. My next stop (crawling on hands and knees) was Mura Place. Nobody there could help either. My next stop was Donagh Place: more people there but knew nothing about first aid either, but just as I was about to give up a Knight of Malta member came into Donagh Place. We went back down (shooting was still going on), and the boy had now been moved up two flights of stairs to the door of the Tenants' Stores. The Knight of Malta examined him and said he could do nothing without hospital aid — so I again went on my hands and knees to the top of the flats looking for a telephone to ring for an ambulance. I couldn't get a telephone and asked a young lad to go and see if he could get any help at all. When I returned to the wounded boy, there was a coat or blanket over his head.

* * * * * * * * * * * *

Helen and Margaret J.
DISPATCH IN BAKERY, AGED 31

We were standing at the mouth of Rossville Street when the soldiers started firing CS gas. I started to move back along Rossville Street and we saw a young boy who had been badly struck by a gas canister on the face. We crossed over to see if we could help. There was enough people there to look after him. So we crossed back to Glenfada (opposite Rossville Street Flats). Then we heard Saracens coming in and we moved back because at the same time we heard gunfire. Then we moved into a small alleyway where there were a number of people already there. From where we were standing we could see the remains of a barricade. Lying at the barricade were three men all on top of the other. Immediately beside them on his back was an elderly man. He appeared to be alive as his arms were moving. I asked some of the men could they not pull him in. They said it was much too dangerous and the other three were dead. Then the chippings came off the wall where the bullets were striking the wall by where we were standing. So we decided to try and move on. We moved to the next alleyway where there were already some people, including Fr Bradley. The fire continued. On the opposite side of the street at the High Flats two boys were crawling along the road. The first one made it up to the doorway. The second one appeared to get shot. He was jerking and when he got to the door he stopped altogether. We were all screaming to the boy inside the doorway to reach out and pull the other lad in, which he did.

Margaret called to me to get down behind the wall and I noticed a small boy sitting against the wall. He had blood all over him. I asked him if he was all right. He said, 'They shot me mate beside me.' He seemed to be in a dazed condition. Then when I looked to the other side of me in the courtyard four men were lying face down. They appeared to have been shot while running away from the army. As I said to Margaret to look at the four fellows, a tiny flat soldier came round the corner. He said, 'Fucking bastards, move'. We immediately moved. One of the soldiers reached for Fr Bradley and Margaret yelled at them that he was a priest. Then the soldiers started kicking us. One made a lunge at me again. Margaret got between him and myself. The soldier immediately beside him struck

Margaret on her head with his rifle butt. One then on my left came
running at me again. Margaret got between the soldier and myself
again, the soldier behind yelled, 'This way!' I turned round and said,
'Which way?' He indicated that we move away from the boys who
had been arrested. We moved away then. We went to Dr Swords and
told him about the men. He went over to where the men were lying.
Then we just tried to help where we could.

* * * * * * * * * * * *

Patrick James Kelly
FARMER, AGED 49

Being a moderate man I can state I have never thrown a stone, nail
bomb or petrol bomb or used an offensive weapon of any kind. I
attended the march on Sunday because it was something positive I
could do to show my feelings against the injustice of internment
with all its consequences. The march was orderly until we reached
William Street where it was halted by soldiers. At this stage I was at
William Street/Rossville Street junction and after a few minutes sections of the front of the march came back dripping with coloured
dye, and after this CS gas was shot from William Street and Little
James' Street barriers. The main body of marchers dispersed, some
back up William Street and the majority over Rossville Street. I stood
with a friend at this point for about ten minutes watching and I
would say there was about 100 youths attacking the barricade in
William Street and somewhat less at the barricade in Little James'
Street. I never saw or heard any petrol bombs or nail bombs being
thrown. My impression was that if they had gathered all the stones
in the vicinity and thrown them, they would not have got close
enough to the barriers to do any damage. The saturation of gas was
so intense that I turned and walked round the corner to the waste
ground to get some fresh air and after a moment I saw people running, and looked up to see at least four armoured cars coming from
the William Street direction. I started to run and one of them turned
down Eden Place behind me. Just as I reached the rear corner of the
High Flats, one of the armoured cars turned into the courtyard

IMAGES

OF

BLOODY SUNDAY

Below: On Sunday 30 January 1972 an estimated 20,000 men, women and children participated in a Northern Ireland Civil Rights Association march in Derry, protesting at the introduction of internment on 9 August, the previous year. The march had been banned by the Stormont Government. **Overleaf:** NICRA had received assurances from the IRA that they would stay away, thus reducing the danger of serious violence. As the crowd assembled in the Bishop's Field, Creggan Estate, they were in a jovial and relaxed mood, enjoying the sunshine.

Below: An army barricade at William Street prevented entry to Guildhall Square. A water cannon used to disperse the gathering targeted press photographers and cameramen (left).

At 4.10 p.m. the 1st Battalion Parachute Regiment advanced, causing widespread panic at the rear of Rossville Flats. The Paras claimed to have come under attack from 'a fusillade of bombs and bullets'. The photographer is behind the Paras and is standing. **Below:** A young man is caught by three Paras while, behind, two Paras open fire towards the Rossville Street barricade from below the ramp at Kells Walk.

Jack Duddy, aged 17.

Paddy Doherty, aged 31.

Bernard McGuigan, aged 41.

Hugh Gilmore, aged 17.

Kevin McElhinney, aged 17.

Michael McDaid, aged 20.

William Nash, aged 19.

John Young, aged 17.

Michael Kelly, aged 17.

Jim Wray, aged 22.   Gerard Donaghy, aged 17.   Gerard McKinney, aged 35.

William McKinney, aged 26.   John Johnston, aged 59, was
wounded. He died in June as
a result of the trauma.

In addition to the fourteen who died, thirteen were wounded by gunfire including Margaret
Deery, mother of thirteen children, and the 15-year-old boy, Damien Donaghy – the first
person to be shot on that day. Many other people were assaulted and beaten by the Paras.

Above: At the Rubble Barricade, Rossville Street. Don Mullan, crouched on the right is just feet away from Michael Kelly who has been hit. **Below:** A few seconds later Michael McDaid enters the scene, top left. Dressed in his Sunday best, McDaid has his back to the Paras. Five or six paces later he was hit in the left cheek by a bullet.

Above: In shock, Hugh Gilmore runs towards the entrance of the Rossville Flats shouting, 'I'm Hit! I'm Hit!' Gilmore collapsed a few paces later at the corner of the Flats forecourt. **Below:** Sheltering close to a telephone kiosk, some of the crowd try to resuscitate Hugh Gilmore by the corner where he fell. To the right of the kiosk and with his back to the camera, a slightly balding Bernard McGuigan looks on. Moments later, as he tried to reach a dying Paddy Doherty, McGuigan was shot through the back of the head.

The above photograph, taken by *Irish Press* photographer Colman Doyle is revealing. Having crossed the Para lines, he is now taking pictures close to the ground since the gunfire is coming from army positions.

Below: The Paras entered the Bogside on the pretence of conducting an arrest operation of rioters. Below are some of their captives including a woman and a priest.

behind me, swung to the right and I saw it strike a man who was lifted up into the air and he fell in front of it as it ground to a halt. I ran on and there was a crowd of us trying to get through the opening where the flats merge. I saw Fr Daly in front of me. When I got through a shout went up: 'There was a man shot in the courtyard.' As I and others turned to go back we saw the soldiers lined along the far wall (Chamberlain Street) on one knee with rifles aimed and a civilian standing in the centre of the square with arms raised. A hail of shots rang out and we dived for cover in the corner by the telephone box. I then saw a man lying at the front corner of the flats, being attended to, and after a moment or two someone said he was dead. At this point Alec Nash came round the front corner of the flats and said to Cullen, 'My son, Willie, is lying round there and he is as dead as a maggot. They shot him.' At this we all got to our feet, fifteen or so. I stepped over to look at the man, he was in his teens and was dead. Another hail of shots rang out and we dived to the ground again. Someone said 'There's another one' and I looked around and saw a man lying two or three yards away, a pool of blood at his head — motionless. There was nothing even remotely resembling a weapon beside him. A man I knew, Paddy Boyle, said to me, 'We are in a bad spot, we'll have to get out of here.' I said, 'If we move out we will be shot for sure and if we stay we could only be shot or arrested.' After a few minutes the shooting ceased and people began to appear and we knew the soldiers had gone. This all happened in the space of ten minutes. During this time I neither saw a petrol bomb thrown nor heard a nail bomb. I did not stay any longer, because I wished to find my teenage son who had been in the march.

* * * * * * * * * * *

Glenfada Park
— James Wray, Gerard Donaghy, William
McKinney, Gerard McKinney Shot

Those sheltering in Glenfada Park courtyard thought they were safe from the shooting in Rossville Street. They were unaware that four soldiers (E, F, G and H) of the Paras Anti-Tank platoon were, at that time, engaged in a pincer movement, cutting off the retreat from the barricade.

As the platoon emerged, everyone sensed that they were in danger. Several people were wounded as they attempted to escape through the alleyway leading to Abbey Park. These included Joe Friel (20), Michael Quinn (17) and Daniel Gillespie (31).* As the shooting began, Paddy O'Donnell (41) threw himself on top of Winifred O'Brien to protect her, and sustained a wound to his shoulder.

Jim Wray fell close to the alleyway, immobilised by a gunshot wound in the back. Nearby, 16-year-old Joseph Mahon lay wounded, pretending to be dead. To the horror of eyewitnesses, Wray was approached by a Para who shot him again in the back, at very close range. It was an execution of an already wounded man.

By now, a small group who had reached the alleyway and were sheltering behind a gable wall were terrified and uncertain what to do. Their intention was to head towards Westland Street, to their left, through Abbey Park. To do so, they would have to expose themselves to the Glenfada alleyway.

Unknown to the group, Soldier G, who may have shot the wounded Wray, was now standing in the alleyway. Seventeen-year-old Gerard Donaghy was the first to move into view, followed by Gerard McKinney (35). Everyone gasped as Donaghy spun around, clutching his abdomen. Gerard McKinney, on seeing the Para in the alleyway, raised his arms and shouted 'Don't shoot! Don't shoot!' The autopsy report on McKinney supported the eyewitness claims that he had his hands in the air when shot. He left behind seven young children. A week after he was buried, his wife, Ita, gave birth to their eighth child, a baby boy whom she named Gerard.

---

* Widgery omitted Daniel Gillespie from the list of injured in Appendix A of his *Tribunal Report*.

Quite unbelievably, William McKinney (26) ran to the aid of Gerard (no relation). As he bent over his namesake, he was shot in the back.

There is still confusion as to exactly where and when William McKinney (26) was shot dead. Medical evidence now suggests that he may have been shot twice. Joe Mahon believes that William fell close to him in Glenfada Park. However, others have suggested that he was shot while running to the aid of Gerard McKinney in Abbey Park.

There are many disturbing aspects to these shootings. Soldier F admitted to firing two shots from Glenfada into Rossville Flats forecourt. Yet four people were shot in the forecourt: Patrick Doherty and Bernard McGuigan, dead; and Daniel McGowan and Patrick Campbell, wounded. Fr Denis Bradley testified to seeing a soldier fire between four and eight rounds from Glenfada in the direction of the Rossville Flats forecourt.

Soldier H testified to firing 19 single rounds (during which he had to change magazines) at a gunman in a house. There were no bullet holes in the window, ceiling or walls of the house. Even Widgery could not make H's story plausible: 'It is highly improbable that this cycle of events should repeat itself 19 times; and indeed it did not. I accepted evidence . . . that . . . 19 of the 22 shots fired by Soldier H were wholly unaccounted for' (paragraph 85).

Widgery does attempt to raise doubts concerning the innocence of those shot: 'It may well be that some of them had been attacking the soldiers from the barricade, a possibility somewhat strengthened by forensic evidence.' 'However,' he continues, 'the balance of probability suggests that at the time when these four men were shot [dead] the group of civilians was not acting aggressively and that the shots were fired without justification' (paragraph 85).

What subsequently happened to the wounded Gerard Donaghy is dealt with in Chapter 10.

* * * * * * * * * * * *

Peter Kerr
DOCKER, AGED 41

On Sunday, 30 January, I was in my home in Abbey Park. A part of William Street is visible from my window. From my kitchen window I saw the Civil Rights march pass Abbey Street going down William Street. After a short space of time I heard the sound of what appeared to be the discharge of rubber bullets and gas grenades. I also saw people run, with handkerchiefs over their mouths, through Columbcille Court from the direction of William Street. The first indication I had that live ammunition was being used was when I saw a young man, who appeared to have been shot, being carried in the direction of my home. It was later established that this young man was Michael Kelly. He was brought into my house and later died in my living room as a result of a gunshot wound. I wish to state that this person was *not* armed in any way. When I saw Michael Kelly I realised that there was considerable danger so I put my children upstairs and told them to lie on the floor. While I was attending to Michael Kelly I heard a volley of shots. I recognised the shots as rifle fire. I then went upstairs to make sure that the children were safe. I reached the landing. A bedroom door was opened and from the bedroom window which looks towards Glenfada Park, I saw a uniformed soldier aim a rifle and fire. At this point I heard my son Sean who was in another room scream hysterically. 'They've shot a man and he had his hands up.' I ran into the room and saw Sean standing at the window. I jumped across the bed and was about to pull Sean to the ground when I saw a figure pass by the window. I heard another shot and my son shouted 'They've shot another man.' I pulled Sean to the ground and told him to stay there. I then checked the other children to make sure they were safe and then went downstairs again. Before I went upstairs I saw a man lying at the corner of Glenfada Park. When I came downstairs again the army seemed to have withdrawn from Glenfada Park. There was a lull in the shooting and a man who was later identified as James Wray was being carried towards my house. They brought him into my house and put him on the floor in the living room. He appeared to have two gunshot wounds in his back and a gash across his forehead. A short time later someone said that an ambulance had arrived in Rossville Street at the entrance to the High Flats. I ran from my house towards the ambulance. When I reached the ambulance I realised that people all around me were taking cover. I immediately did likewise in front of the ambulance (this was recorded on BBC television). The army were firing up Rossville Street towards Free Derry Corner. I did not see who or what they were shooting at. During another lull in the shooting I returned to my home and with the help of a few others I got the two men who were in my house to the ambulance. Michael Kelly seemed to be dead and James Wray appeared to be seriously ill. At no time did I see any person or persons other than soldiers with firearms.

* * * * * * * * * * * * *

Malachy Coyle
SCHOOLBOY, AGED 14

I was at the front of the march on Sunday, 30 January 1972. The steward went forward and was arguing with the soldiers. The officer in charge paid little attention to his words. He turned his back on the steward and the soldiers moved forward. The crowd ran when they saw this, and the soldiers started firing gas and spraying dye. The people at the front of the march were caught by the gas and dye. People were running everywhere, trying to avoid the gas and dye. I went towards Columbcille Court to get some fresh air. When I reached Columbcille Court I heard that a man and a boy had been shot. I stood around for about five minutes, when everyone started running. I ran into Glenfada Park and stood behind a row of garages. I knew at this time that the army had fired live bullets at the crowd. I could hear the gunfire coming closer and I ran for an opening in Glenfada Park. Before I reached the opening a man pulled me into a back yard. We hid behind a dustbin and looked out to see if we could see the army. I could see three unarmed men lying on the ground in Glenfada Park. One of the men had his left eyebrow shot away. He was lying face down on the ground.

I made a move towards this man but the man in the yard with me pulled me back. We then tried to get into this house, but the man said we should not as the door of the back yard was open and the army would be able to see us. We looked towards the wounded men on the ground and the man with the eye wound looked up at us and exchanged a few words with the man in the yard with me. I heard another shot coming from the direction of the soldiers and I then knew that the man had been shot again in the back of the left-hand shoulder. He gave a groan and I could then see that the man was dead. I looked across the court, and saw about eight soldiers running across from my left to right. The first soldier looked around the corner and saw a group of women taking shelter from the army gunfire. He shouted that he was going to shoot them. He also called them bastards. The man in the yard with me said that we show ourselves as the army would shoot us if they had seen us in the yard. I followed the man out, with my hands on top of my head. We stood looking at the soldiers who were still threatening the women. I saw a youth wearing a dark blue suit panic, and start running. One of the soldiers shot him in the stomach, before he had even made a step. The soldier had shot him from almost point blank range. On seeing this, I panicked and ran towards the opening on my right hand side. I heard more shooting but I kept running until I was well away from the gunfire danger.

* * * * * * * * * * * * *

Bridget O'Reilly
HOUSEWIFE, AGED 35

On the afternoon of Sunday, 30 January 1972, I went from my house to Rossville Street. The Civil Rights march was moving down William Street. The army fired CS gas and I went home again. My brother-in-law and some others came to the house and I was making tea for them. A lady in the street sent for me to come down. I stayed talking to her for a little while. I went back home and had just arrived there when the shooting started. We all lay on our faces. I crawled to the front door and opened it and shouted at the people to come in. The firing ceased for a few minutes and I went to the window and saw the legs of a man lying outside. There were five or six people across from him and a youth lying in Glenfada Park. The shooting started again. The boys across the street had their hands above their heads. A man stepped over a low wall to reach the man who was lying down. He had his hands above his head.

At this point I saw the man lying in Glenfada Park raise himself from the ground. I saw a soldier run up to him and shoot him again. He fell in the road again. This same soldier then fired at the man who had stepped over the wall and this man fell. He crawled and the soldier shot him again. A girl from the First Aid post ran to him and a shot was fired at her. She dived to the ground. People came from Lisfannon Park direction with their hands above their heads. One man waved a white handkerchief. People brought the last man who was shot into my home. He was not dead. I ran to get a priest and met a man doing the same. I came back in and went out again and saw Fr Mulvey coming. Fr Mulvey came in by the back door and attended the injured man. The ambulance came to take the man. This man is now dead. I now know that he was William McKinney. I can state with absolute certainty that Mr McKinney had no weapon of any kind.

* * * * * * * * * * * *

Nola McSwine
Housewife, aged 25

Myself and three friends went into the High Flats to get a better view. We saw the Saracens coming into Rossville Street. The soldiers jumped out and started shooting. They were followed up by soldiers on foot. They were all shooting. I saw no petrol bombs, no nail bombs nor any snipers. The people were taken unawares. At that moment we left and went upstairs to one of the flats. We had a first class view from there. We looked out the window and we saw three bodies of boys lying behind the small barricade and there was also a man with a cap. He got up and started shaking the bodies and he realised they were dead. He then got up and waved his arm to tell the soldiers that there were bodies he was trying to help. When he put up his arm, they shot him. When he put up his other arm, they shot him again. He fell to the ground. The Saracen came towards him and picked up three bodies and threw them into the Saracen like raw meat. They appeared to let the injured man go away. Fr Bradley tried to get at the three bodies to give the last rites but with the shooting he could not get out. So he stood at the hall and gave distant absolution. A soldier came up behind him and took the priest and a few fellows and a girl away at gunpoint. Three other boys came out with their hands on their heads. The soldiers shot them and left their bodies on the ground. Another girl — a member of the Order of Malta — came out — nothing happened. She got other boys to help lift away the three dead bodies, that the soldiers shot in cold blood. After that, a boy came into the flat we were in and told us that there was a body of a boy lying on the stairs in the flats. We went to identify him but couldn't. Coming back again to go into the flat I saw a car drive into the car park behind the flats. It was a wine-coloured car — four doors. It drove over to the centre of the car park. A girl was driving. A Knights of Malta girl and another girl, who was hysterical, came out of the car with a boy who escorted them towards the soldiers in Chamberlain Street. They appeared to be trying to tell the soldiers something but they threw the boy up against the wall and searched him. The girl in the car drove towards the soldiers in order to tell them what was going on. She got out of the car and with that three soldiers came towards her: she tried to get back into her car but the soldiers got there first. They took her away and the car was still lying there an hour later.

I actually saw the soldiers kicking the boys who had their hands above their heads.

This is my statement and it is correct and I agree to have it published and the army murdered those men that day.

* * * * * * * * * * * *

Raymond Rogan

On 30 January 1972 I was in my house. During the afternoon I heard firing coming from beyond Glenfada Park. I looked out of my window and I saw two men lying on the ground with people round them on the footwalk which ran at right angles to my house. I opened the door and gestured to the people to bring them in. A young man whose name I later learnt was Gerard Donaghy was brought into my sitting room. He was unconscious and badly wounded in the lower left abdomen. A man who said he was a doctor was present. The doctor told me that he would have a chance of living if he was got to hospital soon. I volunteered to take him in my car and I set off for Altnagelvin Hospital with the wounded man in the back seat. Mr Leo Young accompanied me. As I drove off in my car I was aware of further shooting coming from the same direction as before. I drove down Fahan Street, turned right down Lecky Road, left into St Columb's Wells, left into Lone Tower Street and then into Barrack Street where I was stopped at an army barricade by the Royal Anglian Regiment. I was immediately pulled out at gunpoint, thrown against a fence. I attempted to protest as I had a wounded man but was told to shut up or I would be shot. After half an hour I was made to sit down and after another half hour we were taken to an army compound on the Craigavon Bridge. My car had been driven away but I didn't see this being done. I had asked an officer to contact the RUC but he told me he was contacting nobody and also a soldier told me that if I made a move I was dead as one stiff wasn't enough for them.

At the army compound I was searched and photographed with a soldier named Poole who was put down as the arresting soldier, although this was not correct. I put this to Poole but he just said that he was there. I was then handed over to the RUC and made a statement to Detective Sergeant Mactaggert. The statement related exactly the same facts that I have made above. I was then stripped and searched and tested with a jellysniffer and I heard the operator say it was negative. I was then told by Mactaggert that a bomb had been found on the wounded man in my car and that they had broken open the boot of my car. I protested about this as they had the keys. There was then an explosion and Mactaggert indicated, but didn't actually say, that it was of the bomb found on the wounded man being detonated.

I was then transferred to Victoria Barracks and was kept there for about two and a half hours. I was there told that I was being detained under the Special Powers Act for questioning by the Special Branch and the reason given was that explosives had been found in my car. I then identified myself as the Chairman of the Abbey Street and Area Tenants Association and as such was known to Inspector McCullough and asked for him to be informed of my arrest. After half an hour the sergeant told me I was released and that I had to go to the compound to get my car. I was there met by Mactaggert. He came with me in my car to the police station. He told me my car would have to be checked and he would arrange for this to be done that night. During the time of checking I was told by Mactaggert that the wounded man was dead and I was told to claim for damage to my car.

* * * * * * * * * * * *

William Donaghy
FISH FRYER, AGED 48

We were looking out (from windows of 15 Garvan Place out on Rossville Street) at the time of the trouble and the crowd were going to Free Derry Corner. The soldiers appeared from nowhere (foot-soldiers) and they started firing.

Two men fell at the barricade whom I recognised as my cousin Gerard Donaghy and Willie Nash. Another fell whom I didn't recognise. Alex Nash, Willie's father, came out from Glenfada Park. He went to the barricade and waved his arm, then the soldiers shot him in the arm. About ten minutes later the Saracens came up and lifted the bodies like dead meat.

I saw three young fellows trying to run away and a soldier appeared and shot the three in the back opposite Glenfada Park.

A woman was standing at the corner of Glenfada Park, they kicked her and struck her with the rifle butt.

* * * * * * * * * * * *

Noel Kelly
MECHANIC, AGED 18

I was standing at the junction of Rossville Street and Old Bogside Road when a girl informed us that there was to be a meeting at Free Derry Corner. I then heard what seemed to be rubber bullets being fired (the sound was not of explosions). This was followed by four to five high-velocity bullets being fired. At this point myself and the people around me took cover behind a large tin hut nearby. Jim Craig and a girl friend were also in hiding there. From here we heard heavy firing in our direction which seemed to come from the direction of Derry Walls. We decided that this was not adequate cover and ran to a nearby laneway. From here I could see a man lying on his back, alone on the pavement at the corner of Rossville Flats beside a telephone box. I then ran across Old Bogside Road to Glenfada Park area when I lost track of Jim Craig. I reached the corner where a lot of men were taking cover. I looked round the corner towards Abbey Street and saw two men lying side by side, face upwards on their backs in Glenfada Park. I could see that one of them was still moving. I decided with another youth to go to their aid.

Someone said that we shouldn't go as the soldiers were still shooting but we decided to go on. I pulled out a white handkerchief and held it above my head and we proceeded towards the two men. A few other youths followed, in the shelter of the houses. When we came opposite a laneway facing Rossville Flats, I noticed two young men lying nearby in the laneway; one was trying to crawl in my direction. At this point I saw a soldier leaning against a lamp-post, through the laneway on the opposite side of the small car park. He was facing in the direction of Free Derry Corner. He turned round and saw us. I held the handkerchief with both hands above my head. He seemed to hesitate for a few seconds and then swung his rifle in my direction and fired at least once when I dived to the ground. The other youth who had gone past the lane ran back towards the Old Bog Road. The crowd of youths who had been following had just reached the garden of the middle house of 6 and they ran back too. When the soldier fired there was no one else visible to him as far as I know. I then began to crawl back to the shelter of the houses. A girl, called Lafferty of Creggan Hill, in a Knights of Malta white coat, came running across the gardens from the direction of Old Bog Road shouting 'Red Cross, Red Cross . . .' and came between myself and the soldier. He seemed to panic and ran back in the direction of William Street. I do not know if he fired at her or not. I got up and saw about ten men coming in my direction from Old Bog Road with their hands on their heads. They were followed by the small crowd which had previously run back. Patrick Doherty and Junior McClintock, both from Broadway, were among them. I then went to the aid of the two men in Columbcille Court with about two other youths. One of the men whom we did not know at the time appeared to us to be dead. I was later able to identify him from his photograph in the paper as being Mr Gerard McKinney of Knockdara House. I recognised the other man as being Mr William McKinney of Westway, who was conscious and moving slightly. Four of us lifted him and took him to a house, number 7, nearby. When we were car-rying him he complained of his back. I opened his coat and the left side of his shirt was covered with blood. I pulled my arm from underneath him as I seemed to be hurting him and I saw that it was covered in blood. His coat hung loose and I saw a hole, of about an inch diameter, in the back of the coat on the left-hand side, just above the waist. We took him inside the house and laid him on the floor of the sitting room. He had an open wound just above his right eye. He seemed to have trouble breathing so I opened his tie and belt.

At this point a Knights of Malta girl (I do not know where the Lafferty girl went after the soldier had run off) passed the house. A young man, whose name may be Doherty, who lives on Inishowen Gardens, shouted to her from the window. She came into the house and began to treat the man. At this point myself and another man left the house and went back over to the other man. By this time he was surrounded by a small group of people and was being treated by an oldish Knights of Malta man, with grey hair and thick-lensed glasses — his photograph was in a Monday morning newspaper treating this man, accompanied by another man, Michael McGuinness, Shantallow. The Knights of Malta man called to give him air, so some of us joined hands to hold the people back. After a few minutes an ambulance arrived and several men carried the body to the ambulance.

This is my statement and it is correct. It may be used in investigations and may be published if necessary.

* * * * * * * * * * * *

John P.
CQMS Irish Army, aged 33

On Sunday, 30 January 1972, I was at the junction of William Street and Rossville Street. The Civil Rights march had halted around the corner of what used to be the 'City Cinema'. I observed from the above position soldiers looking out of skylight windows in the rear of Sackville Street facing towards William Street. There was a hole cut from the wall almost midway on the top storey. I remained for approx. five minutes. I heard a volley of bangs at the front of the parade and saw clouds of smoke rising. The main body of the crowd then surged back towards myself and the corner of Rossville Street. Purple-coloured dye was sprayed on the front of the parade. A general panic developed as the CS gas spread. I felt the sting of gas in my eyes. I and most of the crowd then moved in the direction of the High Flats in Rossville Street. I stopped approx. 20 yards up Rossville Street on the right-hand side on the footpath and looked towards the army barrier at the junction of Sackville Street and Little James' Street. I saw a number of youths running towards this army barrier. The army then fired volleys of rubber bullets at this crowd of youths. More youths joined this crowd and attacked the army barrier with a fusillade of stones. A cheer went up from the youths at this stage – the army replied with a heavy concentration of smoke screen. This was very dense – purple-blue colour and rose approx. 40 feet in the air to obscure approx. 25 yards of the street behind the barrier. I then received news that two men had been shot and I went to the area of Kells Walk and Columbcille Court where I saw a television camera crew. Local people were telling the camera men that what they filmed here today should be shown in Britain and not censored. I mentioned to one of this crew that there should be a copy of the Geneva Convention published as well so that the people would know their rights as citizens under this convention. This camera crew wanted proof that two men had actually been shot at this stage so I went with the crew and people to the side of Columbcille Court. A crowd had gathered at a house at this side and a girl came to show a bright red bloodstained handkerchief. The crew filmed this. A young man from the crowd then stopped this. He said 'That's enough of that. You've seen what you wanted to see.'

At this stage I heard the crack of a high-velocity bullet, the report, and the sound of the bullet striking something metal at that side of Columbcille Court. I looked up and saw the strips of gal-vanised sheet metal covering the fronts of these houses. This shot came from the army line from Stevenson's Bakery to Little James' Street from an elevated position. I then moved in the direction of Glenfada Park. Midway between these two I stopped and I heard people telling each other to take cover. I stopped behind a concrete pillar and saw three soldiers wearing gas masks standing on the waste ground in front of the rear of the houses in Chamberlain Street. One soldier was armed with an SLR and the other two were carrying rubber bullet guns. I remained for a few minutes behind the pillar. I then heard the echo of shots being fired (pomp, pomp, pomp, pomp, pomp). I then decided to leave the area. I only got as far as Glenfada Park when I heard people shouting and squealing. 'There's the army. There's the Saracens.' I stopped and looked to my left and saw a group of people running through an arch in front of me. A young man in the group wearing a blue suit had an injury and lacerations to the side of his head. I then turned to run and a woman shouted 'Mister, quick come in here.' I ran in the door and she said 'Close the door.' I kept the door slightly open and looked through the slipway between the houses in front of me. I saw a young man falling and as he fell he hit his head on the sidewalk. I then heard a volley of shots. I closed the door and went to the window. I told the people in the house that a man was injured. I went back to the door and opened it. I looked towards the injured man. His head was raised up looking towards me and I saw a cut above his left eye. He tried to raise himself up but failed and then I saw blood on his wrist. I said to the people in the house, 'My God, there's a man who has been shot.' I ran out the door towards the man and saw a group of men standing in the same area. As I was running I saw one of the men make an effort to go towards the injured man. I then heard three bullets hitting the wall between myself and the injured man. The last was a ricochet. I turned immediately and the men at the corner scattered. I ran back to No. 7 and closed the door. I then went to the window and looked out to my left and saw an elderly man lying face up on the ground. He was not moving. I returned to the door and heard someone shout, 'Get a first-aid man, this man has had a heart attack or something.' I then saw a young man run from the right towards the man, waving a white handkerchief. He stopped between the corner and the man and shouted 'Don't shoot, don't shoot!' The next I saw he was knocked off his feet onto the ground. I then saw a girl run from the same place. She was wearing a white coat with a red cross on it. When she arrived at the corner she stumbled and fell. A crowd of approx. 15 people came forward with their hands raised. Some were waving white handkerchiefs. When the group arrived at the corner a number of shots rang out and some squatted down and some lay down. They immediately scattered again. I then looked back towards the first man who had fallen. I saw a paratrooper appear followed by a second. They took up aimed positions. The first fired two shots and the second fired one shot. These shots were aimed and elevated. They then moved forward a few yards and noticed a group of people shepherding together. The paratroopers then pointed their rifles in their direction and signed for the people to move off. I then saw a paratrooper kick one of the people. When the group moved off a woman wearing a green coat remained. She seemed to protest and was perturbed. She moved and the paratrooper stepped to her right rear. I then saw the para kick the woman. Two more Paras arrived followed by a third. This para turned and followed the group. I then saw the first para of the second group fire four shots from the hip position and fanned the rifle as he did so. The second para almost at the same time fired two shots from chest high. They then moved out of my range of view. I again told the people of the house about the man I had seen fall earlier, and told them he was definitely shot. They warned me to keep away from the window so I moved to an angled position so as to still observe the man lying on the ground. I saw a paratrooper move from the right side of the man to his left. He moved back to the right and crossed again. He was small, dark complexion and could have been wearing a moustache. That is the last I saw of this para. I still did not go outside because I knew the second para was still there. I moved to the centre of the window and still observed the man I had tried to rescue. I then saw him lift his head off the ground and I said, 'That man's not dead yet. He's still alive'. I then saw the back of the man's coat jump up twice about four or five inches in the air and I said, 'Good God, that man's just been shot twice in the back at close range.' I saw some smoke rise from where he'd been shot. A few seconds afterwards I saw the second para move out to clear view. That's the last I saw of that para. He was of light complexion and appeared to have blond-type hair.

We waited a few minutes and the area became completely silent. Myself and a few men rushed out of the houses towards the man. We lifted him and carried him back towards the house. When we had carried the first man into the house before, we lay him face down and while some tended to him I said, 'What about an Act of Contrition?' We lifted his shirt up and he had a bullet wound on his right lower back and also one on his left lower back. As we pulled his shirt further up I noticed the long triangular-shape laceration on his left shoulder. He was still wearing all of his clothes but they were pulled up so we could see his back. Some blood was coming from the wound on his left lower back. I put my handkerchief over the wound to stop the blood flow and a man began to wrap a large wide bandage around his body. I then said that the man would have a wound in his lower right/left arm and I stood up and left the house. At the same time other men were being carried towards the houses as well. I then got worried and moved off towards Eglinton Terrace. On the way a shot rang out and I looked round towards the area of Free Derry Corner and the City Walls and as I did so more shots rang out from the Walls. I then turned towards the houses again and when I arrived I found out that there were five men in the houses who had been shot. I went into No. 7 where a man was being tended by a doctor. Knights of Malta First Aid men were also present.

This is a true and factual account of what I saw and my experiences on Sunday, 30 January 1972.

* * * * * * * * * * * *

Maire B.
SERVICE WORKER IN SHIRT FACTORY, AGED 21

On 30 January myself and three other girls left William Street after the dye and gas was sprayed. We went over to the multi-storied flats. We went up the stairs and looked through the railings to get a better view of what was happening. The Saracens started to come up Rossville Street. Soldiers jumped out of them and aimed their rifles. We ran up into one of the flats and looked out of the window where we got a full view. Three fellows were lying against the barricade when a man came along and started to shake them. He realised they were dead so he tried to wave to the soldiers. It seemed he was trying to tell them the fellows were dead. I saw soldiers with steel helmets on their heads. They shot at him and he was wounded on the arm. He raised his arm and they shot again. The man fell down. Along came a Saracen, four soldiers came out of the back and dragged the dead bodies into the back of the Saracen. They got in beside them and drove off, leaving the man. At that point we came away from the window. I could not look any longer. After a couple of minutes I went into the kitchen. I thought I would take another chance to look, as the shooting was still going on when I saw three fellows coming out from the flats across from where I was. They had their hands behind their neck and were in single file. Suddenly the shooting started again. It came from behind Glenfada flats where the soldiers (men in uniform) were. The next thing was the three fellows dropped to the ground. People tried to get to them but they could not because I saw the same soldiers still shooting. It ceased for a couple of minutes and a girl from the Order of Malta, wearing a white overall came out in front of the three fellows who were still lying down. She raised her two arms out and started shouting to the soldiers, when the shooting started again, and she had to run for cover. After that I could not watch any more. I never heard or saw any nail bombs or petrol bombs.

7: 'We'll Guard Old Derry's Walls'

In the course of reading over 500 eyewitness statements, a fact began to emerge which was totally ignored by the Widgery Tribunal — that the British Army, in addition to firing live ammunition at ground level, was also firing live ammunition from the vicinity of the Derry Walls. This is clear from the following statements.

* * * * * * * * * * * * *

Denis Patrick Oliver McLaughlin
SLABBER, AGED 16

On 30 January 1972, I was part of the protest march from Creggan to the Guildhall Square. On moving down William Street, the lorry and the speakers and others moved over Rossville Street while I with the rest of the crowd remained at the official army barricade at the corner of Chamberlain Street/William Street. Some members of the crowd hurled missiles. A few adult members of the procession and then I and most of the others present called out for the stoning to be stopped. It did stop briefly and, at this point, soldiers behind the barricade began to shoot gas and rubber bullets. The crowd were moving back when the water cannon advanced and the crowd retreated up William Street, and across Chamberlain Street. I moved over Chamberlain Street, down Eden Place and into Rossville Street. While still in Chamberlain Street, I was overcome by gas and two comrades helped me forward onto the waste ground where the old baths used to be.

I recovered slightly and then we moved up to Stevenson's bakery in William Street, going up through Columbcille Court. The army was in the wasteground and old house, beside the bakery where Ritchie's factory used to be. I also saw two soldiers on the roof of the Presbyterian Church in Great James' Street, overlooking William Street. This was where the first victim was shot. I heard a shot and, turning round, while I was running, I saw a crowd gathering round the victim. I stopped to see who it was and if I knew him. Then we went with the body when it was carried to a house in Columbcille Court. A curtain was pulled back from the window and, looking in, I saw a wound in his thigh.

After standing about here for about a quarter of an hour, I moved across Columbcille Court onto Rossville Street again. It was here that I saw the crowds running and screaming. This happened just as I came out onto Rossville Street. I heard the bangs of rubber bullets and gas canisters. At this stage, I could not tell if any lead bullets were being used and took it there was only the sound of gas and rubber bullets.

I saw the Saracens coming up Rossville Street onto the wasteground at the corner of Eden Place. This is where I saw one person hit with a Saracen and knocked six feet into the air. I was standing at the alleyway into Columbcille Court almost directly opposite. When I saw the person being hit by the Saracen, I moved out a bit into Rossville Street. Then a Saracen approached from the William Street direction and stopped ten yards from me while the first Saracen was picking out victims by charging in different directions through the crowd.

Soldiers got out of the back of the second Saracen and came out firing volleys of rubber bullets. As I ran away into the small courtyard behind, I was hit by a rubber bullet. I fell and was helped away by two men. They carried me right across the courtyard to a small alleyway. I sat here for a while to recover. People were running in every direction because, as I also now realised, the army were using live ammunition.

I ran over to the gable wall beside the barricade outside the High Flats. I was trying to find my mates and I was worried about my young brother, Eamon (aged 13). As I stopped at the gable wall to look up Rossville Street, I saw a man dressed in a brown suit and with black hair running over the loose stones of the barricade towards Free Derry Corner. As I caught sight of him, he fell back and rolled over on his mouth and nose on the Free Derry side of the barricade. He was no more than three to four yards from me. He was unarmed in any way. He began screaming and I realised he had been shot. I then saw a friend of mine, George Roberts, who had been running along with the first man, throw himself to the ground and crawl over to his side to see what he could do for him. I threw myself to the ground and crawled over as well. Just as I reached him, the screaming died away to a moan. I began talking to him in a hysterical way, telling him 'Don't worry. You'll be all right. We'll get you in.'

I looked up at my friend, George, and he told me the man was dead. I looked away in fear and saw another person fall, who I later found out was shot dead. He was about four or five yards away on the road while I lay on the pavement. Another person walked out slowly and cautiously towards us. More shots rang out and he fell on top of me.

People over at the flats were calling out and roaring, 'There's men dead', meaning us. I also heard the voice of someone saying they were shooting from the Derry Walls.

I then turned on my back and as I did so I saw a person's head bursting open with blood pouring out. All I saw was red. This body fell on my side and the blood poured all over my hands. I don't know where he came from before this. Each one of these people was, with no doubt, unarmed.

At this point, I became hysterical and began roaring, 'Look at the blood!' I was roaring this to George. He says, 'There's nothing we can do now and we'll get in out of the road.'

At this point, the shooting was really coming heavy. The bullets were bouncing off the clay above our head in the barricade. George started first, crawling backwards towards the gable wall. Someone behind that I know only as Smiler was crouching at the gable wall. He grabbed George's feet and George grabbed my hands. In this way, Smiler pulled both of us in to the wall.

It was here then that I noticed Fr Bradley, who was making an attempt to go out to the bodies on the barricade but the people there held him back. I pulled him down towards me and said, 'Father, forgive me,' thinking I was going to be shot and he said, 'Don't worry. I'm here.'

At this moment, the troops came round behind us from the square where I had rested earlier. They said, 'Right, youse lot, come on,' cocking their guns. It was here that I saw four persons running away. These were part of our group farthest away from Rossville Street and so they would have seen the soldiers first. They got up and ran across the courtyard at right angles to the soldiers. A soldier shouted, 'Stop or we'll shoot.' One, Patrick McGinley, came back but the others were cut down as they ran from the soldiers.

Immediately, the soldiers said, 'Come on, youse lot' and moved us back along the courtyard towards Columbcille Court. I said to one of the soldiers, 'What about the four bodies, over there on the barricade?' and he said, 'We don't care about the Fenian bastards. They can lie there.'

They said, 'Right. Double quick', and marched us up to Columbcille Court.

Here they told us all to get against the wall. I had my hands on my head. A soldier ordered us to stand up against the wall. As I moved to obey, a soldier stepped out and I noticed him point a rubber bullet gun between my legs. I realised that he meant to ruin me by hitting me in the testicles and I moved slightly aside and the bullet grazed the inside of my thigh. (I showed this to the police later in the naval base at the dockyards when they asked for any evidence of brutality by soldiers.)

The soldiers were hitting a few of my companions as they stood against the wall. They were using butts of rifles, their fists and a few were using batons. They were saying things like, 'You boys are [for] the rope. You boys will never learn but we'll teach you.' Fr Bradley was saying 'These boys weren't doing anything. You can let them go.' and one soldier said, 'Fuck off.' I was told later on by one of the fellows beside me that it was at this time they pulled the collar off Fr Bradley.

We then were marched down an alleyway into Rossville Street, over to Sackville Street. We were put up against the wires outside the GPO. Here they took us one at a time, into a big two-ton truck. One grabbed me and said, 'Right, mate, you and me are going for a run.' He ran me down to the bottom of Sackville Street and back up again.

We were then put into the wagon, forced to the front on our knees. We were taken down to the naval dockyard, where we were knocked off the wagon one at a time with a rifle butt and batoned and kicked into the detention centre, i.e. the part surrounded by wire. Here, all our particulars were taken, description of dress, etc., photographed and, later, at 12.00 midnight, released.

The above is a full accurate and TRUE account of my experiences on Sunday, 30 January 1972.

* * * * * * * * * * * *

Brid Donaghy
SECRETARY, AGED 30

I attended the 'Civil Rights' march on Sunday, 30 January 1972. My position in the march was about the middle. When stopped in William Street by the army my position was about twenty yards from Rossville Street junction. I saw that the army had taken up positions right down the left-hand side and along the bottom half of William Street. At this point I and all the marchers with me were showered by gas canisters from the left and from the front of us, some canisters hitting people as they landed. Within some minutes the gas became so concentrated that I and all the people around me were so overcome that I with them had to make our way through every available opening to the right of William Street, the opening for me being that of a derelict building. As I and others clambered over the rubble one high-velocity shot rang out positively coming from the vicinity of the left-hand side of William Street and a man yelled out that a boy had been shot in the leg not very far from us. Some other men told us to lie flat on the ground and after lying like this for some minutes and no other shots sounding, these men helped us over the rubble. I then made my way to Rossville Street and when I arrived there I stood talking with some friends. At this point on looking up I noticed that the army had also taken up positions along Derry Walls overlooking the Bogside. After some minutes someone said a meeting had started at Free Derry Corner. Just as I was moving off, someone yelled, 'They are coming in with the Saracens.' I glanced behind and saw Saracens coming into Rossville Street. Within seconds a volley of shots rang out *positively* coming from the army for even though at this stage I was running looking for cover I can say with *all certainty* that the direction of the shooting was from outside the Bogside, namely junction of Rossville Street and from Derry Walls. Until I got cover from a house inside the Bogside there were at least three or four series of these bursts of high velocity gun-fire still coming *positively* from the directions I have already mentioned.

I can say with *absolute certainty* that during all this time there was *no* crossfire, *no* nail bombs, *no* petrol bombs or *any weapons* of *any sort* used by *any body* in the Bogside area, and I am prepared to swear to this.

* * * * * * * * * * * * *

William Hegarty
BUILDER AND DEMOLITION CONTRACTOR, AGED 43

After the confrontation between the youths and the army we pulled back to the edge of the High Flats. I saw the Saracen tanks come round the corner of Rossville Street scattering the people in front, driving as fast as possible. One of them mounted the pavement on the side of the flats. They circled past each other and did a complete turn stopping at the corner of William Street and Rossville Street and parking broadside along the road. Then I saw a youth fighting with two soldiers at the William side end of the High Flats. They were giving him an awful beating so myself and about seven others ran forward trying to help him. I looked down Rossville Street and saw the soldiers taking up firing positions down on one knee. Before I could say anything I heard the first of the shots fired. Some of the men scattered to the side. Myself and a young boy turned to run straight back. When we got to the gap on the barricade which is in front of Rossville Flats somebody had pulled a barbed wire barricade across the opening. I ran to the right but the young boy tried to step over the wire. He seemed to get caught on the top of the wire because he wasn't tall enough to get over. I ran out to pull him over. I got him off the wire. We were climbing over the top of the rubble on the Glenfada side. Several more shots rang out at this minute.

The boy fell at my feet. I stumbled forward on my mouth and nose. When I got up again the boy didn't rise and he was lying face down bleeding. I called for help to lift him. Several men shouted to stay where I was and that they would get him because a soldier had just opened up from the Wall and split the brickwork above my head.

I visited the wake-house next morning and I learned the dead boy was Gerard Donaghy.

I would swear that this youth had no nail, petrol bombs or guns. The only thing he had in his hand was a small bit of plaster.

I was at the head of the parade and saw no nail or petrol bombs being thrown at the troops.

This is a true and accurate account of the events. I agree to its publication.

* * * * * * * * * * * *

Teresa Cassidy
FACTORY WORKER, AGED 31

On Sunday, 30 January 1972, I was at the junction of William Street and Rossville Street. When the soldiers used heavy CS gas I was forced into Rossville Street. While recovering there, I saw a young unarmed boy shot in the face. He fell and was carried to some waste ground opposite where I was standing. About three minutes later I saw three army Saracens come racing along past me. The crowd ran but I stood there unable to move and prepared to be lifted. One Saracen stopped at the waste ground and three or four soldiers jumped out and began to shoot recklessly into the unarmed fleeing crowd. I saw four boys fall to the ground and one of their bodies was dragged away by two of the soldiers. One of the soldiers actually aimed his rifle at me but suddenly changed his mind and fired instead at the crowd.

I moved to Free Derry Corner where I had to lie flat on the ground as the soldiers fired from the city walls. I then crept on my hands and knees to my aunt's house in St Columb's Wells.

This is a true statement of what I saw on Sunday, 30 January 1972.

I grant permission for this statement to be used in any enquiry into the events on the day.

* * * * * * * * * * * *

Tony H.
CABLE LAYER, AGED 26

I was at the car park of Rossville Flats when the Saracens made their charge. I ran behind the Saracen and it made a deliberate charge at a group of fleeing people. A girl was knocked over. I ran on to the flats where a crowd had panicked and could not get through the passageway. The soldiers were hitting people with the butts of rifles. I climbed over a roof of the outhouse of the flats. There was shooting on the far side coming from the Walls and Glenfada Park. I dived for cover and I saw a boy being shot at a barricade. There was already someone lying there. He seemed to be hit also as there was no movement from him. A bullet hit close by me coming from the direction of Glenfada Park or Columbcille Court. I saw two men crawling out, at the gap between the flats (where the shops are); one was shot. I helped lead a crowd of panicking people along the Walls. A priest pulled up in a Red Cross car. He was looking for injured people. He got out of the car. I told him to take cover. He had hardly done so when a bullet hit the far wall. It came from the Walls. We waited for ten minutes and then went away to safety. I helped to put about seven of the injured into cars.

* * * * * * * * * * * *

J. J. M.
BUILDING CONTRACTOR, AGED 34

I was about ten to fifteen yards from the front of the march; in the approximate area of the Foyle Travel Agency (William Street). At this stage Ivan Cooper came back, and asked me to help to get the marchers to proceed to Free Derry Corner, as a meeting would be held at that point. In the process of changing course I was overcome by CS gas which seemed to rise from ground level. I had a lot of difficulty in reaching open space because of the large number of people in front of me. A lot of young girls were really hysterical and sick as a result of the gas. I finally made my way into open space — between Con Bradley's Public House and the Rossville Flats. By this time I had lost my friends as, at this stage, a large number of people were assembling at Free Derry Corner. I made my way in the direction of Free Derry Corner, when rioting suddenly broke out at the junction of Rossville Street/ William Street/Little James' Street.

I saw gas of various colours. Some youths were stone throwing. There was a number of people, including myself, watching this for several minutes. All of a sudden, the paratroopers snatched two youths, one of whom was trailed by the hair of his head.

At this stage, three Saracen armoured cars rushed up Rossville Street. We all moved in behind the barricade — a small amount of rubble situated in front of Rossville Flats. There was a small breach in the barricade which four or five youths sealed off, using an army-type barrier. At this stage, the Paras opened fire. We ran in the direction of Glenfada Park. As we reached here, two young men fell behind the barricade. There had been at least a dozen shots fired by the Paras as we made for cover. A few seconds later, a youth was shot at the entrance to Glenfada Park. We rushed out and carried him towards the flats for shelter. We came under fire from the direction of Derry Walls, as we sought shelter. In my opinion, the youth was dead and I said an 'act of contrition' in his ear. As I looked up, the late Gerry McKinney was also kneeling beside me, and a priest (Fr Bradley) who was giving the Last Rites to the youth.

At this stage, another youth who had sought shelter was calling on help to recover the two other bodies from behind the barricade. As he ran out, he was shot down by a volley of gunfire. No one else followed us. We had witnessed the callous murder of this defence-less, unarmed youth.

At this stage I saw a youth running towards the entrance to the high Rossville Flats. He was shot down from behind. Lying on the ground, he grabbed one of the canopy entrance supports. He dragged himself approx. one foot, when two shots rang out in rapid succession. The youth appeared to lose his grip on the canopy support and his body went completely limp. There was no more movement. People who were in the entrance to the flats dragged him in. We still sought shelter at the gable wall at the entrance of Glenfada Park.

Some people attempted to run across the entrance to the Park. A few made it across, but three were cut down in cold-blooded murder, right at the kerb. The three bodies were lying parallel to each other.

Ten to fifteen minutes afterwards, a paratrooper appeared at the corner. He brought his rifle to shoulder level, and shouted — 'Move you bastards, or I'll blow your heads off!' He seemed to have gone berserk. One group of us, who had been seeking refuge, were marched off. I told one of the Paras that I was rendering medical attention, who in turn said, 'That's OK, tell my mate.'

I, in turn, told his mate, who told me in no uncertain terms to get in line and get my hands up — 'or I'll blow your brains out, you Irish bastard!' As we were marching off in the direction the soldiers were leading us, a soldier, to my right, struck everyone on the back of the head with the barrel of his rifle. There was at least one woman arrested.

I looked over my shoulder and saw troops behind me, firing in the direction of Lisfannon Park. The last soldier in line (walking beside us) was two or three people in front of me. I made my escape to the left into a flat entrance. I lay under the concrete steps for about ten to twelve minutes. There was a space in the steps through which I could see into Rossville Street. The troops were still firing from shoulder level. I rang the doorbell at the flat entrance next to me. The door was opened by a Mr Doherty and I sought refuge with Mr Doherty, his father and mother. I made my apologies for any inconvenience I may cause them. They assured me I was quite welcome.

They very reluctantly let me leave their house after approx. thirty minutes. I went into Glenfada Park. I met with Charles Meehan, Thomas Bryce and P. K. O'Doherty. I informed them that we were sitting ducks. They all agreed and as we were moving out of the service area of the flats, a volley of shots hit the wall behind us. These were fired from the direction of Rossville Street/Glenfada Park.

We made our way to our car in Westend Park.

Thomas D.
TEACHER, AGED 23

On 30 January 1972, I took part in a Civil Rights demonstration, from Creggan Estate to Free Derry Corner in the Bogside. As the demonstration stopped at the junction of William Street/Rossville Street, I walked towards Sackville Street. Troops were firing CS gas into the crowd. Some marchers retaliated with stones. At one stage they threw gas back at the troops who replied with volleys of rubber bullets and blue smoke. I was aware of trouble further down William Street, but am not prepared to speculate. From this position I also heard 'volleys' of rubber bullets. The gas became so thick that I had to retreat up William Street. I noticed three paratroopers on top of a building overlooking William Street. One child was throwing stones at the paratroops. The soldier nearest pointed his rifle twice at this child. He then withdrew, and I was narrowly missed by a rubber bullet which was fired obviously indiscriminately at the retreating crowd. Overcome by gas, I retreated into the maisonette complex opposite the High Rossville Flats. When I had slightly recovered I heard two shots. Reports quickly circulated that a man and a boy had received leg wounds. This rumour was verified by eyewitnesses.

Throughout the next fifteen or twenty minutes, I heard volleys of rubber bullets being fired. The crowd began moving towards Free Derry Corner, where a meeting had been called. A lot of people were in the vicinity of Rossville Flats.

I would now like to say categorically that there was no gunfire directed at the British. Having lived in Derry all my life, I now recognise the sound of automatic and high-velocity gunfire. There was no gunfire, only the sound of volleys of rubber bullets.

I approached Free Derry Corner. The meeting was about to commence. I became aware of commotion behind me. Looking round, I saw the crowd dispersing into the maisonette complex and into Rossville Flats. I saw three Saracen armoured tanks enter Rossville Flats. They stopped outside the flats. They had stopped to allow troops to disembark. At this stage there was no sound of gunfire. Only the speaker, Bernadette Devlin, could be heard above the sound of fleeing, panicking peaceful people. I was about to run, but I stopped, prepared to meet the troops whom I presumed would be armed only with gas, *rubber* bullets, and batons. I noticed army snipers move into position on Derry Walls overlooking the speaker's platform. Suddenly and without warning, the air was filled with the sound of hails of high-velocity bullets. I heard them hitting walls around me. My fears were realised. The army had opened up on an unarmed peaceful demonstration. There had been no nail bombs, petrol bombs or gunfire. These were army bullets. People dropped to the ground. I could not. I heard bullets whistling over my head. This came from the walls where I had seen army snipers take up position. Everyone was hysterical, people were falling all around me. Men were helping young girls and women. I myself helped a few young girls who were rooted where they stood. I ran towards Westland Street. Bullets were still flying in one direction from the direction of William Street/Rossville Street. People were lying, screaming on the ground. I joined a few friends and left the scene, crawling on my stomach whenever I thought I might be shot at from the Walls. The thirteen people who died were massacred by British Army paratroops. They offered no resistance. They were murdered (as I may have been myself) in cold blood, and with my back to the British murderers.

* * * * * * * * * * * * *

Kevin McCallion
TEACHER, AGED 23

On Sunday 30 January I took part in the Civil Rights march. I was near the end of the procession. When I approached the junction of Rossville Street/William Street I saw gas and dye being fired into the crowd by the troops. A crowd of youths was stoning soldiers just in front of the GPO sorting office. There was another crowd of youths stoning troops further up William Street. The second group of troops was positioned on top of derelict buildings situated in the waste ground beside Stevensons' bakery. Both the troops in William Street and those in front of the GPO sorting office returned fire with volleys of rubber bullets. Many of these bullets were fired directly into the crowd of bystanders who were not in effect taking an active part in the rioting.

While retreating into Rossville Street I heard two shots which seemed to come from the direction of the aforementioned derelict buildings in William Street. I heard numerous reports of two people having been shot. I stood in Rossville Street for about 15 minutes. Then I heard appeals by Civil Rights stewards to retreat and attend a meeting at Free Derry Corner. As the crowd headed from Rossville Street towards Free Derry Corner in answer to these appeals, I heard someone shout 'They're coming in!' I looked round and saw at least two army vehicles enter Rossville Street from Lower William Street. I saw troops emerge from these vehicles and take up firing positions. The crowd, seeing the weapons about to be used by the army, panicked and fled. The rate of the crowd's retreat was visibly retarded by the barricades immediately in front of the Rossville Street Flats. Some people, including women, tripped and fell over these barricades and were visibly trampled on by the general stampede.

As the crowd fled, the troops opened fire at the crowd in general. I took refuge behind a gable of the High Flats. I saw one man at this stage being carried along the foyer of the flats' shopping centre from the direction of Fahan Street. During a lull in the shooting the crowd including myself emerged from the protection of the gable and continued their flight along Rossville Street towards Free Derry Corner. When this section of the crowd became visible to the army, the latter opened fire upon them again.

We all fell to the ground and proceeded to crawl towards an alleyway in Joseph Place maisonettes. The army continued to fire. Approximately 50 people, including myself, crawled into an alleyway in these maisonettes. While we were taking cover in this alleyway the army continued firing. Anyone who dared emerge was immediately shot at. I observed a male figure lying motionless in Rossville Street. Some people in the alleyway attempted to reach this person, but once more were fired upon by the army. Due to the general jostling about in the alleyway, my view of Rossville Street was then obscured, and I heard people in front of me who could see Rossville Street observe that more people (at least two) were prostrate on the ground, seemingly shot.

They also observed that a man attempting to reach one of the prostrate figures was shot, after showing clearly by means of waving a handkerchief that he was unarmed. The feeling in the alleyway grew steadily more tense until eventually one or two young girls became hysterical and attempted to rush forward from the alleyway into Rossville Street. The soldiers spontaneously opened fire again and some people managed to pull the young girls back. It became evident that the only escape from the alleyway was to crawl along it towards Fahan Street and thence behind a wall and off towards St Columb's Wells.

Many, especially young girls, were frightened to do this due to the continual firing. As we crawled on all fours behind the wall, dragging many reluctant people, the soldiers on Derry Walls opened fire and continued firing while the people moved.

We eventually reached the end of the wall at the Fahan Street/St Columb's Wells/St Columb's Street junction. From this point we were ushered one at a time across the street into St Columb's Wells and safety. While in St Columb's Wells I saw two males being carried away seemingly dead *or* wounded in cars. Army fire continued. At this point I left the area via St Columb's Wells and McKeown's Lane, was prevented from going up Westland Street (better known as the 'New Road') due to the continual army fire, took a detour through Meenan Park and proceeded home.

At no time did I observe any of the marchers or people in the area with guns.

This statement is not based on hearsay or conjecture. It is a statement of the facts as I experienced them and, might I add, that I have no doubt whatever that the army fired indiscriminately into a fleeing crowd of innocent people.

* * * * * * * * * * * *

Agnes McGuinness
CLERK, AGED 19

I was on the Civil Rights march which proceeded to Southway then to William Street. I was unaware of any activity until the tear gas came from the army located at the City Cinema in William Street, plus rubber bullets from the Little James' Street direction.

When they fired the tear gas the crowd scattered and went, as far as I could see, in the direction of Rossville Flats. My friend and I decided to go to my friend's grandmother's who lived on the eighth floor of the Rossville Flats, the block above the shops.

In the flat we were in a suitable position to view Chamberlain Street, the waste ground and Rossville Street. In the other direction we could see the Walls, Joseph Place, and as far as Free Derry Corner.

My friend (Phyllis Brown), her grandmother (Mrs Gill) and I were in the flat about five to ten minutes. when we seen the army coming from the William Street area. They jumped out of the Saracens and started grabbing people in the crowd. A soldier grabbed a man on the waste ground near Chamberlain Street. He was running away from the army. A soldier started to beat him over the head with a rifle. The next thing I seen the man was on the ground, very still, near the army Saracens. The army then grabbed another man and pulled him into the Saracen. We ran to the other side of the flat, but just before we did so, we saw the army opened fire shooting into the crowd. The crowd were running towards Joseph Place. At this stage we saw, out the opposite way looking towards the car park behind the flats, a man holding his leg as if he was in pain (presumed shot).

Just after this we saw men crawling along the small wall in front of the shops at Joseph Place. They were protecting themselves because the army were firing from the army posts on the Walls. We then saw a few man dragging a body along at the same place. We looked down on the ground, directly below, in front of the shops and we saw another body lying on the ground very white and very still. One of the men using the small wall as protection came back and tried to reach the man lying in front of the shops. He tried several times to reach him but was forced back because of the shots coming from the Walls. He finally reached the lying man and took his pulse, examined him. At this stage two or three people came over also, they were waving white handkerchiefs, the firing paused at this stage and about 15 minutes later the ambulance arrived. After this we heard fire coming up Rossville Street. We heard no shots until the army opened fire. We never heard any explosions of any sort, except those of shots as mentioned.

This is my statement. It is correct and I agree to have it published.

* * * * * * * * * * * *

Hugh Kearney
AGED 19

Standing in William Street, started throwing gas and dye, moved over to back lane with crowd, then moved back to Rossville Street, five paratroopers were in empty house and were calling 'Fenian Bastards', they started shooting at this time, a man was shot, also a youth, so we got out of the way. By the time we got to Chamberlain Street, the paratroopers had moved in from William to the flats. A man was dragged and kicked around by Chamberlain Street, by soldiers. Shooting then broke out again by army. I ran to top of Chamberlain Street, where about 20 of us were stuck in a corner. A man was lying shot in car park. Fr Daly was giving Last Rites, a youth stood up, put his hands in the air, he was going out to help wounded man, he was shot in leg. We crawled along to Rossville Street Flats. I ran over by St Columb's Wells. Soldiers were then shooting from Derry Walls at Red Cross car. There was a girl stuck in a corner and was hysterical, we tried to help her but couldn't get near her for a while. But we eventually got her away.

* * * * * * * * * * * *

S. B.
SCHOOLBOY, AGED 16

We were walking down William Street and the army sprayed us with dye and gas. We retreated back up William Street and as we were approaching where the Ritchie's factory used to be I saw soldiers on top of the roofs behind the space. Other soldiers, two of them, climbed into a derelict building. Then two or three, definitely not more than three, began throwing stones at these two soldiers. There wasn't more than half a dozen stones thrown altogether when three soldiers on top of the roofs opened fire. Everybody ran for cover and somebody shouted that two men were hit. I ran forward and saw four men carrying a young boy of about 16 who was hit in the thigh. Then I saw another man who was also hit in the leg and I ran to help him. When we had just reached cover another shot rang out and hit the wall behind us. That was definitely the first shooting of the evening — there was no shooting before that. I then moved slowly around towards Free Derry Corner where the meeting was about to begin. The soldiers by this time had advanced into Rossville Street and were shooting rubber bullets and arresting as many young fellows as they could get. Bernadette Devlin had just got up on the platform when we heard an awful lot of shooting which was definitely directed towards the platform on which the meeting was just about to start. Everybody fell flat on their faces and some ran towards the gable of a house. I was at this gable and I looked up and saw soldiers on top of Walls with their guns pointed down at us. Another volley of shots rang out from the Walls on the crowd and a bullet hit a 2-foot high cement pillar beside me. We then realised that they were shooting indiscriminately from the Walls into the crowd and we ran towards St Columb's Wells. The people who had been lying on their faces also got up and ran towards St Columb's Wells. As they did so the army fired constantly into the crowd and I heard that some people had been hit. As the people were running along St Columb's Wells the army still kept firing at them and although more people were hit I kept running on. When I got into the comparative safety of a barricade there was still constant gunfire and I spoke to other people who had seen people shot dead as they were running away.

Margaret J.
FACTORY WORKER, AGED 52

I was in the march from Creggan Estate. As we came into William Street, passing the site of the former Richardson's Factory, we looked towards the now empty site and saw a soldier with a rifle by the rear wall. We proceeded down William Street until the procession was halted. I was then almost at Rossville Street. At this point the army made use of CS gas in great quantities to disperse us. We ran, with streaming eyes, in panic, back up William Street. I heard three distinct shots and a man said, 'They're firing from the helicopter.' The impression was that the shots came from above us. I panicked and ran through the rubble of a burnt-out building and took shelter. A shot then came from the direction of the rifleman positioned at Richardson's Factory site and I saw a young boy fall with his hands raised in the air. I can positively state that this young lad had no weapon of any kind.

I made my way to Columbcille Court and tried to get out of the area. I was helped by a young man and went to the bottom of Fahan Street. Troopers were firing from the Walls at this stage and it was in terror that I finally reached Butcher Gate. There we were told by troops that unless we could climb the barbed wire barricade we could not get through. We went down Waterloo Street to Castle Gate. We were told the same story there and were laughed at by members of the RUC for even attempting to pass. We continued down Waterloo Street to another army barricade where we were again turned back. I went down Harvey Street and met Fr Daly, with others carrying a young boy who had been shot. Fr Daly handed me his hat and we proceeded back into Waterloo Street. We all knelt down and said the Prayers for the Dying and the boy, William Nash, died there. The ambulance came and the body was taken away. A woman and two men accompanied it. I was advised to go down High Street and make my way home via William Street and Strand Road. When I reached Sackville Street one of the paratroopers, on duty there, told me I could go no further. I insisted, and proceeded into Little James' Street and got into Great James' Street where a policeman stopped me. He told me I could go no further. I went down Strand Road to Lower Clarendon Street, along the quays and made my way home. I never, *at any time*, heard any shots from the Bogside area. I saw no nail bombs, no petrol bombs. This is my statement: I heard only cries for help.

* * * * * * * * * * * *

Thomas Ralph Dawe
TEXTILE WORKER, AGED 28

I am originally from Bootle in Liverpool. I have spent ten years in the Royal Navy. I have been living here for two years.

As I made my way from Chamberlain Street to Eden Place I saw to my surprise that the army had come along Rossville Street as far as the High Flats. There was one Saracen which had advanced right into the car park at the back of the flats. Many people including women and girls were trying to get out of the way and running diagonally across the courtyard towards Fahan Street. On my way I saw soldiers who had already dismounted making arrests using batons being covered by soldiers kneeling — their guns at the ready. While I was running across this courtyard I heard an English voice shout: 'Stand still, or we'll open fire.' I ran on and on my way I heard shots behind me. There were hundreds of others running also and the shots seemed to be in our direction, coming from behind. These were the first shots I heard all day. I made my way through the courtyard safely and round to the front of the shops. I stopped at the chemist's — the end shop with its side on to Rossville Street. I turned round facing Fahan Street where I witnessed men carrying a body from the courtyard that I came out of. This boy was taken into the house at the end of Joseph Place opposite the shops. While I was watching this I heard several shots come from my left, i.e. Rossville Street. Two bullets actually hit the pavement in front of me. I fell flat and lay for a few minutes. I then crawled along the front of Joseph Place to an entrance to the back of the maisonettes. The shooting became heavier as I took cover here with many others including women who were screaming. After a few moments I thought of getting out the back but then I realised that there was shooting from the Walls.

A woman was screaming and shouting 'Can no one help that

young boy out there?' I pressed forward to the front of this entrance from where I could see a young boy about 20 yards in front of me on the not yet completed new slipway leading on to Fahan Street. He was lying on his side, crumpled up, with his back to me. His left leg was stiff and raised slightly. I could see a slight quiver in it. I sought the help of another man and with a hankie we both ventured out — the man waving this hankie stepped out. Immediately the shots rang out again and this burst of fire lifted the gravel in front of us. We stepped back in. These shots came from Rossville Street — from the direction of the soldiers. We sheltered for a minute or two; the women were almost hysterical as the firing became heavier from the direction of the Walls above us. We decided to get the women to a safer position — across to the Wells. The women in a single line and in a crouched position sheltering behind the grass bank made their way slowly along the passageway in the direction of the Wells. They had to cross an opening in the embankment on their left — this was a stairway to the car park above. All women crossed the gap safely except for the last woman immediately in front of me. As the firing continued from the Walls this woman panicked and refused to go past the gap. I tried to relax her by giving her a cigarette and telling her to keep calm. She leaned against the wall and straightened up a little — her head coming up above the level of the bank on her left. Just then I heard further automatic fire from the Walls. Bullets landed on the soft earth of the bank above us and clay from the bank showered about the woman and myself. I pulled her down — distracted her for a second and managed to push her across the gap. I followed her and we both arrived safely in the Wells.

This is my statement and it is correct.

* * * * * * * * * * * *

Carol McCafferty
BANK OFFICIAL, AGED 20

On Sunday 30 January I was in No. 49 Glenfada Park opposite the Rossville Street Flats. The people from the march came up Rossville Street past the window where I was sitting. The people on the lorry were calling the people to Free Derry Corner. The people came up to gather there. Most were there standing waiting for the meeting to start. Bernadette Devlin had just started to speak when the people started to run up Rossville Street. At first I thought the people were running from a fresh burst of gas but then I heard shots from the William Street direction. The people scattered and some men and boys came up against the wall of the house where I was, for shelter from the soldiers who fired from the barricade in front of the flats. My aunt shouted to me that she saw a rifle aimed in our direction from the Walls (Derry Walls). I had just time to shout a warning to the fellas to clear when they opened up from the Walls and fired at where they were but they had moved just in time, one may have been hit. I went to the door at the back of the house and called in all the people at the back of Glenfada Park because the soldiers were firing across there also. When I went into the living room everyone was on the floor. I saw from the window a man lying shot at the corner of the Rossville Street Flats, by the telephone. A girl was carried away from there into the first house opposite by a first aider. Another fella was lying injured near the steps up to Fahan Street. Someone tried to crawl out to him when the army opened up on him. He tried a few times and when he did eventually reach him and lifted his head the army fired and shot him. A cameraman came out from behind the Rossville Flats waving a white cloth, the army allowed him to reach the one who had been shot — others followed and reached the one who had been shot. The cameraman then went down to a fella who was lying in the open but when he reached him the fella got up so he must have been all right. He went down to the one was lying by the telephone but he was dead and someone covered the body with the Civil Rights banner. The ambulance was allowed in and they took the stretcher into the first house of the row of houses opposite and brought out two people on the stretcher. The priest (Fr Mulvey, I think) was by the ambulance and he waved a white flag as the stretcher was being brought into Rossville Street from behind the cover of the flats but the army opened fire at them and they dropped the stretcher — all lay flat including the ambulance men. They finally allowed the stretcher to reach the ambulance and it was driven off with a lot of other casualties, some from the flats. After that everything calmed down and the bodies were collected.

8: A Military View

Many Irishmen throughout this century have served in the British forces, including relatives of my own. I recall catching a glimpse of my maternal Uncle William one Sunday afternoon in the mid-1960s on the documentary The World at War. *For a few seconds he was profiled standing on the beach at Dunkirk, with a weapon and smoking a cigarette, awaiting evacuation to England.*

On Bloody Sunday, therefore, it was inevitable that at least some ex-servicemen would be eyewitnesses to the Para operation. These also included English ex-servicemen who had met and married Derry women and had settled with them in the city.

The British Establishment has always claimed a special affection for its veterans. The following statements, and those of others throughout this book, deserve to be given due regard by that Establishment, if only as an acknowledgement of services rendered.

In all cases these men were shocked and appalled by the actions of 1 Para.

* * * * * * * * * * * *

John Gorman
MATURE STUDENT, AGED 42

I took part in the Civil Rights march on Sunday, 30 January 1972. The march was quiet, peaceful and good-humoured. When the march stopped at the army barricade I was beside the Lion Bar about fifteen yards from the barricade. Some stones were thrown at the troops who then replied with CS gas canisters. The water cannon then appeared and sprayed the crowd, including myself, with water.

I then made my way over Chamberlain Street. People were shouting at me to make my way to Free Derry Corner where a meeting was to be held. I crossed from Chamberlain Street to Rossville Street, stopping to vomit as a result of the CS gas.

I went up Rossville Street towards Free Derry Corner on the side of the High Flats. I was at the barricade beside the High Flats when I heard the sound of Saracens. I looked up and saw four Saracens, one whippet car and one four-ton lorry-load of paratroopers. I knew they were paratroopers by their distinctive red berets. The paratroopers deployed left behind the High Flats, right to Glenfada Park and centre ahead up Rossville Street. The platoon in the centre opened fire — three high-velocity shots were fired first of all. Then the whippet car opened fire — this was automatic fire from a Browning machine gun. There was panic among the crowd — men, women and children who scattered. I heard girls say it was rubber bullets were being fired but I knew it was live rounds were being fired and shouted at people to get down. Some people remarked at this time to me that the soldiers wouldn't do that (i.e. fire live rounds) but I told them I knew what I was talking about — the rounds were live ones.

I ran across Rossville Street to Glenfada Park and lay down at the side of a small wall. I saw bodies lying on the barricade. At this stage I did not know if these were dead or wounded. I noticed before people moving towards the bodies on the barricade. I saw an elderly grey-haired man crouched down and moving towards the bodies on the barricade. He put up one arm in the air and was shot through the arm. When he was shot, he was beside three bodies on the barricade on the Glenfada Park side. After this shooting I put my head down and saw no more for about five minutes. All this time the shooting continued. When there was a lull in the firing I went to help the wounded and dead at the barricade. The army had now withdrawn into William Street.

I can say definitely that until the time that the paratroopers opened fire, they were not fired on, and no petrol bombs or nail bombs were thrown at them. From the position I was in when the paratroopers drove into Rossville Street I would have known if any shots had been fired at them. The first shots I heard were three high velocity shots from the centre group of paratroopers.

I should state here that I served for nine years with the Royal Enniskillen Fusiliers in Malaya, Egypt and Kenya and am fully acquainted with the different sounds made by different types of weapons.

I served one year as well with the Ulster Defence Regiment in Derry until I was told to resign as my services were no longer required.

I have seen plenty of action during my years in the army but have never seen such murderous brutality as I witnessed on Sunday 30 January in Rossville Street.

One further very important thing I witnessed. When I was at the wall at Glenfada Park, I saw Michael McDaid alive being put into a Saracen by paratroopers in Rossville Street. Later that night I learned that he was dead.

This is a true statement of what happened.

* * * * * * * * * * * *

John McLaughlin
LABOURER, AGED 39

I was standing at the junction of William Street/Little James' Street when the army Saracens entered Rossville Street. When they stopped, soldiers disembarked and they immediately opened fire into the fleeing crowd. I ran forward towards Mrs Shield's house (Glenfada Park?) They brought two wounded people into the house — an elderly man shot in the leg and shoulder and a young boy shot in the leg. There was a soldier at the corner of the house whom I approached and asked could an ambulance be got and told them that they would bleed to death. They replied with bad language — 'Let the f——— bleed to death.' We told the soldiers that there were no guns here and they told us to move away or they would 'blow our brains out'.

I am an EX-SERVICEMAN with active service in Korea and I have never seen such atrocities committed.

Fr McLaughlin and Fr Carolan could collaborate this evidence — also George McDermott.

This is my statement and it is correct.

* * * * * * * * * * * * *

James Chapman
CIVIL SERVANT, AGED 57

I am a Welshman, a loyal subject to the Crown. I am a Catholic but I have not been intimidated by either Catholics or Protestants. I am not a member of any organisation, political or otherwise. I am a civil servant and do not enter into political activities. I am aged 57 and have lived in the Bogside for 34 years. My wife is an Irish Catholic. I married her in 1938 when I was a regular serving soldier. I retired from the army in 1946 as a Warrant Officer Class I and remained on the army reserve until 1949. I then joined the Territorial Army with which I served for four years. Since then my job as a civil servant has been with the Army department.

On Sunday, 30 January 1972, I was at the window of my sitting room in Glenfada Park. My home consists of a maisonette and I have two floors and the maisonette is above a single flat. My sitting room is therefore first-floor height. My sitting room directly overlooks a rubble barricade which crosses Rossville Street. At about 4 p.m. I saw the Civil Rights marchers coming down William Street and crossing the mouth of Rossville Street. When I first saw the marchers nothing struck me as being unusual. The first thing that really caught my attention was the sight of the crowd fleeing (i.e. running fast) down Rossville Street from William Street and through an alleyway which is between Chamberlain Street and Rossville Street onto the waste ground. At that time I heard rubber bullets being fired at the fleeing crowd from the direction of Little James' Street and also I saw the smoke of CS gas in the mouth of Rossville Street. Before this occurred the lorry which was leading the march had gone past the rubble barricade with a large number of marchers. I would say that about 5,000 to 6,000 people had not got past the rubble barricade when the CS gas and rubber bullets were fired.

I then saw a fleet of seven Saracens preceded by a ferret scout car coming into Rossville at about 40 mph from Little James' Street. Also I saw a Bedford four-tonner follow the Saracens and pull up on the pavement at the mouth of Rossville Street. The ferret stopped in the middle of Rossville Street near the northern end of Rossville Flats. Five of the Saracens took up positions at the northern entrance to the Rossville Flats. The other two Saracens took up positions at the northern end of Glenfada Park. The vehicles reached their positions by fanning out across the waste ground off Rossville Street.

Between 50 and 100 paratroopers dismounted from the Saracens. Other paratroopers were running up Rossville Street and the waste ground in support of the Saracens. On disembarking from the Saracens the paratroopers assumed firing positions from the corner of the Rossville Flats and in Rossville Street itself and from the corner of Glenfada Park. They opened fire immediately on the crowd who were trying to flee through the rubble barricade near my house. I would estimate that about 20 to 30 shots were fired in the first burst and I saw three people fall, I believe, dead or dying. They fell over the barricade. People who were already on the other side of the barricade went flat on the ground and crawled towards Free Derry Corner. An elderly man on the Free Derry Corner side of the barricade got up on his knees and called to the soldiers to get an ambulance. This man was wounded in the left arm or side. The soldiers that I saw continued to fire sporadically in the same direction as before and they ignored the man for 10 to 15 minutes. I then saw an officer speak to a senior NCO who was in a Saracen and the NCO drove his Saracen car through the barricade and 10–15 yards beyond it. The Saracen then reversed to within 7–8 feet of the bodies. Troops got out of the Saracen and lifted the bodies by the hair of the head and legs and threw them into the Saracen. The wounded man whom I mentioned was roughly pushed away from the Saracen. I then heard the NCO shout to those around, 'Get off the fucking streets'. Then the Saracen turned round and came back through the barricade and joined the other Saracens.

After the people were shot at the barricade I noticed several people in the waste ground who had not got to the barricade or found shelter, walk towards the soldiers in an attitude of surrender, i.e. with their hands on their heads and I saw the paratroopers hitting them with the butts of their guns and kicking them. I saw them kick about five or six people to the ground and then drop them into Saracens. I saw no sign of disorderly behaviour or resistance from those people who were arrested.

After the Saracens returned with the bodies there was more continuous firing towards Free Derry Corner by the soldiers whom I could see but by then most people had got away from the barricade. The soldiers retired from Rossville Street at about 4.45 p.m. and I heard no more shooting after that.

At no time did I see any civilian carrying arms or anything that could be even mistaken for an offensive weapon. There was no live firing prior to the entry of the paratroopers into Rossville Street. I saw nobody throw missiles at the soldiers. I never heard any nail bombs or petrol bombs thrown on that afternoon.

* * * * * * * * * * * *

Hugh S.
TURNER, AGED 22

I was at the junction of William Street/Chamberlain Street when army Saracens first moved in across Rossville Street. Deciding that the situation was dangerous, I ran across Chamberlain Street and just when I was nearing the end of this street, the first high-velocity shots rang out from the direction of William Street/Rossville Street junction. At the corner of Chamberlain Street I saw a young girl, who had been shot in the leg, being carried across Chamberlain Street by two people.

Having heard these shots, I checked around the general area of Chamberlain Street to see if there was any further sign of shooting. Then another volley of shots rang out again from William Street/Rossville Street direction and I immediately sought shelter by turning left at the end of Chamberlain Street and positioned myself behind a wall at the children's playground. By this time, the shooting had stopped and from this wall, I noticed a man lying shot in the middle of the car park directly in front of me. This man was being attended to by Fr Daly. One other person who was behind the wall with me decided to assist Fr Daly in his efforts to help the wounded man. He moved out into the open area of the car park holding his hands aloft, thus indicating that he was unarmed. Immediately there was another burst of fire which came from Rossville Street. The man stumbled, hit by the bullets, but didn't fall. Two more men from behind the wall ran to his aid and carried him across into Chamberlain Street.

I remained in the same position behind the wall at Chamberlain Street and I noticed a crowd exactly opposite at a distance of 70 yards approximately from me, gathered in an alleyway which led through the flats into St Joseph's Place. Meanwhile, the army was in Rossville Street and had a direct view of the alleyway and the people in it across an empty car park. I also noticed a green Vauxhall Viva parked about 15 yards from the alleyway and this car was in direct line with the people in the alleyway and the army in Rossville Street. I heard three shots coming from the direction of the soldiers which were aimed directly at the people in the alleyway. The bullets struck the wall exactly behind the people who were definitely unarmed. I heard two more shots which struck the car (which as I said, was in direct line of the people and the army). The people immediately dispersed and disappeared down the alleyway. This shooting seemed to be completely indiscriminate as it is my view that the army shot at anybody they saw moving.

Meanwhile, there was a lull in the firing and three men who were alongside me in the group behind the wall at the rear of Chamberlain Street decided to make their way behind the wall of the children's playground towards the same alleyway at which the army had previously opened fire. I presumed these three to be safe as I saw them disappear down the alleyway. I took the same course of action and proceeded along the wall and into the alleyway. At the bottom of the alleyway, I noticed the last of these three men who had gone before me, lying shot on the ground. He was lying directly in front of the shopping area of the flats (Rossville). From this position, I could see an army Saracen with a soldier standing beside it in Rossville Street at a distance of approximately 80 yards from me and again in the direct firing-line of the wounded man. So I took it for granted that the man was in fact shot from the army Saracen.

Throughout, I can definitely testify that there was no shooting from the direction of the Rossville Street Flats or from that general area against the soldiers. Neither was there any evidence of nail-bombing or petrol-bombing.

* * * * * * * * * * * * *

Brian McColl
POSTMAN, AGED 37

I wish to begin my statement at the time the Saracens entered the waste ground in front of Rossville Flats on 30 January 1972. I saw the two Saracens driving straight at us, we were in groups of four and five and we scattered. I then made for the only exit from the flats — the alleyway leading out to Rossville Street. Behind me I could hear rubber bullets and when I reached the alleyway it was blocked — people jammed tight around it. There seemed to be several hundred trying to get through. I then heard the crack of rifle fire — I am familiar with rifle fire as I have been in the navy for fourteen years. I kept pushing my way out as the rifle fire was coming from behind. I got out and turned right to the wall near the telephone kiosk for cover. I heard that a man had been shot (not sure where he was shot) and was being carried round from the main entrance of the flats on Rossville Street. I then went into Rossville Street and faced downwards towards William Street. I saw about six to seven soldiers around Columbcille Court firing at random up Rossville Street. Myself with two or three others whom I cannot name carried the body of a boy whom I was told was Gilmore around the corner behind the wall. I did not know he was dead but thought he looked serious. He had gunshot wounds on the right side of his chest. I called a Knight of Malta (a man of about 20 with glasses) who said the wounds were too serious for him to treat. Barney Gallagher, Creggan, opened the boy Gilmore's shirt and just then his eyes rolled in his head and I thought he was dying. Barney Gallagher said the act of contrition in his ear. Just with that the army opened fire from the direction of Glenfada Park at an acute angle. I with the others took cover along the wall (towards the telephone booth) and left the body on the ground. I crouched and watched the boy die — he turned grey then waxy white and as I watched his neck muscles stopped and his gums stiffened. There was a young girl about 16 nearby who became hysterical as she watched and when told the boy was dying she screamed and roared. It seemed that the more she roared the more the army fired. After I ran for cover after leaving the body the firing seemed constant. I hit the girl to try to bring her round and she went limp across my knee. (B. Gallagher can verify this.) While this firing was going on I looked up and saw the body of a man lying about two yards away from me. He was dead and looked as if he had been shot around the head — his brains were splattered around. Before seeing this, this man had been in our company trying to help people. I did not see him actually moving away from the wall. A lull in the shooting came after this and myself and Barney Gallagher lifted the girl who was still in hysterics, and who had regained consciousness, into the first house in St Joseph's Place to people the name of McConnells. In their hallway was a body of a man of about 25–30 who had been shot in the arm and the chest. He was bleeding very badly. I left the girl with Barney Gallagher in the house and I went and shouted to the people in the flats for a phone. There was no shooting at this time. Then Mr Barr of Barr's shop came and opened the shop. I went in and dialled 999 and told the operator to send all the available ambulances to Rossville Street Flats. He told me all ambulances had already been sent there and hung up on me. A few priests came to this area and started to give the last rites. When I came back to shout for a phone I noticed a group of people (10 or 12) around both bodies. After this the ambulances arrived.

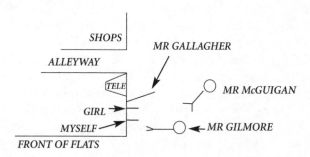

During the time I was lying behind this wall after leaving the body of Gilmore I was able to see up Rossville Street as far as St

Columb's Street and Westland Street. I could see about five young boys lying on the ground on their faces for cover. In spite of this I could still hear the army shooting at them and I saw the bullets hitting the ground all around them. I am now drawing out the positions to clarify where I was during the time I took cover.

This is my statement and it is correct and I am willing to have it published or used in an investigation if necessary.

* * * * * * * * * * * *

William McL.
AGED 45

I took part in the Civil Rights march on Sunday, 30 January 1972. I consider the march to be peaceful and any stone throwing I saw was minor compared to the usual stone throwing. When the march came to a halt, I was at the interjunction of Rossville Street/Little James' Street and the crowd seemed perfectly happy that they had made their protest and that they would not get to the Guildhall Square. At this stage the gas was pretty heavy and I moved up towards Columbcille Court to avoid the gas when I heard what seemed to be a salvo of rubber bullets mixed with rifle fire and the crowd ran. I saw two people being carried up by Columbcille Court. One was a young lad of about 15 years and he had a bullet wound in the top portion of his right leg. The other was an elderly man whom I know now to be John Johnston. He was shot around what seemed to be his shoulder. I'm not sure as he had a heavy overcoat on. There was a lull after this and even then it was like a carnival atmosphere and I was casually leaning against a wall talking to my brother-in-law when about, I would say, three Saracens came across at full speed from Little James' Street into the open ground in Rossville Street. Even at this stage I did not get alarmed as the crowd was well thinned out in Rossville Street and most people were standing in groups conversing. My reaction was that this was the usual sortie to drive the people on up to Free Derry Corner. When the Saracens came to a halt, I have recollections of soldiers jumping out, the next

I heard what seemed to be more salvos of rubber bullets intermingled with rifle fire. I also heard what seemed like an automatic weapon on single fire. The crowd fled in terror up Rossville Street. Everybody ran in the same direction and I ran with the fear of God in me. I managed to get behind a boundary wall at the furthest end of Glenfada Park. I managed to get my head around the corner and saw two bodies lying behind the small barricade. People made repeated attempts to get to the aid of these men by waving white hankies. The army opened fire on the would-be rescuers. I am an ex-serviceman. I served with the Royal Norfolk and the Suffolk Regiment which are now amalgamated to form the East Anglian Regiment now serving in Derry. I swear to God there were no nail bombs, petrol bombs or shooting from civilians that day.

* * * * * * * * * * * *

Duncan C.
ROOF TILER, AGED 39
ENGLISH, EX-NAVY

On the evening of 30 January I intended to look in on the meeting in Guildhall Square. Hearing the commotion in William Street I went down High Street to Chamberlain Street. While standing at the corner of Chamberlain Street and High Street a soldier (paratrooper) approached from Eden Terrace Place and said, 'Come with me, you bastard.' I went with him to Eden Terrace [Place], where there was an armoured car parked. He searched me and told me to get into the armoured car. The only person in the armoured car was an elderly civilian (badly cut and bleeding). About 10 minutes later gas started to come into the car. I opened the door to get air and was promptly hit on the head with a rifle-butt. The cut received two stitches later. The armoured car was then driven to William Street. We sat there and after about five minutes a paratrooper opened the door and said 'What do you think of this, you Irish cunt?' and then fired a rubber bullet into my face (from about five feet). I was badly stunned, and bled profusely. Sometime after this the elderly man and myself were taken from the armoured car and put into a military police landrover where we remained for about half an hour. The paratrooper who arrested me took me from the landrover to the back of an army lorry and told me to jump inside. When I put my hands on the tailboard to pull myself up on the lorry another paratrooper standing in the lorry hit me on the hand with the rifle butt, injuring the middle finger.

In the lorry we were made kneel down facing the front with our hands on our heads, and in this way we were driven to the Dockyard. There we were made run the gauntlet of about ten paratroopers to the place of detention (a large shed). In this shed we were made stand with our hands high against the wall (search position) for between two and three hours. During this period I was photographed and the paratrooper gave his account of the arrest to a military policeman after which I was handed over to an RUC man. The RUC wanted a statement from me, which I refused to give. I was then returned to the detention centre. After quite a long time I was brought to the military doctor. He put five stitches in my nose, two stitches in my head and put plaster on my finger. He asked me to sign a document stating that I had been attended by him. I signed this statement. After this I was brought back to the detention centre where I was allowed to sit or stand in a rather restricted area. Tea was served at this time. I was kept there till I was called by an RUC sergeant who charged me with 'riotous behaviour in the Rossville Street area'. I was allowed out on bail of £50 to be paid to the Crown if I did not appear at court on 3 February. I was then escorted to the main gate and bidden 'Good night'.

* * * * * * * * * * * *

Michael O.
FILM PRODUCER, AGED 49

During the course of the Civil Rights march which I was viewing from the corner of William Street and Rossville Street and taking photographs for possible further use, I saw the lorry at the head of the marchers turn right from William Street into Rossville Street. I perceived an army barricade further down William Street, and I surmised that the lorry had turned right from William Street because of this. Some of the marchers including press or television crews proceeded down William Street to the barricade. The next thing I saw was a spurt of coloured water drenching the marchers at the barricade, and I heard the sound of guns which I knew to be rubber-bullet guns, and the sound of gas canisters, and saw the gas billowing round William Street and Rossville Street. I then saw some youths throwing stones and debris at the army barricade in Little James' Street. The gas became so thick that I retreated approximately 50 yards up Rossville Street. I then saw a girl collapse against a wall on the right-hand side of Rossville Street. I did not know what was wrong with her. People were milling, coughing, vomiting, eyes streaming. The next thing I saw was a youth being carried from the corner of William Street/Rossville Street covered in blood. I assumed he had been shot but could not understand this not having heard any rifle-fire or pistol shots. I pushed my way through the crowd and took three photographs of the youth whilst he was being attended by first-aid men. I was told by one of the first-aid men that he had been struck on the nose by a gas canister.

I heard an announcement by a man with a loud-hailer that the meeting was taking place at Free Derry Corner. I was standing on the pavement on the left-hand side of Rossville Street and about 50 or 60 yards from William Street Corner. I saw two armoured vehicles enter Rossville Street. The crowd shouted 'The Saracens are coming. Run!' I ran with the crowd. As I got over the barricade opposite the High Flats I heard some youths shouting 'Don't let the bastard British in.' Three youths pulled a make-shift wooden barrier across the gap in the rubble barricade. Everybody was running up Rossville Street, and I then heard the sound of shots. People started screaming and shouting. 'They are shooting at us!' 'Lie down!' I saw hundreds of people dropping to the ground, and I saw puffs of dust rising from the road and the whirr of bullets. I did not lie down. I continued to run and attempt to take photographs. I reached some houses past the High Flats, and I saw a wounded man being carried into a house in Joseph Place. I was pulled into a house. The people who pulled me in told me it was for my own safety. People were still lying on the ground in Rossville Street at this time. I took photographs of them. I looked down Rossville Street towards the barricade and I saw soldiers running to both sides of the road and shooting. I then saw two people, one appeared to be dead, the other was lying across the body in a protective position, with his left arm raised above the rubble. I took four photographs of these two people: I saw his left arm fall to the ground, and he then raised his right arm. An armoured vehicle came up Rossville Street and broke through the barricade. The soldiers emerged and dragged the man to his feet. While one soldier covered him, two others dragged the body of the person I assumed dead to the rear of the vehicle and took the other man to the rear of the same vehicle. Of these incidents I took photographs. While this was going on rifle fire was still being directed up Rossville Street. I was then pulled bodily into the house by three men who were in the hallway. The shooting then stopped. I then proceeded past Free Derry Corner.

On the following day (Monday, 31 January 1972) at 4.10 p.m. I had just opened my car door at Newmarket Street when I saw three soldiers coming towards me on the opposite side of the street. I heard the last man in the patrol (wireless operator) shout something, and look to his left down some steps. Thinking there was some trouble I directed my camera towards the soldiers and took three separate photographs of the wireless operator bending down, picking up a stone and throwing it down the steps. The soldiers carried on walking in my direction. Whilst they were passing me on the opposite side, I took two photographs of each soldier. They turned left into Orchard Street. I walked to the steps myself, and saw about six children and I asked them what had happened. They said that the soldier had called at them 'You Fenian bastards'. They informed me the soldier had thrown a stone at them. I took two photographs of these children, walked back to my car, and got into it, turned left into Orchard Street to go to the City Hotel. Seventy yards down Orchard Street I was stopped by the same patrol. I wound the window down and had a rifle pointed through the window at me by a corporal. I asked what they wanted — was not answered. The other soldier (not the wireless operator) opened the car door and dragged the camera from around my neck, opened the camera and pulled the film out. I protested and was told to shut up or I'd be shot also. They threw the camera in my lap, slammed the door and left quickly. I went to the City Hotel and protested to some pressmen. I was advised not to waste my time complaining at Victoria Barracks.

After lying for five days on Dunkirk Beach in 1940, serving in His Majesty's Forces, this is my second experience of mass murder, as no petrol bombs or nail bombs had been thrown in my opinion — prior to the British Army opening fire.

* * * * * * * * * * * *

Patrick C.
PETROL PUMP ATTENDANT, AGED 56

I am an ex-serviceman and I have served in Palestine (two campaigns), Malta, Africa, Dodecanese. I was a soldier in the 2nd Battalion of the Royal Irish Fusiliers. I was marching in this very peaceful march on Sunday 30 January. We came to the junction of Rossville Street and Chamberlain Street. I stopped in Chamberlain Street when the dye and gas was first thrown. This caused me to move back to Rossville Street. At this stage I was told that a man and a boy were shot. I then saw Saracen tanks moving into Rossville Street with troops behind and alongside them. I then saw the troops open fire, without any warning, as everyone was running to get out of their way. There were no shots or nail bombs thrown or shot at this stage as I am familiar with the sound of both from my own experience. I saw the troops stand in an open position and fire into the crowd. No shots were fired at them. If shots had been fired by snipers, as the army allege, they could not have missed these soldiers. I saw two men shot, lying in the open. They were not armed nor were they in a sniping position. They were members of the crowd which were there at the march.

9: 'A Fusillade of Bombs and Bullets'?

Jane Winter, in her Preface to this book, recounts under the heading 'Official Versions of the Events' the British Ministry of Defence's account of Bloody Sunday. This account was issued to the world media by the British Information Services, New York, on 1 February 1972. This was on the same day that Prime Minister Edward Heath met with the Lord Chief Justice of England, Lord Widgery, to discuss the proposed Tribunal of Inquiry into the Derry killings. A few hours before that meeting, and in spite of the government's announcement that an Inquiry was to be held, the British Minister of State for Defence, Lord Balniel, insisted on having the army's version of events written into the parliamentary minutes. He stated that 1 Para '. . . came under fire from gunmen, nail bombers and petrol bombers, some in the flats and some at ground level'.

In 1990, David Reynolds in his book, The Paras, 50 Years of Courage, wrote of Bloody Sunday:

> The Paras moved in to make arrests using batons. . . . But the crowd turned on them and, caught in a clever trap, IRA snipers opened fire on them. . . . Two Paras were hit by machinegun fire and two more seriously burned after acid bombs were dropped off the top of Rossville Street flats. Thompson sub-machine guns, Garand sniper rifles and Armalites were fired at the Paras in a series of separate fire fights which lasted over an hour. The Paras engaged armed terrorists in what was a straightforward ambush by the IRA, who attempted to use the cover of the crowd for protection. When the shooting had stopped, 13 gunmen were dead and another 16 injured. . . .

It is widely believed that as many as 20 gunmen died during the fire fight, but were taken away to be buried elsewhere for fear that forensic science would have proved that they had been firing weapons. The Widgery report exonerated the Paras from IRA claims that they had fired indiscriminately at a crowd and of opening fire before they themselves were fired on. . . .

For the Battalion they had simpl[y] done their job. Having been ambushed, they returned fire and the world's press dubbed the event 'Bloody Sunday'. It was a day the IRA would never forget.

If the IRA was present in force, it must be the best-kept secret in the history of the Bogside and Creggan communities.

Of the several hundred eyewitness accounts of people who were there on the day, almost all state categorically that they neither saw nor heard gunfire, nail bombs or petrol bombs fired from the civilian side. If a fusillade of bombs and bullets had been unleashed, the communities of the Bogside and Creggan would, at least, have spoken to one another about it. In twenty-five years, the collective memory has been consistent on the following facts:

- *Once the army had begun to open fire on the fleeing crowd, one man, positioned close to the gable of Chamberlain Street, stepped forward from a group of three or four people and discharged two or three shots from a revolver. He was immediately told by civilians nearby to 'Fuck off!' for fear that he would draw army fire on them. Italian photographer Fulvio Grimaldi photographed this man.*

- *Bottles were thrown from the Rossville Flats which may or may not have had acid in them.*

- *There are a few isolated reports of one or two other shooting incidents and these may be supported by some of the following eyewitness testimonies. However, even if these are accurate, they certainly do not constitute a fusillade of bullets and bombs.*

- *One eyewitness who watched events from the fifth floor of the Rossville Flats said that he heard one nail bomb explode, but this is not corroborated by any other eyewitness, or by detailed analysis of sound recordings of the day.*

- *Two or three car-loads of gunmen did arrive on the scene after 1 Para had withdrawn from the Bogside. A number of these gunmen did open fire on army positions. This, however, was after the events we now call 'Bloody Sunday' were over.*

In the final analysis, neither the Paras nor their elephant-sized armoured vehicles sustained injuries or damage from bullets or bombs. The claims by David Reynolds that two Paras were hit by machine-gun fire and two more seriously burned by acid bombs are unsubstantiated. In the circumstances, such casualties would have been a godsend to Lord Widgery and the British government.

Lord Widgery, who Reynolds correctly states 'exonerated the Paras', concluded that '. . . the soldiers escaped injury by reason of their superior field-craft and training' (paragraph 95).

* * * * * * * * * * * *

Charles M.
DRIVING INSTRUCTOR, AGED 36

At approximately 4.10 I joined the end of the parade in William Street. I was in the company of Jack Quigg, a next-door neighbour. As we proceeded down William Street I met my cousin Dan McCafferty whose clothes were spattered with a dark substance which I assumed was dye used by the army. He confirmed my assumption. He told me that the army, to quote his words, were 'having a field-day', and that 'the situation looked rather nasty'.

Then I proceeded further down William Street, and when I came opposite the remains of Richardson's shirt factory I was completely overcome by gas. I could see however that stones were being thrown in the direction of the army in Little James' Street. I was then approached by another friend, Patrick O'Carolan, Glen Road, who is an excise officer in H.M. Customs and Excise.

We stood for a while trying to clear our heads and eyes from the effects of gas. There were very few people in our immediate area. The bulk of our people had by now proceeded along Rossville Street to a meeting at Free Derry Corner. On looking across towards the rear of the church in Great James' Street I saw two soldiers lying on the flat roof alongside the church. Something I thought rather strange occurred to me on looking in that direction. I saw two windows on the gable side of the disused building, previously occupied by Abbey Taxis Ltd, which had formerly been blocked up by the Derry Commission, were now lying open. I saw movement inside the shadows of the building and was amazed to see two paratroopers crouching in a sniping position, pointing their rifles in the direction of myself and my friends. Their headgear showed them to be paratroopers.

I said to Pat O'Carolan: 'We are in a very exposed and dangerous position if anything like shooting does start.' I had hardly finished this sentence when one of the paratroopers in the building lifted his rifle to the shooting position. I pulled Pat O'Carolan into waste ground on my left and as I did so still looking at the soldier, he fired one shot and hit a youth* who had moved into our position. The youth fell and was dragged across the waste ground towards Columbcille Court. As we ran in that direction a second man* was shot in the shoulder as he ran alongside me. He also fell and was assisted out of the line of fire. I must make it absolutely clear that no one, where I was standing, was involved in riotous or disorderly behaviour.

There was panic all round as people scrambled behind buildings which would give them some cover. I then made my way to Glenfada Park. During this time, which was only minutes, there was a lull. Suddenly fire sounded to my right and bullets thudded into the masonry above my head. Again more panic with people lying flat and seeking whatever cover they could find. Shots came from the direction of the walled part of the city, which is patrolled solely by the security forces. I saw two men running towards where I was taking cover. One of them I knew personally. His name is Gerard McKinney, Waterside. He was running across an open courtyard in Glenfada Park. I saw him stop and fling his arms in the air. He shouted: 'No, No,' and was shot by a soldier who appeared at the corner. McKinney fell to the ground on his back and lay still. The other who fell was moving, trying to pull himself towards us, but then seemed to lose consciousness.

---

* I have since learned that the man was J. Johnston of Marlboro Road, and the youth was named McCallion and came from Circular Road.

Several attempts were made to get to the fallen men, but each time anyone exposed himself he was fired on. A man called John McLaughlin, carrying a white handkerchief and with his hands clasped above his head, eventually succeeded in reaching them. I may add that several attempts had already been made by people and myself, carrying and waving white handkerchiefs, to get to the fallen men, but these earlier attempts were repulsed by rifle fire. I assume therefore that the army had pulled back from this area.

During the period described in my statement, I only heard two low-velocity shots coming from the area of Rossville Street. I wish to emphasise that the army had already fired many rounds before I heard these two low-velocity shots. On viewing the bullet-scarred gables the following day, it was obvious from the strikemarks that the shots came from the area which was held by the army.

* * * * * * * * * * * *

Sean McCarron
MILLWRIGHT, AGED 19

Yesterday, 30 January, I took part in a Civil Rights demonstration. There was definite stone throwing from the demonstrations but after the use of CS gas and water cannon the crowd was dispersed. I ran in the direction of Rossville Street Flats where I saw one man lying wounded on the ground. He was being attended by Rev. Fr Daly. Gunfire was being directed at the crowd from the direction of the army personnel carrier. I witnessed two army marksmen fire definite automatic fire into a crowd of ten or fifteen people; no one fell. I then saw a young man who ran to help the priest being shot in the leg, there then followed fifteen minutes of indiscriminate shooting from the army, all the shots came from the army. I think I heard one shot that may have come from the direction of the crowd. There were no nail bombs thrown, no petrol bombs were thrown. I would say that the army fired at least fifteen hundred rounds. After walking across a children's playground with a section of the crowd, six or seven of whom were waving white handkerchiefs, I arrived in front of shops in front of the flats. Three men were lying dead, one of whom had been shot through the eye, another must have been shot from the direction of the City Walls.

* * * * * * * * * * * *

Anna O'D.
Housewife

I was within sight of the head of the march, at McLoughlin's furniture store, when the first attack of gas and dye came. The crowd panicked and turned to run. I told them not to run. There were girls in hysteria. People where choking with the gas and tears were streaming from their eyes. Some younger boys began throwing stones. Gas and rubber bullets continued as people retreated from the army into Rossville Street and Columbcille Court. Just then, a shot was fired from the Presbyterian Church wall in Great James' Street, where at least two British soldiers were positioned. This shot injured a youth in the legs. It was the first shot fired, and it definitely came from the British Army. A man appeared with an old rifle behind the taxi office in William Street, and fired one shot — hitting nothing. Other bystanders advised him to put the gun away, as it would only draw fire — which he did immediately. I saw no sign of this man after this incident. I am certain that no nail bombs or petrol bombs were thrown at any stage, nor was there any evidence of gunmen other than the British troops.

* * * * * * * * * * * *

F. Lawton
Unemployed Lorry Driver, aged 33

The following pages you are about to read are an eyewitness account of the events on Sunday, 30 January 1972, in Rossville Street, Londonderry.

But first let me state that I am an English ex-serviceman (10 years

R.N.) married seven years to a Londonderry girl and have lived in Ireland for a number of years. Since the start of the troubles in Ireland I have always looked at events with an open mind and an unbiased opinion. I've always kept myself to myself with no political views and am a convert R.C. but do not attend services regularly. But after Sunday I feel it is my duty to speak out and if need be attend any inquiry to swear a statement as to the events witnessed.

Those events as I saw them follow.

I watched the march from the fifth floor of the High Flats in Rossville Street, from the time it appeared at the Bogside Inn and round the route to the corner of William Street and Rossville Street. At this point I saw and heard CS gas and baton rounds being fired. The lorry and people leading the march turned down Rossville Street towards 'Free Derry Corner'.

The man on the lorry was calling for the people to meet at 'Free Derry Corner'. This subsequently happened. But at this time I did hear *one* nail bomb explode. I stress the *one* and this appeared to be at the Grandstand Bar in William Street. There were no further explosions.

By this time the meeting was under way at 'Free Derry Corner'. There were still quite a lot of people between that point and Kells Walk, most were holding their faces with the effect of the CS gas. Up to this point I'd heard no small arms fire of any description. (There is a distinct difference between baton and live round fire.) I've been here long enough to distinguish the sounds. (Incidentally I may point out that my job in the R.N. was Sonar. My hearing was above the standard required for this job, also pitch and quality of sound is needed. My service included time spent at Suez, Cyprus and Borneo. The sound of gunfire isn't new to me.) At this stage I noticed three army personnel carriers coming round the corner by 'Bradley's Bar'. They drove down Rossville Street towards the flats, the first of these turned into the car park at the rear of the building, two stopped at the end of the block by the entrance of the car park. Soldiers leapt out and ran in all directions, one I noticed wearing a respirator ran towards Glenfada Park. It was then I heard small arm fire to the rear of the flats. I ran into the bedroom and looked out of the window. There I saw a young man lying face down in the car park. He had been shot. A priest who I recognised as Fr Daly crawled to him and started administering the last rites. The gunfire didn't stop. I then ran to the front of the building and saw three men shot at the barricade in front of the flats. An elderly man who was lying beside them pulled at them. He appeared to be getting them closer to the barricade for shelter. None of these three men were able to assist themselves. The elderly man was later identified to me as Mr Darnion (this will have to be verified). I saw him look over the barricade and raise his hand, a shot struck the slab of concrete beside him and passed on to the area of 'Free Derry Corner'. He ducked, then again put his hand up. By this time the fire had stopped. He beckoned to the troops to come forward. They did this in an armoured car and removed three men who appeared to be dead. The armoured car then went back to its position. The shooting started again for a few moments, then stopped. Some of it now appeared to be coming from above me in the flats in retaliation. I then saw Fr Daly again. He went to the armoured car and got in. A few moments later he got out again. People were then getting up and walking about with their hands up, some with their hands on their heads. At this point I noticed the troops had their helmets off and I noticed the 'red berets' (Paras).

My first thought on seeing the initial rush of troops was 'Snatch Squad'. This wasn't to be. I was shouted at and told to get the window shut. Fire had been directed up at windows in the flats that had been opened. I later found out by radio that an Italian cameraman had been shot at for doing just that. At no time during the shooting did I see anybody other that the security forces carrying guns.

I took particular notice when they removed the men shot at the barricade, nothing was picked up from beside the bodies; all that was lying there when they had gone was one shoe belonging to one of them.

What you have just read is an unbiased, non-sectarian, true and accurate account of what I saw, whilst in sane mind, on 30 January 1972, which is now known as 'Bloody Sunday'.

* * * * * * * * * * * *

Kevin M.
AGED 18

Yesterday, I was in the march and was caught in the ensuing violence. When the army charged I ran down Chamberlain Street, along with several hundred others. I saw a Saracen and doubled my efforts to get out, I made it. I then ran down beside the shop side of the flats. It was then that I heard the shots, I think I know gunfire well enough to recognise SLRs. I saw one IRA man with a pistol, he opened fire. I must stress that this was after the army opened fire. There were no nail bombs, or petrol being thrown at that time or any other time before the incident that day. I ran across Rossville Street to a gap in the Glenfada complex. We, i.e. about 30 youths, then reorganised and tried to make a charge, we ran into the open when about five successive shots rang out. A young boy who was beside me fell, blood streaming from his side. He only had a stone in his hand like the rest of us. More shots rang out but I was eating dirt, I could not tell if any more were hit. I helped some men drag the boy in the Wrangler jeans and jacket, who fell beside me, around the corner. Somebody took him into a house. I tried to get out of the way, shots were ringing out everywhere, I was sort of dazed, then half stumbling I made my way to the comparative safety of the New Road. I then saw some more casualties being brought up. One man aged about 17 was hit and blood was streaming from his jaw. It was half shot off. He was carrying no weapon either. I saw a girl who was hit in the leg. I was very lucky and then went home. I knew further fighting was useless.

* * * * * * * * * * * * *

Francis P. Dunne
TEACHER, AGED 29

By the time the section of the march I was with had reached the junction of William Street and Rossville Street the army already had used gas and purple dye. Confusion was caused by the mass of people retreating up from the water cannon into the oncoming marchers. At that time the rear of the march was not aware of the confrontation at the front of the march. Many teenagers in the march then broke towards Sackville Street and had a go at the military barrier there with stones and waste from the waste ground there. The army replied with rubber bullets and gas. One of the rubber bullets broke a window above McLaughlin and McLaughlin's shop.

This action lasted for nearly ten minutes. Then the army used tear gas — firing it into the roadway at Rossville Street just beside Con Bradley's Pub. I got a fair dose of this and staggered back to where the old City Baths used to be. There I paused to recover and met Adrian Healy, a former pupil, and Brian O'Kane, a boy at the school. They told me they had heard that a man and a boy had been shot in William Street during the march. I didn't pay too much heed to these stories as they tend to fly about during riots.

I was looking round for Morris Kelly and some others I had seen on the march when I saw Fergal McCarthy and a group of men carrying a man with blood flowing from a head wound. I asked McCarthy what had happened to him and was told he had been struck by a CS canister. Just after this there was a rush of people along Rossville Street — a sort of mass retreat. I didn't know what was causing it but I joined the rush and ran towards the High Flats. When I got to the gable of the flats I stopped and looked behind. I saw two or three military vehicles tearing up Rossville Street towards where I stood. I hurried back to the courtyard behind the three blocks of flats. Here there was a lot of confusion with the two exits at the junctions of the blocks jammed with fleeing people.

I paused again — I was thinking at the time that to be arrested in a riotous situation and to get a six-month sentence would be embarrassing and inconvenient. There were a few people throwing stones towards the Chamberlain Street side of the court. I looked back there and saw three soldiers along the wall at the rear of the Chamberlain Street houses. At this point the shooting started — the soldier at the front of this group was firing from the hip into the courtyard towards the Fahan Street opening. The one behind him was down on his knee in an aiming position but I couldn't say he fired. I saw a boy up towards my left fall. A taller fellow in the middle of the court was standing with his hands up and spread wide. He was shouting 'They are shooting, they are killing.' He went down also. I ran towards the Bogside exit and got through the alley. As I ran I saw a man edging along the gable of the Chamberlain Street houses — I think but I couldn't say for sure that he had a hand gun. When I got through the alley I saw a man wearing a brown coat and tan trousers standing just beyond it. He was telling people to take cover along the gable of the flats and the frontage of the shops. I stood at the edge of this wall and peeked back around the corner. The soldier at the Chamberlain Street wall fired along the alley. I was aware of shots passing fairly near me. It dawned on me then the full realisation that the troops were really firing real bullets. I ran across the open space in front of the flats and along the gardens of the houses. A man in one of the houses called me in. I watched on my knees from the front window of the house. I could see the people at the gable of the shops attending to two wounded people. There were some bodies lying at the near side of the flats barricade. Some people who went towards them were fired at. One man fell as if hit — he was smallish, wearing brown and had his hands in the air. A Saracen then moved forward and bumped across the barricade. Two soldiers jumped from the Saracen and threw the bodies into it. Soldiers then moved up along the maisonettes diagonally opposite where I was and arrested people sheltering along the gable of those maisonettes. A soldier hurried a woman at the rear of the line by kicking her. There was a lull in firing then and people moved out of the houses — I did also. I saw Fr Mullan from Pennyburn moving along the road from the direction of Free Derry Corner. I called to him that there were injured near the gable of the flats. I followed him and at this time saw the body of a man lying near the front of the shops. He was wearing a brown overcoat and tan trousers and had been shot in the head. He was lying on his back. I had seen him earlier when I had run through the alley. He had certainly not been armed. There were further outbursts of shots at this time and priests, ambulance workers and helpers had to take cover. At this stage some shooting may have come from behind me, i.e., from the line of the former Wellington Street. This was the only time I was aware of any shots towards the army except for the occasion I have already mentioned. At no time did I hear automatic fire, nail bombs or see petrol bombs being used. I saw two people fall in the courtyard, neither of them was armed.

Mrs M.

I am blind, but my hearing is very good. I would swear to you that there was not one nail bomb.

* * * * * * * * * * * *

William K.
UNEMPLOYED, AGED 34

I was in Glenfada Park area, home of my mother-in-law, on Sunday, 30 January 1972. I saw troops come in at the end of the square. They were behind a red van. I had brought three girls into the house a few moments before. I heard banging at the door and went to see. It was three men — they were lying on the ground at the doorstep. I brought these men in as well — one had a badly cut hand. There were two men lying dead or dying outside the garden fence and one lying further up at the corner. I couldn't get out to help these people as the troops were still firing. It was only when a young Knights of Malta girl in white came with her hands up that the shooting seemed to stop. About 35 people were arrested at the right-hand side of the square. One woman was hit high on the back by a rifle butt. There was definitely no shooting at the troops from the direction of these houses. The houses that were fired upon are occupied by old people. The position of the bullet holes can prove the kind of indiscriminate shooting these murderers carried out. I challenge the statement that troops only fired back when fired upon themselves.*

* * * * * * * * * * * *

---

* [On legal advice, the last sentence has been omitted — Ed.]

William McC.

UNEMPLOYED, AGED 19

My brother and myself ran into the Rossville Flats area. By the time we got to the stairs the Saracens had pulled into the back of the car park. The paratroopers jumped out and shouted to the fleeing crowd 'If you move, you're dead.' About 50 per cent of this crowd were women and children. We ran up the stairs and we heard a shot. Afterwards we discovered a man shot dead on the stairs. I went into my mother's flat, No. 9 Mura Place, and watched from the bedroom window. People in the flats threw milk bottles and the paratroopers opened up fire on them. There are bullet holes in the windows and ceilings of these flats. I could see a wounded man lying in the car park. Fr Daly and the Knights of Malta were giving him aid. Paratroopers were lined along the wall opposite the back of the flats and they opened up fire on the group. A man stepped forward with about half a brick and threw it at the paratroopers. He then opened his coat and roared 'Go ahead and shoot me', and the paratrooper did, in the leg. Across the street in Glenfada Park, paratroopers rushed behind and took the people by surprise. They put them under arrest and marched them out with their hands above their heads. Three of them made a break in one direction and three others in the opposite direction. No order was given to halt and the paratroopers shot to kill. One was shot through the head and was dead before he reached the ground for he didn't bleed. Another two were shot in the back. The paratroopers marched the others away and left the three men lying there. An old man ran over to the three men and when he reached them he was wounded in the shoulder. He tried to signal the paratroopers to get help. They ignored this and instead opened up fire on him. Eventually a Saracen did come to pick up the three men. One of the men was dragged along by the hair and the other two were dragged by their ankles on their faces through the rubble. They arrested the old man. There were eight shots fired from an M5 Carbine at the Saracen. The paratroopers then moved out except for one that stayed in Chamberlain Street.

10: Hindering the Healers

The actions of 1 Para, and those of other regiments on Bloody Sunday, most notably 1st Royal Anglians, will forever leave doubts as to whether some lives could have been saved.

In Chapter 11, paramedics and nurses tell of their own experiences during this half hour of military madness. But one case, that of 17-year-old Gerard Donaghy, is worth highlighting.

After young Donaghy was shot, he was carried to the home of Raymond Rogan at 10 Abbey Park. He was attended by Dr Kevin Swords who, according to the statement of Rogan (see Chapter 6, Glenfada Park), said that he had a chance of survival if immediately rushed to hospital. Rogan volunteered to take him in his car since ambulances were scarce and having difficulty in moving about because of the heavy concentration of gunfire.

At great personal risk, Rogan, accompanied by Mr Leo Young (who at that moment did not know that his brother, John, lay dead on the barricade nearby) set forth with the wounded Donaghy. Rogan drove while Leo Young nursed the dying youth in the back seat.

At a military blockade on Barrack Street their car was stopped and, in spite of protests, both men were arrested and the car with the wounded but still-living Gerard Donaghy was taken away.

Donaghy was eventually delivered dead to Altnagelvin Hospital. While in military and police custody, four nail bombs were 'discovered' on his person, stuffed into the pockets of his tight-fitting jeans. Police photographs were produced to substantiate the security forces' claims of a weapons find.

* * * * * * * * * * *

Thomas M.
CABLE JOINTER, AGED 44

I walked in the march as far as Little James' Street where I stopped
to watch the stone throwing at the junction of Little James' Street
and William Street. When I saw three Saracens coming across Little
James' Street I ran across and up Rossville Street. The first two
Saracens overtook and passed me. The third swerved in my direction
but was going so fast that it actually swerved in front of me and
missed me. I saw all three stopping, two on the right-hand side facing towards the Bog and the third stopped at the gable of the High
Flats, facing into the enclosed area. I saw two soldiers jump out of
this last one and immediately they began shooting. They didn't seem
to be aiming at anything. There were people sheltering in the
enclosed area and a crowd was running towards Free Derry Corner.
I saw one soldier shooting into the enclosed area and the second
shooting from the hip in the direction of the fleeing crowd. I ran into
the enclosed area as I was too exposed where I was in Rossville
Street and as I ran I felt the swish of something passing my head. I
ran into a corner where there were already about 15 people trying to
shelter. I saw a boy fall but didn't know at that time that he had been
shot and I ran back into Chamberlain Street. There was a Saracen
coming up the street with soldiers coming on either side of it and
they were shooting up in the direction of the flats. At this stage a
door in the corner house of Chamberlain Street opened and someone called to me, 'Come in for God's sake or you're going to be shot.'
Inside, a young woman, Mrs Deeny I think the name was, was lying
with a very bad leg wound, on the sofa, and I saw a man in the back
yard with a leg wound also. Although we knew the soldiers were
outside, we knew help was needed immediately for the woman, so
we had to open the front door to call for an ambulance. I heard one
of the soldiers say — and I'll not forget it till the day I die — and I'll
remember the soldier's face always — he said 'Let the bastard bleed
to death.' But the ambulance was called.

At that point all of us who had taken shelter in the house were
arrested. There were 22 of us counted as we were taken out (Otto
Schlindwein was one of the number, a Campbell man and John
Morrison were with us). We were taken to the dock yard. A sergeant

stood guard over us with his Alsatian dog and on several occasions another sergeant nodded towards us and remarked to him — 'Plenty of pig meat for the dogs today!'

My wife and family had been searching for me over the city and had phoned all of the police barracks. The police in Victoria Barracks, Strand Road, phoned the dock yards and were told that I was not among those arrested — this happened twice or three times. I was arrested at 4 p.m. and released at 10 p.m. No charges had been brought against me.

I want to stress in the strongest possible terms that no shots were fired before the soldier opened fire, and there was *definitely no shooting* either from the flats or from the courtyard. There were *definitely no* petrol bombs or nail bombs fired from the marchers — or fired by anyone at all.

This is my statement. It is true and I grant permission for it to be published or used in any investigation.

* * * * * * * * * * * *

Hugh Leo Young

On 30 January 1972 I was in William Street looking for my young brother at about 3.30 p.m. CS gas caused me to run back up William Street in the direction of the cathedral. I then moved through Columbcille Court where I heard two or three rifle shots. I then ran through Glenfada Park to Fahan Street where I found Joe Friel lying against a wall having been shot in the chest. I and two other people took him over to a house in Lisfannon Park. From there I saw two bodies lying on open ground in the Glenfada Park area. My attention had been drawn to them by several people. I and a Knight of Malta girl called Laverty who lives in Creggan Road crossed Fahan Street to these two men. As I ran to the bodies a soldier who was about twenty yards on my right fired at me and just missed me. The shot was very near the ground and I heard it ricochet. I took one man to the house of Mr Rogan in 10 Abbey Park. He was unconscious and his intestines seemed to be protruding out of his stomach. I tried to find his identification from anything in the two top pockets of his blue denim jacket but found nothing. Mr Rogan got his car in order to take the man to hospital. I went in the car with Mr Rogan driving. We went to Barrack Street via Fahan Street and St Columb's Wells in order to make our way to the Altnagelvin Hospital. In Barrack Street we were stopped at an army barricade and pulled out of the car. I said to a soldier 'What about that dying young fellow?' and he said, 'Let the bastard die.' I said 'You are just an animal.' He then put me up against some railings, pointed his gun at me and told me that if I blinked he would blow my head off. There was another private car there with the wounded Joe Friel in it. I didn't actually see Friel but the men who got out of the car told me that it was him. Two soldiers drove these cars away and I never saw the wounded men again. We were then taken to an army post in Foyle Road near Craigavon Bridge and kept there for an hour and a half. Before we were taken there in a landrover I heard further shooting from the direction of Rossville Street. At the army post I was made to remove my clothes and a jelly-sniffer was run all over me including my finger nails. My clothes were also tested.

After testing I was asked to make a statement to Sergeant Taggert of the RUC who told me that it was for an inquest. I was then taken to Victoria Barracks and then to Ballykelly and not released until the following Monday. It was only then that I heard that my brother John had been killed.

At no time on 30 January did I see any civilians carrying a weapon and I never heard the explosion of nail bombs or petrol bombs.

* * * * * * * * * * * * *

Celine Brolly
MOULDER IN ESSEX, AGED 35

We went into the second floor of the Flats to a friend of ours. We looked out the frontroom window and the people were proceeding to Free Derry Corner for the meeting. Just as the crowd thinned out we saw the Saracen tanks charging up and we started to shout to the people to run. Then we heard the gunfire and we all ran into the back bedroom. Then there was a lull. Then as we were watching out of the back window into the Market we saw three soldiers grab hold of a middle-aged man. They kicked, punched and battered him and took him away over the 'Fish' Lane. There was a First Aid boy running to the aid of this man but he was also punched and kicked and thrown on the ground and they shot a rubber bullet at him. He was still lying on the ground and Fr Daly called him. As prior to this I saw a soldier with a black moustache shoot the boy dead that Fr Daly was attending and Fr Daly held up a cloth with the blood dripping from it to try and get them to stop shooting. They shot at him. My husband and I looked down at three soldiers at the Saracen tank to try and draw their attention that Fr Daly wanted them as the other soldier against the wall was shooting away. A small blond stout soldier directly behind the tank aimed the gun and my husband threw me to the ground and they fired right in at the bedroom window. My husband was hit in the head with glass and a rubber bullet and was unconscious for half an hour. I thought he was shot dead. I ran out to get a priest and an ambulance and as I ran along the balcony they started to shoot at me. I didn't realise this until two men threw me on the floor at the lifts of the Flats. I was shocked as I didn't realise they were shooting at me until the men told me. They kept me there then along with forty or so other people lying on their stomachs as the soldiers were just firing at anything that moved. Then my sister-in-law came out looking for me with a white flag to take me back as the First Aid man went into my husband. As we were crawling along, the soldiers were still shooting and a woman opened her door and pulled my sister-in-law and I in. She was in a terrible state crying. Then I went to the window in the front sitting-room to call up the photographers as we saw them passing and a soldier shot a rubber bullet at me and Mrs McGill who was in the flat helping to attend my husband and the owner of the flat, as she had taken a heart attack.

This statement can be corroborated by my two sisters-in-law, Peggy Brolly and Mrs Curran, also Theresa Clarke and Mrs Cunningham (owner of the flat).

* * * * * * * * * * * *

Damien Friel
APPRENTICE JOINER, AGED 19

On Sunday 30 January when the soldiers were advancing towards Rossville Street I went into No. 2 Kells Walk. From here I saw a young man running from Chamberlain Street down through Eden Place. He turned left through the waste ground. He saw a Saracen in Rossville Street. He stopped about five yards in front of this Saracen and headed towards the High Flats. After running about two yards he saw a group of soldiers at the left-hand side of the flats facing directly onto Rossville Street. He stopped. He was confronted by one soldier from the Parachute Regiment who had a bayonet on his rifle. The soldier attempted to thrust the bayonet into the upper part of his body but the young man jumped back although the bayonet injured him below his arm on his right side. As the young man attempted to run in the direction of William Street he was captured by soldiers in Rossville Street. As these soldiers put him into the Saracen they kicked him and hit him with their batons and rifle butts on his head and shoulders. They also thrust his head three or four times against the edge of the back door of the Saracen.

A French cameraman was in this house also. He stepped outside the door onto the terrace, facing directly onto Rossville Street. After about thirty seconds a Sergeant in the Parachute Regiment looked up towards the terrace. A soldier holding a rubber bullet gun was standing beside the Sergeant. They were both standing at the back of a Saracen with another three soldiers, two of whom had SLR guns and the other had a rubber bullet gun. The Sergeant grabbed the left arm of the first soldier and turned him round to face the terrace of Kells Walk and pointed at the cameraman. The soldier fired one rubber bullet, missed the cameraman by about one foot and smashed the window pane, struck the frame and bounced back onto Rossville Street. The broken glass severely cut the face of a girl in the room inside. Her name was Margaret and she was about seventeen years old.

The soldier from the Parachute Regiment was standing on the terrace at No. 2 Kells Walk. People were running across Rossville Street towards Free Derry Corner. I saw this soldier shooting indiscriminately towards these people. I saw him reload his SLR rifle with a magazine five times. There was no return of fire towards him. He walked away very calmly.

As I looked towards Columbcille Court I saw about 15 to 20 people including one priest standing with their hands against a wall with their legs apart. There was a soldier standing on either side of this group with his gun aimed directly at the group. Meanwhile four other soldiers beat the group with batons and rifle butts. They also kicked and punched the people. I saw one soldier striking the priest continuously for about five minutes.

I heard the priest, who was young and wore glasses, tell the soldiers that he wished to make his way to people who had been shot but the soldier pulled him back and pushed him so that his left side hit the wall. The soldiers arranged the people in groups of two and all marched towards Rossville Street. As they marched with hands on top of their heads the soldiers brutally assaulted them and also used abusive language. These facts are true.

* * * * * * * * * * * *

Patricia H.
HOUSEWIFE, PART-TIME MACHINIST, AGED 30

I was in the top floor of the Rossville Street Flats and I saw the beginning of the march going down William Street. I saw the panic and the people running when the gas and water-cannon was used on them. The people were running up Rossville Street and coming into the waste ground off the flats. Things became normal as the crowds made their way toward Free Derry Corner. A few people had been hanging back round Eden Place and a loud-speaker from the lorry at Free Derry Corner hailed them and asked them to come up as the meeting was about to begin. Somebody also walked down with a megaphone in his hand calling them to the meeting at the corner. When I looked out I saw with gratitude that everyone was heading towards the place of assembly. A very short time after that I looked back down Rossville Street and I saw at least two Saracen cars at Eden Place moving in the direction of Free Derry Corner. A little above Eden Place they stopped and soldiers jumped out the back and came round the sides and started shooting. They weren't taking aim but were just shooting into the crowd. I then went to the back bedroom which overlooks the Market Square and there were some soldiers at the Eden Place end of the flats and two or three Saracen cars. The soldiers there were also shooting. A man was lying on the ground apparently badly injured and he was being attended to by Fr Daly and another man who seemed to be giving him the kiss of life as he was very close to him. I saw a lot of blood on the ground. When I looked again towards the soldiers they were still shooting. They seemed to be firing at Fr Daly and the other man who was assisting the injured man. Over towards Chamberlain Street I saw a man dressed in a Knights of Malta uniform crouched against a wall at the back of the houses. The soldiers batoned him and when he fell the contents of his bag spilled out on the ground. Fr Daly and his helper were signing to him to come to the assistance of the injured man. He got up and made his way towards them, crouching down as he went. He managed to reach them. I also saw a soldier lifting his rifle and hitting a man on the head with it.

At this stage I went back to the front room. There was a small barricade between the Flats and Glenfada Park and when I looked down there were three young men lying across this barricade. They were obviously dead. My friend Monica Hegarty who was with me in the flat said she saw them before we went into the back bedroom, and they were lying there face downwards and they seemed at that stage to be talking to each other. When I saw them now the two men on the outer sides were still lying face downwards, the man in the centre was lying on his back across the barricade. The man lying nearest the High Flats had his back covered in blood. I could see this as his coat was raised up at the back. Shortly afterwards a Saracen car pulled up beside them and I saw three or four soldiers there. They picked up the bodies by the arms and legs and tossed them into the back of the Saracen.

Before the three bodies were removed from the barricade, I saw five bodies lying in Glenfada Park — three on the path and the other two were further in. Some people from an alleyway off Glenfada Park were trying to pick up one of the bodies but the soldiers were shooting from the corner and they had to retreat. Some of these rescuers wore Knights of Malta uniforms.

The shooting was very bad at this stage and I couldn't watch what was going on any longer. I lay down on the floor in case I would be caught in the line of fire.

I can definitely say that there was no gunfire nor nail bombs before the soldiers opened up on the crowd of people.

11: Last Rights and Last Rites

The Knights of Mercy Speak

In addition to the killing and serious wounding of unarmed civilians on 30 January 1972, 1 Para also hindered, intimidated, brutalised and arrested pastors and members of the Ambulance Corps of the Order of Malta, attempting to carry out their duty.

The behaviour of 1 Para on that day was in direct contravention of the Geneva Convention, which states, concerning the protection of civilian persons:

> In the case of armed conflict not of an international character occurring in the territory of one of the High Contracting Parties, each Party to the conflict shall be bound to apply, as a minimum, the following provisions:
>
> 1) Persons taking no active part in the hostilities, including . . . those placed hors de combat by sickness, wounds, detention, or any other cause, shall in all circumstances be treated humanely, without any adverse distinction founded on race, colour, religion or faith. . . .
>
> To this end, the following acts are and shall remain prohibited at any time and in any place whatsoever with respect to the above-mentioned persons:
>
> a) violence to life and person, in particular murder of all kinds, mutilation, cruel treatment and torture;
>
> b) taking of hostages;
>
> c) outrages upon personal dignity, in particular humiliating and degrading treatment;
>
> d) the passing of sentences and the carrying out of executions

without previous judgement pronounced by a regularly con-
stituted court, affording all the judicial guarantees which are
recognised by civilized peoples;

2) The wounded and sick shall be collected and cared for.

An impartial humanitarian body, such as the International
Committee of the Red Cross, may offer its services to the Parties to
the conflict. . . .*

* * * * * * * * * * * *

Bernard Feeney
KNIGHTS OF MALTA WORKER, AGED 17

As the procession was going down William Street, on Sunday 30
January, I went up to the army barrier. The army stopped the crowd
and moved in the water cannon without any warning. The crowd
started to scatter and as the crowd moved away the army fired gas.
This caused a panic and the crowd scattered and started to run in a
hysterical fashion. A couple of shots rang out at this stage. I did not
know where these shots came from at this stage. I was then called to
Rossville Street, in my capacity as a Knights of Malta worker, where
a few people were overcome with CS gas. One of these people had
been hit on the mouth with a canister and had later to receive two
stitches from Dr McCabe. It was while I was treating this bloke in
one of the houses of the multi-storey flats that the Saracens moved
into Rossville Street. The soldiers jumped out of the Saracens and
fired one rubber and the rest were real bullets. They fired volley after
volley in towards the barricade where the crowd were scattering for
cover. This is where I saw three men fall on to the barricade. I knew
to look at these men that they were shot.

I was then called from here to a house along the corridor where
a man was said to be shot in the head. However, on arrival, it turned

---

* *Geneva Convention Relative to the Protection of Civilian Persons in Time of War of 12 August 1949*, Part 1, General Provisions, Art. 3.

out that a rubber bullet had come through the window and glass had embedded in his head. It was here that I met Fr Irwin and he came along with me to a woman who was hysterical. I diagnosed that the woman was hysterical because she had seen three bodies being roughly handled and thrown into the back of the Saracen.

Fr Irwin and I went along to the Saracen and here we met an R.S.M. of the paratroopers. He wore stripes, a crown and wings on his uniform and he wore a red beret. When Fr Irwin asked to see the bodies he was told that there were no bodies in the Saracens. This story was supported by an officer with three pips on his shoulder.

We then went back to the flats where we saw the same woman who had told us about the bodies. She became more hysterical when we told her we did not see the bodies. She then took us to a window where she pointed out the Saracen. We went back again to the officer. Fr Irwin took the number of this Saracen and called on Fr Mulvey. The three of us went along with the officer and when the officer pulled back the door of the Saracen we saw the three bodies lying inside. Fr Irwin and Fr Mulvey went inside the Saracen to administer the last rites. I was told to get in by a soldier but I refused. Photographers gathered around then and started taking photographs of the bodies. Fr Irwin and I went looking for the sergeant and finally found him. We asked him why he had not shown us the bodies when requested at the beginning. He just laughed at us.

We then went back into the flats and it was here we found somebody shot on the second floor of the flat. He had got gunshot wounds in his stomach and his back was blown out. He was dead and we covered the body. As other people were calling out for first aid we had to move on. I left a civilian with the body. I went to treat a heart-attack case. I told an ambulance driver that there was a body on the second floor, and he went and got the body removed and I went on to the case. It was here that I met Captain Day (Knights of Malta), he told me to go with Jim McDaid, an officer in the Knights, to attend to this heart-attack case. It was here that Jim McDaid sent me for the Order of Malta Ambulance. This was to be at the Infant School at Francis Street. I met Charlie McMonagle (fellow member of the Knights) and he came along with me. As we were moving out of Abbey Street towards William Street we met another squad of paratroopers, who told us, in an ignorant fashion, to get against the wall, despite the fact that we had the uniform of the Knights of Malta on. A soldier told us to get our hands against the wall and he kicked our legs apart. Another soldier came along then and he frisked us. He then told us to go across the road to a Saracen which was parked at Stevenson's Bakery. We told him we were going for an ambulance but he told us to get our hands against the Saracen and shut up. The soldiers at this Saracen frisked us again and examined our kit-bags. One soldier pulled stuff out of my kit-bag and threw it at the wheel of the Saracen and told my mate to pick it up. As he stooped to pick it up they kicked me on the legs and jabbed my back with a baton. They radioed in and said they had 'two Fenians'. A soldier inside the Saracen opened the slot at the side of the Saracen and stuck the baton in and knocked off my peaked cap and started to laugh calling us 'bastards'. He asked us how many they had shot and we refused to answer. He said that he would tell us and he said that at this stage there were eight dead. He laughed and his mates laughed with him at this 'joke'. We were roughly treated until an army padre came along, whose name, I think, was Rev. Bailey. We recognised this priest, who is attached to the Anglian Regiment, because we had met him previously in June 1971. He asked the soldiers what we were doing here and the soldier told him that it was a routine check. The priest gave us permission to go on but the paratrooper told us to stand against the Saracen, 'You Fenian cunts.' The priest then went away to see someone in another Saracen. It was while he was away that the soldiers began again to jab us with their batons. The priest returned and told us we could go.

When we went away with the priest up William Street, towards the first-aid post, the priest advised us to try and forget all about it as we were quite upset. The Saracens then started to move off except one at the top of William Street. About an hour had elapsed since the time we had set out for the ambulance this time being 4.30 to 5.30 approx. We saw one of our fellow members at the Saracen at the top of William Street, and he was being abused by a radio operator of the Parachute Regiment. The paratrooper accused him of calling him an 'English Pig'. The priest came along, at our request, and the paratrooper asked who the priest was. The paratrooper then radioed in saying that he had one, Jim Norris of the Knights of Malta, and he was told that he could be released. The soldiers then got into this Saracen and moved off and that was the last we saw of them.

The priest then sympathised with us and told us to try and forget about them.

• • • • • • • • • • • • •

Frank Mellan
STUDENT NURSE, AGED 18

Me and my mate were standing at the corner of flats opposite Glenfada Park. John [sic] Gilmore jumped into the air shouting 'I've been hit' and he started running towards the cover of the flats where we were standing. My friend and I grabbed Gilmore by each arm and dragged him around the corner. Just beside the telephone box, Gilmore collapsed to the ground. I got down beside Gilmore, my friend stood by to ward people off. I commenced to open his jerkin to find where he had been hit. The bullet had gone in on the right side just under the lung, I think. I took off my jumper and tried to stop the bleeding. I felt around the rest of his body to see if he had been hit anywhere else and found that on his left side the bullet had come out taking most of his intestines with it. There wasn't much bleeding at this point. It seemed that he must have been bleeding internally. Blood started to come up his mouth. I wiped the blood away and tried to give artificial respiration. Each time I did this I heard a sound indicating that his lung had been punctured. All during this period there was shooting around us. Mr McGuigan stood up with his hands in the air trying to tell the army *not* to shoot. Mr McGuigan fell to the ground — blood pouring from his head. We knew immediately that he was dead, due to the amount of blood he lost. This man was unarmed. Due to the fierce shooting we were forced to leave Gilmore knowing that he was about to die.

Five of us pinned ourselves against the wall beside the phone box. At the steps leading up to Fahan Street, I noticed that another man had been cut down. This man, I found out later, had also died. People began to wave white hankies in the air. There was still shooting, then a lull during which we managed to get out and into a flat.

By now a fleet of ambulances had arrived and were attending to dead and injured people. Priests had also arrived at this point. Ambulance men and priests were carrying the people to the ambulances when shooting again broke out. Eventually it began to lull and finally died out. It was the most terrifying experience I have ever encountered, especially knowing that all these peaceful demonstrators were without doubt *unarmed*. The army at *no* time came under any fire from Rossville Flats or any other area.

* * * * * * * * * * * * *

Ursula Clifford
THEATRE SISTER, AGED 30

I, Ursula Clifford, having taken part in the massive Civil Rights march from Bishop's Field, Creggan, to William Street, would like to make the following observations.

A) There were 15,000 to 20,000 people marching in peaceful demonstration before any violence occurred.

B) Due to the saturation of the area of William Street by CS gas I made my way to Glenfada Park, where I was attracted by an organiser of the march, using a megaphone, who called for a meeting of the people at Free Derry Corner. I answered the call, made my way to the place of meeting. On making my way through, I observed that there were thousands of people going in the same direction, from the Rossville Street end.

C) On the 'platform' were B. Devlin, Cooper, Lord Brockway and approximately 12 teenagers. Bernadette Devlin took the mike and told the people that they were now holding a perfectly legal meeting, and therefore not to panic. She then introduced Lord Brockway who waved to the assembled crowd who acknowledged his greeting and were quietly awaiting Bernadette's next words when there was a volley of shots from behind. Everyone, including myself, immediately dived to the ground. It was then that I observed three military vehicles stopped at the William Street end of the barricade at the multi-storey flats. There were soldiers in front of and in between the vehicles.

D) I made my way in stages between volleys of shots back to
Glenfada Park which took approximately five minutes. On
entering Glenfada Park I saw a man who was being given artificial respiration. I went forward, looked at his colour, took his
pulse, noticed his lack of respiration and decided that he was
dying. As he was already being treated I then made my way into
my aunt's flat which overlooks Rossville Street. On looking out
the window I saw two bodies lying beside the gable wall of the
multi-storey flats — the Lecky Road side.

My aunt and I took blankets and went across Rossville Street. The
first casualty we encountered was a youth named Philip [sic]
Gilmore who had a bullet wound through the left side of his chest.
On further observation I concluded that he was dying. I covered him
with a blanket.

There was another casualty lying at an angle to him. I observed
that he had been shot on the side of the head, with approximately
three pints of blood lying around the head area. He was definitely
dead. A man had a coat over this corpse. I replaced it by a blanket.
I heard a shout from Glenfada and observed Lawrence Doherty who
enquired if a priest was required. I ran across the street and observed
Fr A. Mulvey and replied that a priest was urgently required. Fr
Mulvey placed his hands on his head and crossed the street.

Shortly afterwards two ambulances arrived. One was directed
into the courtyard of Glenfada and the other pulled up at the corner
of the flats. I called to the ambulance man to bring a 'minute man'
and they followed me to the patient lying in Glenfada Park. I helped
to carry him to the ambulance and at this stage I was accompanied
by Dr Kevin Swords. There was a patient already in the ambulance.
Someone shouted that there were more in a house behind us but on
the way to the house we encountered a youth who was shot in the
legs so we had him placed on the floor of the ambulance. The ambulance then went off.

We entered a house and there was a youth lying face down on the
floor. He had been shot through the scapula. He also appeared to be
dying. Dr Swords then remained and I went back to my aunt's house.
Shortly afterwards we observed another ambulance pulling up at the
flats and it was driven by the ambulance controller.

They started bringing out patients from the maisonettes adjacent to Joseph's Place. While they were putting the patients in the ambulances, accompanied by Fr Mulvey, shots were fired from the direction of the army, and they had to dive for cover in front of the ambulance which was facing Lecky Road.

My overall comment was that the army obviously knew that people were injured due to the fact that they saw me with the blankets, first-aid people clearly marked and clergymen going back and forth, and they offered no assistance whatsoever and then they callously stood by and watched us in our distress. Some of these people needed blood transfusions and drugs (e.g. morphine) which we had not got and which the army could have got in record time.

* * * * * * * * * * * *

John C.
MALE NURSE, AGED 26
ON DUTY WITH KNIGHTS OF MALTA

I left my home at 1.30 p.m. on 30 January, myself and two neighbours, Mr John Mailey and Mr Michael McLaughlin. We made our way to the assembly point, Bishop's Field, Creggan Estate. I was informed I was officially on duty with the Knights of Malta First Aid Organisation.

We reached William Street. As I was arriving the army started using a water cannon and firing CS gas. I helped two or three old people to Upper William Street. As I treated these old people I was informed by Volunteer Charles Glenn (Knights of Malta) that there was a lady who had been hit by a missile on the forehead. She required stitching which I performed. While I was so engaged I was told by a woman volunteer Maureen Gallagher (Knights of Malta) that two people had been hit — believed to have been shot.

The first casualty I saw was a young lad of 17 or 18. He had been hit by a rubber bullet on the left side. We got him moved to safety. By this time the second patient had been moved by some of his friends; I do not know the extent of his injuries. Just then there was a roar from the crowd that the Saracens were coming. The crowd seemed to disperse. As I looked round I saw four paratroopers down on their knees. Three were shooting rifles, and one a rubber-bullet gun. At this moment volunteer Rosemary Doyle joined volunteer Maureen Gallagher and myself. The crowd parted and I saw two Saracens tanks coming straight at us. I pulled the two girls clear of the tanks and I heard one of the soldiers shout, 'We'll get them on the way back.' I tried to get the two girls to safety, when Rosemary Doyle said 'Robert. I've been hit.' (Both girls were wearing overalls with a red cross and carrying white kit-bags.)

Her hand went to her face. I pulled her hand away. There was no blood but her face was starting to swell. I presumed she had been hit by a rubber bullet. This incident occurred on the waste ground at Eden Place off Rossville Street.

We crossed Rossville Street to Kells Walk. As we were crossing, the soldiers were firing. There was a corporal at the wall firing a rifle and a soldier behind him with a rubber-bullet gun. At no time did I hear nail bombs, petrol bombs or gunfire being returned. I saw a small group of people sheltering in an entry at Columbcille Court. I perceived the soldiers moving toward them. I shouted to them to move out of the road. We ran to a house in Columbcille Court where Dr McClean, Captain Day (K. of M.), Lt. McDaid (K. of M.), Serg. Lafferty (K. of M.) and a few other members of the Knights of Malta, as well as pressmen, were present. In the house was an elderly man and a young boy, both suffering from gunshot wounds.

I saw that my services were not needed so I made my way to the front of the house. I had just a lit a cigarette when two women shouted to me from a house that there were two men lying in front of their house. This was in front of the houses in Glenfada Park. Myself and another member of the Order ran to the two men. At the same time but from the opposite direction Woman Volunteer E. Lafferty was running towards the two men. I saw a rifle protruding from a passageway between the houses in Glenfada Park. I shouted at Eibhlin, 'Don't move. Stay where you are.'

I heard a ping and saw Eibhlin's hand go to her leg. That was the last I saw of her until later on in the evening, as I went straight to the two men. The first man I looked at was dead, the second was unconscious and as far as I could judge was dying. I recited the Act of Contrition in his ear, and made the sign of the cross on his forehead with the indulgence crucifix. I then proceeded to check the extent of his injuries. I could see no blood and it looked to me as if this was the victim of a heart attack. I told my companion to give cardiac massage while I proceeded with mouth-to-mouth resuscitation. This occupied a space of about half an hour or more until the ambulance arrived.

One of the ambulance attendants brought the minute-man machine which we used on the patient. I then proceeded to give cardiac massage until we reached the hospital. There were two other patients both suffering from gunshot wounds in the ambulance.

I since know the man Gerry McKinney, whom I had treated as a victim of a heart attack, was in reality shot through the side. When the ambulance was on its way to Altnagelvin via the lower deck of Craigavon Bridge the soldiers on duty there were laughing and jeering and I distinctly heard the remark passed by one of them, 'That's a few less in the Bogside.' When we finally reached the hospital there was an army ambulance at casualty reception. The driver of this ambulance refused to move and had to be pushed to allow access for the wounded. He said laughing, 'I can't get it started.'

This is my statement and it is correct.

* * * * * * * * * * * *

Fr Edward Daly
PRIEST

About 3.00 or 3.15 p.m. on Sunday, 30 January 1972, I walked from where I live at St Eugene's Presbytery, down Creggan Street and William Street. The Civil Rights march was going along at that time also. It is my custom, and has been for the past three years, to stay in the Rossville Street area when there are disturbances there, or if there is a situation which might bring trouble about. I have been attached to this parish and to this area of the parish for ten years. There is a large concentration of elderly parishioners, many of them living alone in the Kells Walk, Columbcille Court and Glenfada Park area. I have usually moved about in this area during any disturbances to allay their fears, and on occasions have helped in evacuating people to safer areas when excessive quantities of CS gas were used.

I noticed on my way down William Street a soldier with a rifle and a red beret on the near wall of Great James' Street Church. I could see him across the vacant site of Richardson's factory. I remember this well because several people in the parade jeered and catcalled at him. That was what attracted my attention to him. I continued down the street until I came to the doorway of Porter's television and radio shop. The crowd had built up to there from the barrier that the army had erected near the old City Cinema site, a little past the junction with Chamberlain Street. I could hear some jeers and shouts at the army. There were some comments made which brought about cheering and laughter. Then some missiles, stones and bottles were thrown. I could not see from where I stood exactly how many were involved in this but it wasn't a very intensive barrage by Derry standards. I would reckon that about 30 to 40 people were actually throwing missiles. There was no reaction from the army for a time, perhaps three or four minutes, and then CS gas and purple-dye water cannon was used to disperse the crowd. The crowd dispersed and there was some panic where I was, people at the front wanted to get back and people at the back wanted to get forward. The street was packed with people. After some minutes, however, the crowd dispersed up Chamberlain Street and along Rossville Street, and up William Street. After a few minutes hardly anyone was left in the area between the junction of Rossville Street and the army barrier in William Street. I took up a position in the Rossville Street area near Kells Walk, where many of my old people live. I remember a man, I think it was Kevin McCorry, the Civil Rights leader, asking people to move away from the area and go to a meeting that was to be held at Free Derry Corner. Most of those in the Rossville Street area moved in the direction of Free Derry Corner, presumably to attend the meeting. I had not intended going to the meeting, so I stayed where I was. There was also a steady stream of people moving up William Street towards the Cathedral, presumably on their way home. During this time I remember being concerned about the conduct of a few young people behind the shops in William Street. I spoke to them and mentioned my concern to Patrick Duffy, a much respected Civil Rights steward. I was worried that they might interfere with the rear doors of these premises. I also remember speaking to Mr Stephen McGonigle and other people. At this time in the Rossville Street area, there were still a good few people, mainly standing around talking, discussing the march, and expressing relief that it had passed off peacefully. There was sporadic stoning of a very limited nature by a few individual young people during this time. The army repelled them with the odd canister of gas. I wish to state categorically that I never once heard a nail bomb explode during that whole afternoon.

The first intimation I had that there would be any further trouble came when I heard two or three rifle shots that came from the direction of William Street. At this time I was in Rossville Street, about midway along Kells Walk. I knew they were not rubber-bullet or gas guns. The crack was much too sharp for that. These shots came about 15 or 20 minutes after the army had dispersed the crowd with water cannon. A few minutes after hearing the shots a woman came running to say that two men had been shot in the vicinity of the Grandstand Bar. I made my way through the alleyway in that direction, but, as I did, two people came along to say that two priests were already there. After discussing the affair with these people I returned to my previous position on Rossville Street, roughly opposite the entrance to Eden Place. I cannot give a very accurate estimate of time from this point on, either time on the clock or periods of time elapsed.

Perhaps ten minutes after the first two or three shots rang out, I heard the sound of the engines of the Saracen armoured cars revving up. I must state once again, from the time of the first shots until now, I did not hear any shots fired . . . there was hardly any stoning or 'aggro' at this time . . . the odd gas canister was being fired . . . people in the Rossville Street area were mainly a peaceful crowd standing around chatting like myself, prior to going home.

When I heard the sound of the engines, I looked over along the waste ground in Little James' Street. I saw three or four Saracen cars heading towards us at increasing speed towards the mouth of Rossville Street . . . there were also footsoldiers running along behind them. I decided, like the rest of the crowd, that it was best to run, and I did so. I raced with the others for the courtyard of the multi-storey flats. As I ran I looked back from time to time, to see if the soldiers and cars were still following. They kept coming on. I remember coming level with a young man just as I entered the courtyard of Rossville Flats. He smiled at me, I think he was amused at the sight of me running. Like me and everyone else he was running away and looking back over his shoulder from time to time. I don't recall seeing anything in his hands and he was not shouting or remonstrating in any way. The next few seconds are quite confused . . . so many things happened that I will always remember. The order of events, however, is not quite clear. I remember seeing a person, I don't know whether it was a man or a woman, being thrown in the air by a Saracen that was driven straight at that person. I remember seeing the body being thrown in the air. That was just inside the high wire fence at the edge of the courtyard near the back wall of Chamberlain Street houses. I remember hearing the first shot, and simultaneously the young boy already mentioned, grunt or gasp just beside me, he was only a few feet from me and a little behind me, like me he was running . . . he fell to the ground . . . I don't think the reality of it sank into me at the time . . . a split second later there was a dreadful fusillade of gunfire. It all seemed to come from the one direction, behind us, from the direction of the soldiers. The reports of the guns were all the same. I threw myself to the ground just at the edge of a little wall that runs along behind the back stores of the shops . . . I remember a terrible panic and screaming as people tried to escape. There was a huge crowd trying to get through a narrow opening at the corner of the Rossville Street and Joseph Place side of the flats . . . I remember while lying on the ground seeing men trying to tear the door of the flats open with their bare hands. Apparently it had been boarded up. There were people lying, creeping, running and screaming everywhere. I then looked back over the courtyard and saw this young man earlier referred to lying on his back, with his head towards me . . . I could see blood coming out over his shirt. I decided I must go to attend him . . . I took out a handkerchief and held it up and in a crouched position went to him . . . There were still bursts of gunfire from time to time, though it was not continuous . . . I first knelt beside the boy, and held my handkerchief to his wound . . . then a young Knight of Malta whose name was Glenn came out to the other side of the boy . . . some others came out and stood beside us; I asked them to go away, that we would be safer on our own . . . they did so . . . I must state that this boy had nothing in his hand nor was anything lying beside him, and

I was first to reach him after he fell. After a few minutes the gunfire got worse. We both lay down beside the boy as I gave him the Last Rites of my church. I felt he was dying. Just as I had finished giving him the last rites, a young man dashed out past where we were lying towards the soldiers . . . I screamed at him to get back. He danced up and down in front of the soldiers, shouting something that I could not understand. He had his hands held up at full stretch over his head. I saw a soldier at the corner of the flats take aim and fire at this man . . . he staggered and ran crazily around for a moment. I don't know where he went then . . . I am certain that he was hit . . . I think his name was Bridge. In the meantime we were still lying flat on the ground in the middle of the car park with this young boy, whom I now know to have been Jack Duddy. After a period of time, I don't know how long exactly, perhaps ten minutes during which there had been quite a lot of gunfire, all from one direction, in single shots and bursts, two men crawled out behind us. One of them was William Barber. They offered to help to carry the boy to a position where he could receive medical aid. They suggested that I should go in front and carry a white handkerchief and they would carry him behind me. Then there was a discussion as to whether we should carry him to the flats or through the army lines to the centre of town. We decided on the latter. Just as we were about to get up and make a dash for Chamberlain a civilian gunman appeared at the gable of the last house in Chamberlain Street. I first of all saw the man move along the gable of the house. I thought his movements were strange and suddenly he produced a gun from his pocket . . . it was a small hand gun and made a very different bang from the soldiers' rifles . . . he fired two or three shots at the soldiers at the corner of the flats . . . I think they fired back although I am not sure. I shouted at him to go away or he would get us all killed. He looked round at us lying out in the middle of the car park and then he moved away. After lying for a few more moments, I got up on my knees and was just about to rise when the army opened fire again. We all dived to the ground again and lay there for another while. Eventually we got up, I went in front, the others carried the boy and we made our way into Chamberlain Street, and then turned into Harvey Street, where we were challenged by soldiers and met the BBC camera crew with John Bierman. We proceeded to the junction of Harvey Street and Waterloo Street and there laid the body of the boy on the street, on Mr Barber's coat. Soldiers further down the street ordered us to clear off, and some woman came out of a house and screamed at them that he was only a child and they had shot him. A woman called Mrs McCluskey phoned for an ambulance. People came out of the houses and we all knelt and said a prayer. I think the boy was now dead. The ambulance came after a time and then a Mrs McHugh came and asked me into her house for a cup of tea. I took it and then went up Waterloo Street and down Fahan Street and down the steps to Joseph Place. The sight there was terrible. There were dead and dying and wounded lying everywhere. I attended to many of them. I don't know how many. The firing seemed to have stopped at this time. After some time an ambulance or two came, and with the help of Fr Mulvey, some of the Knights of Malta, and many other people, we got them to the ambulances. On several occasions I recall gunfire during this operation. We felt that it was coming along Rossville from the direction of the army positions there. I remember John Bierman of BBC television asking me to do an interview, and as we were about to begin a shot rang out. We moved to what we considered a safer position. I still have no idea as to what time it was then.

I spent some time then trying to console people who were stunned by it all. I was quite overwhelmed myself. I eventually made my way home via the Little Diamond. My hands and clothes were covered in blood. A patrol of soldiers made to search me at the Little Diamond. I protested and then they did not go through with the search. I came to my house and felt upset and frustrated. I reached for the phone and called Inspector McCullagh of the RUC who was a contemporary of mine at school. I asked him what on earth was the meaning and purpose of it all. He answered that it had only been a minor disturbance and that his latest report said that only two people had been slightly hurt and there were several arrests. I then informed him that I had seen at least six dead bodies and many other people who were seriously wounded. He expressed disbelief. He said he would phone later. He phoned me a few minutes later to tell me that there were 11 dead bodies so far admitted to Altnagelvin Hospital.

12: The Para Removals

John Young, William Nash and Michael McDaid lay dead and dying on the Rossville Street barricade for almost twenty minutes. No one was allowed to go near them. Alexander Nash, on seeing the wounded body of his son, William, ran to his aid. He was cut down and lay wounded.

Then a Saracen armoured vehicle slowly advanced towards the barricade and all three bodies were man-handled by Paras and thrown into the Saracen.

Curiously, the bodies of Hugh Gilmore, Bernard McGuigan, Paddy Doherty and Jim Wray, which lay nearby, were not retrieved. It was over an hour before the three bodies were delivered to Altnagelvin Hospital.

* * * * * * * * * * * *

Mary Harkin
MACHINIST, AGED 41

When the Civil Rights march of Sunday, 30 January 1972, was halted at the army barricade in William Street, I was near the entry to Chamberlain Street. Gas was fired by the army and the marchers were sprayed with dye. I ran into Chamberlain Street and reached the corner of Harvey Street. I made my way towards Columbcille Court, where there was a reported shooting. I saw the youth who was shot. He was wounded in the leg. I left and went home to Mura Place which is part of the Rossville Flats. I heard shots and went to the door. I saw a youth falling. He was running away and had no weapon of any kind. The shots were coming from Chamberlain Street where troops had lined up with rifles. Fr Daly, waving a white handkerchief, went to attend to the dying boy.

I went into the house, to the living room, and called to people below that a boy had been shot. As I looked, the Saracen tanks came into Rossville Street. Troops jumped out firing as they came. The crowd was at this time going towards Free Derry Corner. Three boys fell beside a home-made barricade outside the Flats. I heard a man call, 'That's my son. He's dead. Get an ambulance.' It was Mr Nash. As he raised both hands to show he was unarmed, more shots came from the army and he was wounded. One of the three boys at the barricade was Mr Nash's son William. He was dead. Ten minutes later, a Saracen came. Troops dragged the three bodies by the feet and dumped them like refuse into the back of the Saracen. They drove off. After that there was stunned confusion. I saw Fr Mulvey escorting an ambulance with wounded or dying.

I state positively that I neither heard, nor did I see, any shots, nail or petrol bombs from the Bogside area.

* * * * * * * * * * * * *

Susan and Betty Coyle
FACTORY WORKERS

On 30 January 1972, I, Susan Coyle, saw the marchers pass my house peacefully. I then was aware of four Saracens and two covered army trucks come from the direction of Little James' Street. They drove directly at the crowd and the people scattered. Some of the Saracens stopped at the High Flats and the soldiers got out and opened fire immediately on the crowd who at the time were running towards Free Derry Corner. At this stage three youths and a man were running over the barricade at the entrance to the High Flats. I heard gunfire from the army and two of the youths and the man fell. The third youth took cover by one of the other bodies. As he lay there I actually saw the bullet hit the boy in the head and from his position I assumed him to be dead. The other two youths, when shot, had fallen, one on top of the other and never moved, so I thought they had died immediately. The man raised himself and beckoned to the army and called to them that the boys lying beside him needed an ambulance. A Saracen was then driven to the barricade. Two soldiers got out and lifted the body in the middle (that is, the one lying on top of the other). He was wearing a brown suit and was bleeding from the side. They, at no stage, looked to see if any of those shot were alive. They threw this young man into the back of the Saracen. They then went to the boy who was shot in the head. Each soldier took an arm and a leg and they flung the body into the back of the Saracen. One soldier dragged the third body by the scruff of the neck and threw it also into the Saracen. In the meantime the man had got to his feet and went to the Saracen; he appeared to want to get into it but the soldiers pushed him in the direction of the High Flats. One of these two soldiers shouted towards the direction of Abbey Park. He told the people to get off the streets. I then heard shooting at the back of my house; my daughter went to the kitchen and from the kitchen window she saw three bodies lying in front of the three pensioners' houses in Glenfada Park. I went into the kitchen and I also saw the bodies. Just then there was another shot, also from the army, at the same time one of the bodies shuddered as though struck by a bullet. There were no other people present in this part of Glenfada Park at the time. A girl in a white coat with a red cross on it appeared from the direction of Abbey Park. She had her hands in the air and was calling to the soldiers, 'First Aid, don't shoot'. The army permitted this girl and two or three men all of whom had their hands above their heads to come forward and remove the bodies. They took the bodies in the direction of Abbey Park. My daughter and I went back to the front of the house and from the front window I saw a body to the right of the entrance to the High Flats; another body lying in a pool of blood at the alleyway between the High Flats; one lying at the bottom of the steps leading to Fahan Street. At this time an ambulance came across the waste ground and stopped in front of the High Flats. Priests, First-aiders and other helpers put the bodies into the ambulance. This ambulance left and another one arrived. More people were put into this one. They appeared to be wounded people who had sheltered in people's houses. While people were being put into this ambulance more shots were fired from the direction of the army. A First Aid boy at the ambulance lay down, at first I thought he had been hit but he got up when the firing stopped and we knew him to be okay. Fr Mulvey came from the direction of the High Flats waving a white hankie. He walked towards the army. He spoke to the soldiers and then came back. He was joined by Fr Irwin and they both went back to the army. Another ambulance arrived and I assume Fr Mulvey had come back because after a few minutes he stepped from behind this ambulance and waved a white hankie while another body was carried to the ambulance. There was a lot of confusion and more ambulances were departing and arriving continuously, taking away the wounded and the other bodies. All during this time the army remained in the area around the High Flats. We were not aware of the army actually leaving but they were still there when the last ambulance left.

I, Betty Coyle, witnessed everything my mother Susan Coyle has said in the above statement.

* * * * * * * * * * * * *

Chris B.
AGED 25

I was on the Civil Rights march and when the shooting started I was outside the flats. I saw seven people, men and young lads, shot dead. I saw them with my own eyes.

The meeting at the Free Derry Corner was just taking place when the army came charging up Rossville Street in tanks and cut a lot of the people off. The army started firing immediately, at first I thought it was rubber bullets but then I recognised the distinct twang of their rifles. I managed to get in through the door of the flats. The first thing I saw was a young fellow running and jumping over the barricade. The next moment he was lying on the ground with his back all covered in blood. They had shot him in the back as he went over the barricade. There were two other lads lying beside him. They also had been shot. They must have been dead, because the army came up and dragged them away. They dragged one of them by the head and the other two by the feet and threw them into the back of a Saracen.

There was a man at Molly's shop. Molly's shop is the one near the telephone box. There was a man lying dead against the wall. There were two more people dead. One was on the bottom floor of the flats and another one on the second floor. The crowd all went out then and there was a priest waving a white flag. The flag of truce and the army shot at him and he had to run for cover. Then there was a lull in the shooting and the ambulances began to arrive and all the dead put into the back of the ambulances. A few of the boys became very angry when they saw all the bodies and they began shouting at the army and calling them murderers and the army opened fire at them again but I don't think they hit anyone. I never heard any gunmen, nail bombs or petrol bombs during the whole time. The army just came in and shot people for just being there.

* * * * * * * * * * * *

Pat C.
CHEMICAL OPERATOR, AGED 28

I was in Chamberlain Street on Sunday 30 January, when the stone throwing was going on at soldiers in William Street around 4 o'clock. Someone shouted 'Saracens are coming in Rossville Street' and the crowd immediately started running up Chamberlain Street towards the High Flats. Some of us stopped at the junction of Eden Place and Chamberlain Street to see exactly where the Saracens were. At this exact moment I was on the left-hand side of Eden Place in the corner and the first thing I saw then was an elderly man standing inside a confectionery shop in Eden Place (what is left of it). Now soldiers appeared round the corner of the alleyway joining Eden Place, one of whom grabbed the old man. He hit him over the head with a baton and dragged him round the corner into the alleyway. Immediately a rifle spout appeared from the alleyway corner firing a shot which hit the gable wall of the house in the corner — at the junction of High Street and Chamberlain Street.

There were no gunmen or gunshots in the area where I was standing. The rifle was fired without the soldier putting his head round the corner. I then started to run up Chamberlain Street towards the High Flats and looked back and saw soldiers running up William Street, some of whom stopped and again started shooting up Chamberlain Street.

On reaching the square or court behind the High Flats — which I had crawled up to on my hands and knees — I saw a friend lying flat on his stomach attending someone who was lying flat on his back in the middle of the courtyard. Another man was beside this man and was also attending him.

At this particular point I was able to see British soldiers in firing positions and shooting over the head of the priest at other people who were taking cover behind a low wall at the rear of the shops in the High Flats. I made my way round to the passage at the lower intersection of the two blocks of High Flats —and here I came upon a member of the Knights of Malta in attendance on another injured person. He asked for assistance. We were unable to determine there and then what was wrong with him as he did not seem to have any wounds. I knew the man to be Pius McCarron. Another fellow and myself started to carry him to one of the nearby houses, and while doing so some shots were also fired at us, hitting the wall above our heads.

When we got him into a house we found out that he had been hit in the head by a piece of masonry from a ricochet. This he told us himself when he recovered. In that same house was a young girl who had been hit by a Saracen and was in great pain from back injuries.

I then left the house and made my way to the corner of the shops where the telephone box is — the Rossville Street side — where some other people were crawling about and trying to take cover. Some more shots rang out and I then saw the body of Barney McGuigan, although I did not know at that time that it was him. Another young man lay at the very corner of the flats and two more young men were lying on the small barricade in front of the High Flats. There were eight or ten people who were huddled with myself at the gable wall of the High Flats. While we were there the shooting continued and an army Saracen slowly came through a small entrance in the barricade and stopped. A group of soldiers got out of the Saracen, lifted the two bodies of the young men lying on the barricade and threw them like carcasses into the rear of the Saracen. While this was going on rifles were trained on us from the Saracen

Above: The Saracen in the picture has just collected three bodies from the rubble barricade. In the foreground lie the bodies of Hugh Gilmore and Bernard McGuigan. There were at least two other bodies visible to the soldiers in the vehicle. *Below:* The Saracen returns to its position. On the high ground are derelict buildings, just outside the Derry Walls, in whose attics British army snipers were positioned.

Waiting with the dead — white-coated Knights of Malta para-medic waits with others by the covered remains of Hugh Gilmore.

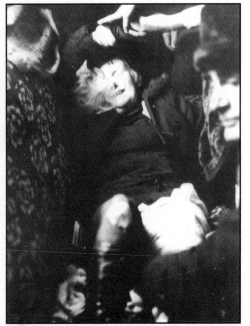

A mother of 13 children, Mrs Margaret (Peggy) Deery, is assisted. She was the only woman shot and seriously wounded on Bloody Sunday.

A horrific image of death and desolation as the body of Bernard McGuigan lies on the concrete pavement. The Bogside, which ten minutes earlier had been thronged with an estimated 15,000-20,000 people, is now deserted.

Above: The six bullet holes in this third-storey window in the Rossville Flats were fired by a Para at Italian photographer Fulvio Grimaldi who was attempting to photograph the bodies of William Nash, John Young and Michael McDaid, which lay across the street on the rubble barricade.

Below: People huddle in shock and terror by the telephone kiosk. Close by are the bodies of Hugh Gilmore and Bernard McGuigan.

Above: Caught in the open three unarmed men try to crawl to safety. The one kneeling on the left and wearing a handkerchief for protection against the CS gas is Paddy Doherty. Moments later he was shot dead.

Below: 31-year-old father, Patrick Doherty, lies dead on the Rossville Flats forecourt. A brave man crawls towards him in an effort to render assistance.

Above: The commander of 1 Para, Lt. Col. Derek Wilford, watches his soldiers fire in the direction of Free Derry Corner.

Below: In direct violation of the Geneva Convention, a young Knights of Malta para-medic is left in a crumpled heap having been attacked by two members of 1 Para.

Above: The scene which was to become the icon of Bloody Sunday. Fr Edward Daly, waving a bloodstained handkerchief, leads a small group of men who are carrying the body of young Jackie Duddy. See also, overleaf, the same image reproduced on the famous memorial murals at Free Derry Corner.

Below: Thirteen coffins rest side by side in St Mary's Church, Creggan.

Derry today. At Free Derry Corner, two powerful murals by Bogside artists Tom Kelly and Kevin Hasson remember and remind of Bloody Sunday. The ominous gasmask worn by a child dominates one apartment block gable end, while the other depicts perhaps the most remembered icon of that terrible day – Father [now Bishop] Edward Daly waving a white handkerchief as he leads rescuers carrying Jackie Duddy, a dying victim through the still threatening bullets (see photo on previous page) with, behind, the truck which led the demonstrators on the parade (see photo on first page of first picture section), with the gathered citizens of Derry in their thousands. The bloodied Civil Rights banner is trampled underfoot by a member of 1 Para looking at his dying victim. According to Don Mullan, 'Bloody Sunday also effectively killed the Northern Ireland Civil Rights Association.'

which remained in this position for about ten minutes. Apart from soldiers who had taken up positions behind the garden walls of the maisonettes no shooting was taking place in this area. The soldiers shouted to all, 'Move and you are dead!'

I covered up the body of Barney McGuigan with my jacket, removed his shoes and straightened his legs from the crumpled position he was lying in. At this particular point an elderly lady came towards me with a blanket and seeing that I had used my jacket to cover Mr McGuigan turned towards the gable wall of the High Flats where she used the blanket to cover the body of young Gilmore. Another lady came with a second blanket. This I then used to completely cover the body of Mr McGuigan in place of my jacket. By this time the army had pulled back to the William Street end of the flats and had taken up a position there.

After that a number of ambulances appeared and we started to get the injured people into the ambulances. After that I walked around trying to find who was dead and I found out that a friend of mine, Willie McKinney, had been killed. I then went up to break the news to Mr McKinney's family.

I agree to the publication of this statement and to its use in any investigation. This is my statement and it is correct.

* * * * * * * * * * * *

Alice Long
SHIRT WORKER

On Sunday 30 January, being a superintendent in the Knights of Malta Ambulance Corps I took part in the march as a first-aid worker. When the march stopped in William Street, I was opposite the former site of Richardson's shirt factory, standing with three other members of the unit, 1st Lieutenant Jim McDaid, Adjutant Joe O'Kane and Volunteer Angela Coyle, when the gas started coming into William Street. I put on my gas mask and with Joe O'Kane and Angela Coyle went to the assistance of a girl who had been overcome with the gas. We took the girl back out of William Street through a gap where houses once stood into Columbcille Court to a house there.

While we were treating the girl in the house, shots rang out and
somebody in the house shouted that someone had been shot outside. I came out of the house and ran across Columbcille Court to
Shiels' house where a crowd was gathered. When I made my way
into the house Fr McLaughlin was giving the last rites to a young
boy. Dr McClean and Jim McDaid whom I've already mentioned
were attending to a wound in his leg. I helped them with this.
Another man was being treated for gunshot wounds by Sergeant
Johnny Lafferty. While I was still there, shooting started. Someone
called Dr McClean and Fr McLaughlin and said someone had been
shot in the Columbcille Court area. They left and I finished attending to the wounded boy. During this time shooting was still going
on. When I was finished I went out and headed across Columbcille
Court towards the passageway at the back, near to Glenfada Park.
The shooting had now stopped and there were few people about. A
man was standing in the passageway with Captain Leo Day of the
Knights of Malta and he told Captain Day about civilians in a
Saracen. He gave us the impression they were hurt and Captain Day
said that as I was wearing a white coat I should go with him and see
what we could do for them. I went with Captain Day along the passageway to Rossville Street and we approached the soldiers who
were at the end of the passageway, with our hands in the air. We
asked if there was anything we could do to help them or the civilians. They said there was not. We moved off across the barricade in
Rossville Street towards the High Flats. There were two casualties
there. We were standing outside the shops in the bottom of the High
Flats when somebody said that a man had been shot a short distance
away at the Fahan Street corner of the flats. Mr Day and myself went
up there and met Volunteer Paul McLaughlin on the way. When we
got there a man was lying on the ground beside the steps with several people gathered round him. I felt for his heartbeat and pulse.
There was a slight pulse but I could feel no heartbeat. I found a
wound on the left-hand side of his rib-cage. A priest was giving him
the last rites. Mr Day had left to go to another casualty. I considered
working with his heart but Fr Mulvey arrived in a mini car. I told
him the patient was a stretcher case and could not be put into the
car. A woman had called to me that an ambulance was in
Chamberlain Street. Volunteer Antoinette Coyle came with me

across the courtyard of Rossville Street High Flats to try to get the ambulance. We were in the middle of the courtyard when a soldier in the Chamberlain Street area shouted at us to halt. We stopped and I shouted to him that we were first-aid workers looking for an ambulance. We continued to Chamberlain Street and were stopped by a Saracen armoured car. A soldier asked what we wanted and I replied that we were looking for an ambulance for a casualty that was seriously injured. For some time, nobody answered. There was an ambulance there and a woman called Anna Nelis who was there told us that the ambulance was required for two women who had been injured. Eventually a soldier told us to go to William Street for an ambulance. He was about 5' 7" tall, stout, with the winged badge of the paratroops on his shoulder.

We went to William Street, at the end of Chamberlain Street. William Street was full of soldiers and I could see no ambulance. We came back along Chamberlain Street to the soldier who had sent us. He started to laugh. I told him I didn't think it was funny. He began to work the bolt in his rifle. He told me that our white coats were a good target. I told him I needed an ambulance because there were two casualties whose lives could be saved. He said that he was not finished shooting yet. I became angry and asked him if he thought he was a hero. He replied that he knew he was. Throughout this exchange he was laughing all the time.

About then I saw an ambulance come into Chamberlain Street. I went to the driver and told him where the casualties were. I left the ambulance and went back across the courtyard of the flats to the casualty. When I got back to the casualty I examined him and he was still alive. There was a priest and some other people around him.

I left again and went towards the two casualties I had passed outside the shops. I knew at first sight that the elder man was dead. Blood was coming from a wound in his head. I was told he had already been attended and I asked a woman in the flats for a blanket to cover him. I got the blanket and covered him and turned to the younger man. There was a man crying over him and he wouldn't let me near him. At that time Mr Day who was standing at the barricade called me to come with him to the army to get assistance. The ambulance had not arrived.

We went across Rossville Street to the army on the waste ground opposite Eden Place. Mr Day asked to see an officer. There was no reply from any of the soldiers. A photographer had approached Mr Day. He asked Mr Day if he needed any help. Mr Day said that we needed stretchers. He explained to the photographer about the casualties needing transportation.

At this point Captain Day noticed three soldiers guarding a Saracen. He asked if he could see who was inside it. A soldier opened the door. An officer appeared and shouted not to let anyone come near the Saracen. The soldier closed the door again. I got a glimpse inside and saw three bodies lying in a heap. The one on top was wearing a light-coloured coat and seemed to have a wound in the face. The body at the bottom had his head thrown back with his mouth open and blood seemed to be pouring from the back of his head or neck.

We turned away and Fr Mulvey and Fr Bradley had come across to the army. They wanted to get to the civilians in the Saracen also. Mr Day made some more inquiries about assistance and I picked up three empty cartridge cases from the ground. A soldier approached and made me hand them over. Captain Day and myself then left and went back to the flats.

While we were at the shops in the flats again, the army opened fire again. About five or six shots were fired by the army in Rossville Street toward Free Derry Corner. The shooting stopped again. A few minutes later several ambulances arrived on the scene. We started to move the casualties. While a priest was administering the last rites to a dead body in one of the ambulances the ambulance was almost struck by a rubber bullet. Lead bullets were fired at this time also — about thirty or forty rounds perhaps. We lay on the floor of the ambulance.

The shooting stopped again. I got out of the ambulance and waved my hands in the air. I shouted to the army not to shoot, that we were only moving bodies. We put the casualty that I had attended into the ambulance. Some soldiers got down on their knees and took aiming positions and I shouted again to them not to shoot.

The ambulances moved off, the soldiers pulled back and everything was quiet and we gathered in Glenfada Park where we treated some women for shock.

13: Gloating on Death

From reading the eyewitness accounts below, there seems no doubt that Paras did gloat over the deaths they had caused on Bloody Sunday. This gloating was carried out by highly trained and professional soldiers — soldiers whose demeanour and truthfulness at the Widgery Tribunal of Inquiry greatly 'impressed' the Lord Chief Justice of England (paragraph 97).

* * * * * * * * * * *

Margaret O'Reilly
HOUSEWIFE, AGED 42

Standing in Chamberlain Street with my sister, Mrs Mooney, and Mr Mooney. Mr Mooney was standing getting dressed by first-aid help after being hit on the cheek with a rubber bullet.

Three Saracens came up to the waste ground beside Rossville Flats. People ran in panic. I fled back to Chamberlain Street. Someone took me into a house. Just entering the house people shouted that someone, a girl, was shot. I ran out to assist, thinking it was my own child. Mrs Deery was the person that was shot in the leg. A few people were in the house at the time including Mr Michael Canavan and Mr McDermott, Westway. When first-aid help arrived the army entered the house and stood in the house for 15 minutes. The army asked who shot the injured people. I answered, 'the army'. At that the soldier grinned. I told him I thought that Mrs Deery would bleed to death. Mr Bridge was in the back yard at the time after being shot in the two legs. The people in the house requested that they bring help quickly. Then the army left and went to the street. When leaving the house to go to the hospital a soldier laughed, I asked him why laugh at such panic. He answered 'It is a laugh.' I went on into the ambulance with Mrs Deery waiting on Mr Bridge. As Mr Bridge was helped into the ambulance by men in the house the army put the men against the wall with their finger tips against the wall and hit them on the legs. I lost the head and cried at them to leave the men alone. He turned to me and said 'There will be more of you pigs dead before the morning.' The ambulance men told me to get back into the ambulance.

I know for fact the men in the house were like myself in for shelter.

When they marched the men over Chamberlain to the Barrack they kept punching Mr McCloskey in the back and also abusing Mr McDermott after coming out of the house.

This is my statement and it is correct and I grant permission for it to be published or used in any representation.

* * * * * * * * * * * *

Jean Donohue
HOUSEWIFE (EX-NURSE), AGED 30

On Sunday, 30 January 1972, a young girl came to my door and asked me if I was a nurse. I told her 'Yes' I was. She told me to come quickly, a woman had been shot. When I went to the bottom of the street I approached a soldier and explained that I was a nurse and that I wanted to go to the aid of an injured person. I was then subjected to obscene language. I continued on past the soldiers to the end of Chamberlain Street where an ambulance was just arriving, a woman was just then carried out on a stretcher from No. 33 Chamberlain Street. As the stretcher was being carried past a soldier he called to another soldier opposite him, 'I've never seen a stiff.' To this the other soldier replied, 'You'll see plenty today.' The other soldier then said, 'The more the merrier, thirty the limit.' I asked the soldier if he was human and would he let me through to the other injured people as I was a nurse. To this he replied, 'It's not nurses they need.' 'It's Blood Donors,' he said laughingly.

A large number — approx. 12–13 people — were brought from No. 33 Chamberlain Street. They were pushed face against the wall and made stand hands against the wall with outstretched legs. They were then kicked on the legs. I complained strongly and was told that I would get the same treatment. Once more I was subjected to foul language and was told 'Today we got the Bogsiders.'

* * * * * * * * * * * *

William B.
BREAD SERVER, AGED 24

I was in my mother's flat in Rossville Flats, overlooking the barricade. As I was looking out the window I saw the 'Paras' entering the courtyard of the flats. One soldier caught an elderly man, standing against the wall with his hands in the air. The elderly man who was arrested was beaten severely by the butt of the soldier's rifle, over the head. I could see clearly the blood as the man was bald. Two members of the march went to his aid with no success and fled when they saw other soldiers approaching them; a soldier took aim and shot one of the fleeing men; after this incident, I took cover in the flat as army bullets were flying in all directions. I proceeded to the front room of the flat, where I saw another civilian lying at the barricade who had been shot dead. Two other bodies were lying beside him. One of these bodies was lifeless, but the other person only appeared to be wounded as he was writhing in agony and waving a handkerchief in a hand. Seconds later, more gunfire rang out, I took cover. When I looked again all three bodies were lifeless. A Saracen tank approached the bodies, soldiers got out and tossed the bodies into the back of the Saracen like coal into a bunker, showing no respect for the dead. I could see soldiers smiling over the dead. After this incident, I could no longer go near the window because each time I did, a soldier trained his gun on me, smiling as he did so.

All this time I never heard a nail bomb go off or saw a petrol bomb being thrown.

* * * * * * * * * * * *

David Melarkey
WELDER, AGED 28

I was standing with my brother Noel at the junction of William Street and Chamberlain Street and decided to move up it to avoid the water cannon. A gas grenade landed in front of me and, choking, I made my way via Eden Place to Rossville Street to a point opposite Kells Walk.

I then saw two Saracens enter Rossville Street from William Street. The crowd had broken and were running at this time. I realised that the crowd might get jammed in the narrow entrance behind the flats so I made my way by the front of the flats to the Free Derry side of them. I decided to stand on one of the bollards to have a view of what was happening and was surprised to see the Saracens very close to me. During all the time I was moving from opposite Kells Walk to this point I heard several shots from the Saracens. As the soldiers came out of the Saracens they kept shouting. Two or three of them took up firing positions on the William Street side of the barricade. The rest were shooting from round the side of the Saracens, except one. He was pointing his gun towards the roof of the flats — as I thought at the time. (Next day visiting the scene I noticed six bullet holes in the first-floor windows.)

The soldiers motioned the crowd to come towards them during a short lull — about 15 seconds — in the firing. While some were going and some were not I crawled across the street to an empty builders' hut. Two other young lads came in after me.

We were afraid that if shots came from the walls the hut could be riddled so we left the hut and got into half-built houses. I went from one house to another, then reached Cable Street. All this time shooting was going on all over the place from somewhere in the area of the Credit Union Building.

I made my way to Great James' Street and came down as far as Little James' Street. In Little James' Street I saw a number of soldiers who appeared to be discussing what tactics they had used. One of them — a small man — was showing how he got someone in the back and mimicked how his target had staggered and fallen.

A commanding officer came across the street and told the radio operator, 'Recall all your snipers.' Two soldiers with shopping bags came down from a deserted building. They walked over to the eight or nine standing in Brewster's doorway. About 15 seconds after I saw one push another in the back and the group appeared to be nearly coming to blows. A shot rang out and everybody ran for cover.

I headed home to be there before my wife would hear the 6 o'clock news and get worried.

I can definitely state that in all the time covered by this statement I never heard a nail bomb nor a Thompson machine gun.

This is my statement and it is correct.

* * * * * * * * * * * *

Patrick Kelly
CLEANER, AGED 34

I arrived at the meeting in Free Derry Corner via Cable Street and stood about 10 yards from the platform in Rossville Street. The time was ten minutes to four. Just as Bernadette Devlin began to speak I heard the sound of firing. I thought it was rubber bullets. She asked the people to keep calm and stay where they were. I decided to move to the edge of the crowd to see what was actually happening. I was told 'they', meaning the army, were firing real bullets. I made my way to Lisfannon Park. I looked towards the Rossville Flats and saw the Saracen cars, about four, stopped. Soldiers with rifles facing the crowd were deployed around and some had taken up positions on the walls of the maisonettes. People were fleeing from the soldiers who were down on their knees in a firing position. I ran in the direction of Lisfannon Park and on looking in the direction of the Rossville Flats I saw the body of a man lying on the ground beside the telephone box. I realised at that moment the bullets were real. People were panicking and screaming. I took out my handkerchief, held my hands above my head and looking towards the army post on the Walls, I proceeded across Bogside Road, towards Glenfada Park. The first thing I saw was a boy of about 17 or 18 years who had been shot in the leg being helped by two other people. People in the area told us that there were more casualties round the corner in the Mews Lane. I and another man went round to pick up a casualty we saw lying on the ground. There were three soldiers armed with SLR guns who threatened to shoot us if we went forward into the area. We went back and after a few minutes we decided to try again. This time the soldiers did not stop us and we advanced to pick up the wounded man who we later discovered was the older man, McKinney. As we lifted him from the sort of alcove where he lay we saw three other bodies lying still, without movement. They were very close together. We carried up the first man who was still alive, round the corner to safety. The Knights of Malta took him over and attended him. Another man and I went back to where we had seen the bodies and lifted the first one — a boy who seemed to be dead. We carried him into a house. A doctor and priest had arrived at this time. The other casualties were carried by other men into the house next door. I can swear that the two men I personally helped carry had no weapons of any description on or near their bodies. Neither could I see any weapons lying near the other bodies.

By this time the shooting had stopped. I made my way to the telephone box at the Rossville Flats where I had seen the body of a man earlier. He was still there with a crowd of about forty people gathered round him. As I approached, someone covered him with a cloth. The crowd shouted in frustration at the army. I saw one soldier making signs at the crowd and seemed to be gloating at the crowd. I moved in to have a closer view of the casualty and I heard two bangs which seemed to be rubber bullets. Then a fusillade of shots rang out and the crowd scattered. The shots had come from the army who still kept on firing, as the crowd scattered round the two corners. The ambulance had already arrived to pick up the casualty and even as the body on the stretcher was being preceded by a priest carrying a handkerchief in front, towards the ambulance, the firing continued. The ambulance men had to seek cover behind the ambulance. When this shooting was over I saw a wounded girl being carried from behind me. The ambulance men shouted, 'There is room for one more.' At this stage, I turned away as I realised I was in a vulnerable position and made my way home.

14: Arrest and Assault

During their operation the Paras arrested twenty-two men from 33 Chamberlain Street. Some of those arrested had carried the injured Margaret Deery and Michael Bridge into the house for shelter and medical attention. Others had simply taken refuge from the army gunfire and aggression.

The Paras rounded up and arrested about twenty men and youths, and one woman, in and around the Glenfada Park/Kells Walk area. Several people were also arrested by 1 Para in the open ground of the Rossville Street car park. These were initially held in armoured personnel carriers. In addition, isolated arrests were made by other British Army regiments manning barriers on the outskirts of the Bogside throughout the afternoon.

Most of those arrested were taken to a holding centre at the Navy Dockyard on Strand Road, Derry. They vividly recount physical abuse and degrading treatment, especially at the hands of 1 Para.

Charges of 'riotous behaviour' were issued to several of those detained. However, all charges were subsequently dropped, on the recommendation of the DPP and British Attorney General.

* * * * * * * * * * * *

Kevin L.
POSTMAN, AGED 30

At bottom of William Street the main group broke away to go to Free Derry Corner — I stayed behind in William Street/Chamberlain Street where stone throwing at troops was going on — about 100 involved in this stone throwing for about half an hour. During that half an hour the soldiers fired rubber bullets and coloured dye. About then I saw the Saracens going in to Bogside — in Rossville Street. So everybody turned and some shouted to get stones — this was their chance of stoning the Saracen. We ran a short distance down Chamberlain Street and cut right into Rossville Street. I was behind the main group. I heard a single shot ring out then, and heard a lot of people shouting, 'They are firing real bullets this time.' I turned back down Chamberlain Street towards Rossville Flats. When I got to the flats I heard several single shots ring out and saw a young fellow fall dead in the courtyard. Fr Daly turned back to help him. I was frightened so I took cover against the wall in the courtyard. During this time I heard a lot of people crying and shouting, 'They are shooting them down and murdering them.' I also saw Fr Daly waving a handkerchief coloured with blood. The soldiers continued firing into the courtyard. I could see the bullets breaking the windows of a car in the area. I also saw a man run across. I spoke to him later on — he was shot in the leg. He told me that he tried to run across to help the person that was lying in the yard with Fr Daly. The situation was now worsening — some decided to make a break for it — I stayed. I saw a half dozen running along the left-hand wall from where I was — four shots rang out — I saw the bullets hit the wall and I saw the men fall to the ground. I thought that at least one of them had been hit as they lay there for a couple of minutes. When next I looked towards Fr Daly a Knight of Malta was lifting the body from the ground and carrying it down Chamberlain Street waving a white handkerchief. The shooting seemed to stop for a couple of minutes at this time — then the men who were lying by the wall made a break for it to the safety of the flats. I saw two other men lifting the man that was shot through the leg — I went over and helped to carry him into a house, No. 33 Chamberlain Street. There was also a woman in the house with a gun-shot wound in the leg but I did not see her getting shot. We decided they, especially the woman, needed hospital treatment at once. When I opened the door to go out I could still hear shooting and I shouted up to a woman in the flats on my left to get an ambulance. She did not seem to understand so since I couldn't leave the courtyard to go any further I went back to No. 33. At this time I saw two armoured Saracens at the bottom end of Chamberlain Street (William Street end). When I went into

33 a Knight of Malta was bandaging the man's leg. Since we had no way of getting an ambulance we decided to get the army up to see if they could get us an ambulance. When we went out, there was one Saracen and 10 soldiers coming up the street kicking over buckets of water left outside doors. The woman who owned the house spoke to the soldiers about getting the ambulance. They did not seem to be very helpful at this time — they said, 'Who are they?' The woman explained about the two injured people in the house. They said they would come in and have a look. The woman replied, 'This is my house. I don't want any trouble and one of you is enough to see them.' However four of them pushed their way past her in; they saw the two injured and then they continued to search the house — upstairs, searching bedrooms. The officer in charge shouted into the street to other soldiers to phone for an ambulance. After this he told all the men to get outside and we received very rough treatment from them while we were being put out, even though we were willing to go. We were made to stand up against the wall with our hands against the wall. We were searched. It was during this time that I was kicked by a soldier searching me several times. After being searched we were made to march with our hands on top of our heads to the waste ground off William Street. We were receiving so many different orders from the soldiers that we did not know which to obey and were being batoned for this by the paratroopers. Then I heard someone saying, 'Make them all sit down on the ground facing the wall.' Then they questioned us individually, asking us what we were doing in the area and I also heard a soldier using abusive language about what he would like to do to Bernadette Devlin — trying to provoke us. After sitting in this position for 20 minutes we were told to get up into a three-ton truck, army lorry, that had arrived at this time. Again I was hit while I was getting into it. We were made to sit facing the front of the truck. At this time I did not know where I was going but when we reached our destination I realised it was the Naval Dockyard — I knew it well since I spent 12 years in the Navy. When we got out of the truck the dogs were barking at us and I heard one soldier say, 'We brought them some fresh meat.' We were then put into the building where I saw about 20 more men who had been arrested, with their hands up against the wall. By then we had an identification parade — the soldiers were picking out men that

they alleged they recognised as stone throwers. I saw them grab one boy in particular and said, 'We want you — you were at Magilligan.' I spoke to this boy later and I said to him that he should have said that Magilligan was not an illegal march and that they therefore had nothing to hold him on. Out of about the 40 men there they decided not to charge seven of us. I was one of the seven. So we were taken behind more barbed wire in the building and told to stay there with a soldier and dog on sentry. The conditions in the building were very cold. I was there for about five and a half hours (4.15–9.50). After about four hours they brought us two heaters in and gave us a cup of tea but during this whole time the other men had to remain against the wall. I saw a lot of men who had been beaten up and badly cut and they told me that the paratroopers had run mad on them. After being charged the other men were put into the same compound as us. At 9.50 I was called out — asked to sign a paper stating that I had no valuables taken from me — This I done and was then let out into the Strand Road, and told to make my way home.

* * * * * * * * * * * *

John Noel Devine
MACHINE OPERATOR, AGED 38

On Sunday evening, 30 January, around 3.30, I was in Glenfada Park and I was on my way to Free Derry Corner. Then the shooting started (this is why I turned into Glenfada Park to seek shelter). Paratroopers came running round the corner, and in Glenfada Park took aim from about 10–15 yards and I saw them shoot three people. Crossfire was coming from the waste ground into Glenfada Park also.

I threw myself behind a car — there were about 27 of us taking shelter there. The troops came across, put guns to our heads and told us we were arrested, threatening to shoot us. We were taken away, kicked along the street, and hit with batons and guns. They batoned us into a wagon and made us kneel on the floor of the wagon, and anyone who moved was batoned. We were taken to the shipyard down by the Buncrana Road, and we left the wagon, still being batoned and kicked by the paratroopers. The Coldstream Regiment then took us over from the paratroops, and I was made to stand faced to barbed wire for about three hours.

When the paratroops came to identify the people they had arrested, we were picked out, one or two at a time, searched, and I saw them removing money from others. We were abused and kicked in the knees and groin — this again was the paratroops. I was struck twice in the stomach by one, and twice kneed in the groin. Another paratrooper continued this treatment. We were asked if we would join the UDR — if we didn't answer they kicked us. I was charged with throwing stones. I was then handed over to the RUC, who took a statement from myself and the paratrooper charging me. I was not ill-treated by the police — it was exclusively the paratroopers who did the damage. I was released at 11.55 p.m.

Before being arrested, I witnessed heavy shooting from close range by paratroopers, and four dead bodies in the street. The shooting seemed entirely indiscriminate, aimed at anyone who moved, which is why I stayed put.

* * * * * * * * * * * *

James Gallagher
Apprentice Electric Engineer, aged 16

On Sunday 30 January I was coming from Mass at St Columb's Church. I was picked up by the military — they had moved in to the area and taken up positions. A soldier was lying on the ground outside the People's Hall with a rifle pointing towards the church. He was positioned under a car. The path was crowded and I had to walk along the road. I did not see the soldier until I was on top of him. To avoid him I had to jump over his rifle. A soldier then came up behind me and struck me in the back with his rifle butt. I turned to defend myself and again I was struck in the stomach with the butt of the rifle. A man then came forward and stated that he was the owner of the car, his name being Seamus Boyle of Westland Street.

The same soldier struck the muzzle of the rifle into the car owner's stomach and said to him, 'Get away you bastard unless you want to be shot.' One of the soldiers then cocked his rifle, the car-owner then moved back. A second soldier came forward and was instructed to arrest me and this he did and took me to a Saracen truck which was parked on waste ground at Bishop Street where Gilmartin's store used to stand. I was placed between two soldiers in the Saracen truck and ordered to sit on the floor. The soldier who arrested me then left to take up his position. One of the soldiers in the truck left the remaining soldier in the truck, pointed a sub-machine gun at me and told me to sit on the bench where he could see me, then he keep clicking the magazine out and in. He then started to point it at the people outside the truck, waving it about making a sound like a machine gun. He then turned to me and said, 'You are lucky to be out of this. You will not be marching today. You are going to be taught a lesson. You will have no more females.' I made no reply. He then sat watching the people for a few minutes. I said to him, 'Why am I being held as I have to go to work at the Derry City club?' He made no reply. I then heard a conversation on the radio. 'We have picked up one of them and he has been arrested for kicking Pte Last while being positioned in Barrack Street.' A few minutes later two soldiers came forward and ordered me out of the Saracen and led me to the jail in Bishop Street. On the way up there was conversation passed between the soldiers. They were asked 'Had you got one already?' and they asked, 'What did you get him for?' and they replied, 'We are going to get him for kicking Pte Last.' When I had been led into the entrance of the jail an official said, 'Good work, Corporal', and he said, 'Thank you, sir.' I was then led into the centre of the jail area, I stood there for a few minutes while they made up their mind what to do with me. At this the officer came up and said, 'Get him up against the wall. I do not want to see his ugly mug.' Another officer then came forward with a blue slip of paper and asked the corporal if he could read it. The corporal said, 'I think so', and the officer said, 'Can't you read yet?' The corporal replied, 'Yes, sir.' He stuttered and stammered a few lines on the slip informing me that I was being arrested for assaulting a member of the security forces. I was then put in the back of a landrover after about 20 minutes, during which I was made to stand up against the wall. It was bitterly cold. I was then driven to the detention centre under the bridge. While being driven there, the two soldiers said that I was a lucky boy. They both agreed. Before leaving the landrover I noticed a stretcher marked B. Coy Royal Anglians. I was taken to the RMP hut. The sergeant said, 'What, one already?' Corporal Smith was then addressed by one of the Military Police. They then began to take particulars from Corporal Smith. They then took particulars of my name, address and occupation and age. They took articles from my pockets and particulars of my clothing and one said, 'That is a paramilitary-style uniform — where did you get it? Can we not get him, Sarge?' I was then led over to the far wall and had my picture taken twice alongside of the arresting soldier. The names were written above us with chalk on black material. I was then made to stand at the door away from the heat. They would make it rough if I tried to escape. They mentioned that there were two war dogs outside the door and said that they may put me in the compound with them. After that I stood there for an hour and a quarter. Then the police arrived. They took the same particulars and asked for the photos. I mentioned to the police that this was not the same soldier who had arrested me. He then went forward to the policeman at the typewriter. He said something to the other policeman. He came back and sat down and read the newspaper. After about 10 or 15 minutes they were instructed to take me to the Police Barracks. I was then put in the detention cell until my father came for me at 4.20 p.m. My father then made a phone call to Mr McDaid to inform John Hume MP that he would be up to see him. We left the GPO phone box to go up Ship Quay Street to get down the Long Tower and down the Bullring to Free Derry Corner. We heard gun fire from the Walls and a woman called to us, 'Watch, there is shooting in Rossville Street.' The woman said that three or four were shot dead and anyone trying to reach them was being shot at. She said that a man with a white cloth had already been shot dead at the base of the High Flats. On looking up Rossville Street I could see three or four bodies in the barricade area. I then saw a detachment of three or four paratroopers enter the Glenfada Park. Almost immediately there was a volley of shots. My father said to come along to John Hume, MP's house to get out of the line of fire. At this time a bullet struck the brick between us. We then hurried into Westland Street as fire still continued in our direction. We went to John Hume. We then saw John Hume and then went home.

This is my statement and it is correct and I am prepared to let this be used so that the truth will be achieved.

* * * * * * * * * * * * *

James Doherty
MILLER, AGED 24

On Sunday, 30 January 1972 around 3.30 p.m. I was in William Street at the corner of Rossville Street. A crowd was coming marching down William Street. Near McCools shop (newsagents) there was an army barricade across the road. The crowd were pushing forward and some teenagers were throwing stones at the army. The army brought a water-cannon from the direction of Waterloo Place and started to spray the crowd. A few minutes later tear-gas canisters began to land and the crowd began to surge back from the water-cannon and gas. The crowd scattered across Chamberlain Street and back up William Street. I myself ran back up William Street. As I got to the waste ground on the corner of William Street and Little James' Street (opposite GPO sorting office), about a dozen youngsters were pushing sheets of corrugated iron towards a soldier's barricade at the top of Sackville Street. The soldiers shot more gas and the crowd scattered. Most headed over to the waste ground near the high Rossville Street Flats. Rubber bullets were being shot from the Sackville Street barricade and from William Street as well as CS gas.

I was now standing round the corner of a burnt-out dry-cleaners. I saw a Saracen armoured car coming across Rossville Street. I thought it was only coming to scatter the crowd and then do a U-turn. But it turned to face towards High Street — and soldiers jumped out screaming with batons and rifles flying. I tried to run but two more armoured cars pulled in front of me. I was caught in a group hemmed in by these armoured cars. The crowd tried to escape, some towards High Street, some tried to climb back-walls. I ran towards the car park of the High Flats but fell. As I tried to rise, one soldier struck me on the back of the head with a baton, while another kicked me on the back, arms and head. I lost consciousness for a second, and when I came to, I was being dragged by the hair, and by the coat by these two soldiers. Each time I tried to get to my feet, I was kicked as they shouted, 'Come on, you pig, it's the paratroopers you're dealing with now.' I was dragged into a Saracen — there were five soldiers there as well as the two who brought me in. They kept shouting, 'Just you wait, you pig, we're going to kick you to death.' They kept striking me with batons and mouthing obscene remarks. Another man, about my age, was dragged in with his face covered with blood. A soldier kept hitting him across the face, butting him with his helmet — and bruising and cutting his mouth and nose. I saw through the open door a line of teenagers and men — all prisoners of soldiers — go past, with their hands on their heads. I heard a command and we were pulled from the armoured car. We were dragged across Rossville Street and made to stand against a wall with hands and legs spread wide and our whole weight resting at a painful angle. Then we were dragged around the corner into William Street and had to stand the same way while seated soldiers swore at us and jabbed at our ankles with their guns.

Out of the corner of my eye I saw a man being caught and bustled into an empty house. I heard him screaming — then a voice said 'I'm a priest, he's a bullet through his arm.' I didn't dare look round but the person who said he was a priest was pushed away, and a voice which sounded like an officer's said, 'Are you sure it's a bullet-wound?' Again the man was dragged into the empty house; then we were dragged by the hair against a lamp-post and across to the wire fence which guards the GPO sorting office. I was ordered to count the squares in the wire — when I said I didn't know how many there were I was struck and ordered again to count them. There was a long line of prisoners against this fence.

We were dragged by the hair to an army lorry in Sackville Street. We sat down on benches but were ordered to our knees, sitting back on our heels. We were squeezed up till about 30 of us were in the front half of the lorry. There was one woman in the lorry — she kept shouting, 'Leave them alone', and was threatened by the soldiers. By this time my hand was bleeding badly, and she kept scooting my blood on to the soldiers. The lorry started but we weren't allowed to look where we were going. They threatened to throw us out on the road and shoot us as trying to escape.

The lorry stopped and we heard voices shouting. We were kicked from the lorry, I fell and was kicked in the stomach to make me get up. I looked up at a whole line of soldiers and we were made to run the gauntlet between two lines to a door, as they struck and kicked at us. Inside was a large room, all concrete with a barbed-wire fence dividing the room in two. We were lined again against the wall, the woman as well, and were searched for the third time (one at the Saracen, one at the GPO fence and the third in this building). They kept prodding us with batons, saying, 'Who are English pigs now?' and we had to stay like that for three hours. Then we were marched over to the barbed wire and made to stand with our hands on the wire and our legs apart again. My hand was still bleeding all this time.

I asked an officer to have my hand dressed, but they said the medical officer had gone for tea. I asked to go to the toilet but was assaulted by a soldier who said I had been complaining about him. This happened when he took me out to the toilets, and there was no-one to watch him. He punched me in the stomach and said that I and a fellow with long hair had complained about him. Then he took out the long-haired fellow and asked him the same questions.

While at the wire we were ordered, 'Hands on the wire!' 'Hands on your heads!' for about half an hour a time. The woman was released earlier, after an officer had come in and demanded to know what she was doing there.

An officer then came in, told us we could put our hands down and relax, and promised us tea. They brought us tea in plastic cups, and we could smoke if we wished. Finally a sergeant gave us ten cigarettes when we ran short. The paratroopers came back. The one that had arrested me grabbed me again, took me to a door and into a room where there were soldiers, police, and a photographer. We were made to stand against a board one at a time. On the board was written my name, and the name of the soldier who arrested me; the soldier stood beside me, under our names, and the two photographs of us were taken.

Two young soldiers were sitting there. They took our names and addresses and asked the soldier what the charge was. He said 'Stone-throwing, he struck me, and he resisted arrest.' I said, 'That's a pack of lies.'

I was then taken to an RUC man, who took my name and all particulars and asked me if I wanted to make a statement. I said my statement was that all the charges were lies. I was then taken back to the compound and chairs and a heater or two were brought in.

After a time we were called out to an RUC sergeant who charged me and ordered me to appear in court on Thursday, 3 February at 10.30 a.m. I was then released. It was after 11 p.m. and I was taken to a first-aid centre. There my hand was dressed for the *first* time, and my head was treated also. I made a statement into a tape-recorder of what happened.

This is a true record of what happened.

* * * * * * * * * * * *

John G.
UNEMPLOYED, AGED 33

On Sunday, 30 January 1972, I was in William Street in the middle of the crowd when the water cannon opened up and the tear gas followed. Everybody was forced to move back into Rossville Street by the gas. Then I heard two shots. I enquired where the shots came from and was told the shots came from further up William Street. As I went around the back of Kells Walk I saw an elderly man being carried from William Street direction. Then I helped to carry a younger man into a house. I came out of the house and was standing at the door to prevent the crowd entering the house. I saw the paratroopers appear at the space where Duffy's bookies used to be. I ran in the direction of Glenfada Park. I saw three bodies lying in Rossville Street and I came back, going towards Kells Walk to try and get a first-aid man. I saw two first-aid men and a white-coated girl whose face was bruised. I asked them to go to the bodies in Rossville Street. Another man came round and he said, 'There's three men lying round there dead.' He asked the girl for her white coat and she refused. I went into a hallway of the house where the two wounded men had been taken. I told Fr McLaughlin CC, Creggan, not to go out as there was still shooting. I left the house with the man who had asked for the white coat and could see the paratroopers all around. A man called from the house, 'Stop your shooting, there's no fucking guns here.' The paratrooper at the corner of the house called to myself and the man with me to 'Halt!' Another paratrooper appeared and struck me on the back of the head three or four times. As I was falling, a different paratrooper struck me in the face with a rubber bullet gun but I still fell to the ground. I was kicked in the ribs while on the ground. When I got up I was pushed forward and told to put my hands on my head. As I ran forward I was repeatedly struck. I was taken with a group of other men and put into the back of a truck. As I was getting in I was hammered on the back. I was told to get on my knees and to stay there and if I moved I would get hit again. I was taken to what I now know to be the dockyard.

When the wagon stopped we were taken separately from it. When it came my turn I was dragged by the hair and slung out onto the ground. When I got up I was made to run twenty yards between two parallel lines of soldiers who kept hitting me. Inside I was told to stand with my hands against the wall and my legs apart. We stood that way for what I would estimate to be about three hours. We were then told to put our hands on our heads. We stood that way for about an hour. The building was very cold and my hands were numb. We were finally told to stand as we pleased and to have a smoke if we wished. As I finished my cigarette eight troops appeared and ordered us back against the wall. I was punched in the ribs with a baton, punched in the stomach with a fist and kicked in the ankles, received a cut knee and tore my trousers as a result of kicks from the troops. These attacks occurred at different times. I had a slight hole in my trousers which a soldier made bigger by ripping them. He asked me had I got any cigarettes and I did not answer. He put his hand into my pocket and took my cigarettes and matches. He lit one match, put the lit end to my nose and said, 'Your Hail Marys will do you no fucking good now.' I was photographed with a soldier. I was next taken to a table where a plain clothes man asked my name, address and who lived next door to me. I was led outside, put back into a line and eventually taken to the police along with a young boy from Rinmore. The one soldier took both of us. The RUC man asked the paratrooper what was the charge. The soldier replied, 'Throwing stones and bottles.' He claimed to be the one who apprehended me. He then asked me where had I been arrested. The policeman said to me, 'You are charged with throwing stones and bottles — what have you to say?' I replied, 'Nothing to say at the moment.' He asked me did I wish to make a statement. I replied, 'No.' We were taken back to the big room and kept there until I was released at about 12.30.

* * * * * * * * * * * * *

James McDermott
LABOURER, AGED 52

I was in the march on Sunday 30 January.

I retreated from William Street from the army tear gas and along Rossville Street, and was near to Chamberlain Street. I saw a woman shot in the thigh. Further along Rossville Street I saw someone shot lying on the ground. At this point little shooting had occurred. I saw soldiers bending and taking aim at the far end of Rossville Street. I bent down and held the shoulders of the shot woman and pulled her round a corner, and handed her into the care of two men who took her into a house in Chamberlain Street. Due to my liability to heart attacks I could not take her any further single-handed.

I then went into the house to see how she was. Two or three of the men went out to find an ambulance — a couple of paratroopers entered the house and saw the shot woman, and then two ambulance-men came who took the woman away. A Scots soldier said all men in the house (roughly twenty) were under arrest. This was about 4 p.m. We were all taken from the house by a large number of soldiers, with our hands behind our heads, and stood up against the wall for ten minutes, and searched. A wagon came, and we were told to get in. Some of us were bodily lifted and thrown on to the wagon, and we were taken to the (former RN dockyard) detention centre, where there were many other men. In the hut, I was lined up with others, and told to grip barbed wire, with three Alsatians guarding us.

I was searched again by paratroops and kicked in the ankle. While there I saw a teenager (I don't know his name) with a cut hand asking for first aid. He was ignored. At 11 p.m. I was released by the police, into whose custody I must have been passed at some time. The teenager with the cut hand was with me, and had his hand dressed in Creggan. I had been given two cups of tea during my seven hours in detention.

I give my permission for my statement to be used in any investigation whatever.

This is my statement and it is correct.

* * * * * * * * * * * *

Hugh O'B.
DuPont Operator, aged 24

I joined the procession at Bishop's Field, Creggan, stayed in the procession until it reached William Street. Some youths began stoning the troops. Troops returned with rubber bullets, CS gas and purple dye. At this point I moved to the car park behind the flats. Shooting started for the first time. I looked towards Chamberlain Street and saw a man being arrested and also one of the Knights of Malta, who seemed to be badly hurt, crouching on the ground. The army scout cars began moving up Rossville Street. I ran into Rossville Street, going towards Free Derry. At this stage more shooting broke out from the soldiers positioned in Rossville Street. I ran for cover to the gable house in Glenfada Park. The shooting was still going on and I saw the first civilian shot in the stomach — he was calling for help and saying, 'I've been shot.' Some youths ran out and dragged him into the gable of the house and the shooting continued. I ran for cover behind a car because I was visible to the soldiers stationed on the Derry Walls. There were four other people with me behind the car. I looked to my left towards Abbey Street and saw three men shot in the back as they ran. The fire must have come from the William Street area. I said to the man beside me, 'How do we get out of this?' He replied, 'We don't, we just pray.'

The soldiers then came in from the Rossville Street direction and told us to come forward with our hands above our heads. There were about ten people at the gable of the house in Glenfada Park, including a woman and they also accompanied us with the soldiers.

We were marched for about 50 yards in the Sackville Street direction when we were told to stand facing a wall with our hands up against the wall. The soldiers then used obscene language such as 'You Fenian bastard, blood will run tonight, Fenian blood.' They physically abused us also. A priest, Fr Denis Bradley, arrived at this stage and said to the soldiers, 'These people are innocent.' We were then marched to the fencing around the post office in Sackville Street where we were told to stand with our hands against the wall again. I was then searched and thumped on the back with either a baton or a rifle. At this stage we were taken to an army lorry and shoved in. We were driven to the Naval Barracks on the Strand Road and ordered one by one out of the lorry. I was batoned and kicked out. There were about eight to ten soldiers waiting and we were batoned, kicked and we had to run a gauntlet. We were taken into the building were we were told to stand against a wall with our hands above our heads. Police took statements after about two hours — details of name, address, etc. We were then made to stand and hold onto barbed wire for a period of time. They gave us a cup of tea after about four hours and chairs to sit on and heaters were brought in. When we were batoned coming out of the lorry I received a severe injury to my knee for which I received no medical attention until I reached the first-aid post at St Mary's Intermediate School about seven hours later at one o'clock in the morning.

When I attended Altnagelvin Hospital today (Tuesday) for treatment I had to have my back, and side and knee X-rayed.

15 : The End of Innocence

As children, we did not understand the political corruption of the Stormont government, which sowed the seeds of the unrest that we were now experiencing.

I have so many memories from prior to 1968 of doing the things of childhood with my friends: catching butterflies and bees in a jam jar during the long summer holidays, standing with bare feet in a cold stream near Rosemount, catching tiny fish with an old sack; collecting chestnuts in September; playing marbles and corks. Some of my happiest memories are of walking from Creggan to the ancient Celtic ringfort of Grianán of Aileach, six miles across beautiful hills and dales in neighbouring County Donegal.

When my street, Leenan Gardens, played Dunmore Gardens in soccer derbies, young Michael Kelly lined out against us. Our heroes were the men of Manchester United, Tottenham Hotspur, Chelsea and Glasgow Celtic. As a goalkeeper, my idol was the great England goalkeeper, Gordon Banks.

Bloody Sunday changed everything. A new and frightening era dawned, as the innocence of our generation died. Standing in the grounds of St Mary's Church, Creggan, having walked past thirteen coffins, I heard some of my peers speak of joining the IRA. Many did. Bloody Sunday was to cast a long shadow over the decades to come.

Micky Devine, for example, was 17 when the events of Bloody Sunday took place. He went on to join the INLA, and on 20 August 1981, he died in Long Kesh on the sixtieth day of his hunger strike. The following is his recollection of Bloody Sunday and the effect that it had on him:

> I will never forget standing in Creggan chapel staring at the brown wooden boxes. We mourned, and Ireland mourned with us. That sight more than anything convinced me that there will never be

peace in Ireland while Britain remains. When I looked at those coffins I developed a commitment to the Republican cause that I have never lost.

I and many of my peers did not join a paramilitary or illegal organisation, and there is no implication that any of the eyewitnesses whose statements appear in this book did. However, as I look back on Bloody Sunday I often wonder why not, and can only conclude, 'But for the grace of God . . .'

* * * * * * * * * * * *

John Carr
SCHOOLBOY, AGED 13

On Sunday, 30 January 1972, I was in an upstairs front bedroom of my home, looking out, when I heard shots from the direction of William Street. I saw one Saracen come up Rossville Street from the William Street junction. It stopped and reversed behind the small flats and the soldiers got out. Some soldiers crossed Glenfada car park and started shooting at the men who were at the corner of Glenfada Park opposite my house. I then saw a youth lying on the edge of the kerb; a soldier ran towards the corner where the youth was lying, he put his boot on top of the youth and pushed him off the footpath. Then he ran forward towards several men at the corner of the house and stopped 15–20 yards from them — the men ran except one man who put his hands above his head and faced the soldier. The soldier put the gun to his shoulder and shot at this man who fell on his face and turned over. Another man ran to him from the next house — the soldier was still standing there and as the man bent over the injured man the solider shot him too and he fell. The soldier then ran away through Glenfada Park.

* * * * * * * * * * * *

A. McGuinness
SCHOOLBOY, AGED 13

I was standing about a yard from my friend Damien Donaghy. The next moment he fell to the ground and the blood was pouring out of him. He had been shot. He wasn't doing anything at all. He never even had a stone to throw or anything. He was just standing next to me in Kells Walk.

This is my statement of the events that I saw in Derry on Sunday 30 January and is to the best of my knowledge a true account of what happened. I agree to this statement being published.

* * * * * * * * * * * *

Don Mullan
SCHOOLBOY, AGED 15

After the Paras entered the Bog I began to run with the rest of the crowd up Rossville Street. Suddenly there was an outbreak of shooting and as I ran past the small barricade at the High Flats I saw a boy fall. Men ran from behind a wall at the maisonettes to help the boy who I had seen fall but they had to dive for cover as the soldiers opened fire on them. Bullets struck the wall above my head and along with the others I ran behind the maisonettes and I eventually managed to make my way out of the area.

This is my statement and it is correct and I agree to have it published.

16: In the Line of Fire

During 1996 Madden & Finucane Solicitors, acting on behalf of the families of those killed, obtained from the Public Records Office, London, several classified documents on Bloody Sunday, which had been closed for twenty-five years.

The Public Records Office presented Madden & Finucane with a cover sheet, detailing all the documents they were releasing. Curiously, one document, referenced as HO 219/56**, was left blank. A footnote simply stated 'Closed for 75 years'.

When pressed by the solicitors to reveal what document HO 219/56** was, the Public Records Office informed Madden & Finucane that it was the medical reports on the injured.

Perhaps the wounds of the injured might provide important clues as to what was really happening on Bloody Sunday. Perhaps information on the lines of trajectory of some of their wounds might throw light on who was firing and from where. The unresolved question remains: were 1 Para the only soldiers doing the killing on Bloody Sunday?

The dead cannot speak. The wounded still can. When seventy-five years have passed, they too will be silenced.

* * * * * * * * * * *

Alana Burke
ACCOUNTANT CLERK, AGED 18

On 30 January 1972 I joined the Civil Rights march at the Grandstand Bar in William Street. The march continued down William Street to the military barricade at the City Cinema. I was in the front rank of the crowd. Some teenagers began stoning the soldiers. The stewards linked arms to try to keep the crowd back. After some time the line of stewards broke and the next thing I saw was the water cannon spraying everyone with purple dye and people tried to escape. About this time too, there was a lot of CS gas being fired.

I made my way towards the bottom of High Street just off Chamberlain Street. I was drenched to the skin with the dye, my clothes were soaked and heavy and I felt sick from the gas. Some people from the Knights of Malta came out of a house in Chamberlain Street and attended to me. I stood in Chamberlain Street for some time and by then rubber bullets were flying. I went into the waste ground at Eden Place and went over to where a man was lying on the ground after being struck on the stomach by what I was later told was a rubber bullet.

Someone advised me to get away home and so I set off towards Rossville Street. I went across the waste ground behind Chamberlain Street and came through an opening in a wire fence and out into the car park behind the High Flats. I was standing talking to Frankie Campbell, the Long Tower Youth Club leader, when suddenly he shouted, 'Quick, Alana, run, the Saracens are heading this way!' I tried to run, but my wet clothes held me back. Lorney McMonagle, who was nearby, caught me by the shoulder and pulled me along. Somehow or other he let go his hand on me and I got left behind. An armoured car came quite fast into the car park behind me and as I watched, an elderly man who apparently thought his best way to escape was to try to get out to Rossville Street past the soldiers, was blocked by a few soldiers on foot. I saw one soldier raise his rifle and strike the man with the butt full in the face. He seemed to sort of rise up in the air for a split second and fell to the ground with blood streaming from his face. I don't know this man. He looked elderly and was wearing a dark grey coat.

Meanwhile there was general panic in the car park. People were rushing madly towards the two exits. As I said, I got left behind, and a Saracen came up behind me and struck me with a thud, which I can still remember vividly, on the right side of my back and leg. What exactly happened next is somewhat confused in my mind, but I remember moments later lying against a low wall behind the shops at the far end of the car park. I then crawled through the alleyway on all fours and came out near the telephone box. There a girl supported me and called to Frank Campbell who came over and carried me to one of the maisonettes in Joseph Place. Here he laid me on the floor and the Knights of Malta took care of me. About an hour later I was taken by ambulance to Altnagelvin Hospital.

While in hospital I was under the care of Mr Fenton, and was discharged on Wednesday 2 February. I am still attending hospital twice weekly.

* * * * * * * * * * *

Michael Bradley
PAINTER, AGED 22

On Sunday, 30 January 1972, I was part of the large crowd which had been stopped at the army barrier in William Street. Gas was fired by the army and I retreated into the alleyway at Quinn's Fish Shop, which leads from William Street into Eden Place. After remaining there for some minutes I decided to make my way home as the gas was affecting me fairly severely. I was making my way across the waste ground, going in the direction of the Rossville Street Flats. People began shouting that the army was coming in. I immediately began to run. I ran across the forecourt of the flats and through the south-eastern alleyway which leads into Joseph Place. While I was running I looked to my right and I saw three Saracens coming along Rossville Street. When I got to Joseph Place I stopped to catch my breath and then I heard shooting. At first I thought it was the sound of rubber bullets being fired but then someone shouted that someone had been shot. Someone then said it was Jackie Duddy who was shot. I knew Duddy personally and I decided to go back into the forecourt of the flats. I jumped over the small retaining wall at the back of the shops in Joseph Place and went towards a small crowd which was positioned near the children's playground on the north-eastern corner of the forecourt. I noticed blood on the ground where the people were standing. I was not able to see the body at this stage as the people were surrounding it. I was about five or six yards from this crowd when I looked over towards the waste ground at Eden

Place. I saw two Saracens in the forecourt. One was near the rear of the houses in Chamberlain Street and the other was positioned in line with it but more towards Rossville Street. I saw soldiers come out of the Saracens and take up position around the vehicles. I noticed that they did not appear to have visors on their helmets. Just as they had taken up these positions I heard shooting. Then I felt a heavy thud on my left arm. I clutched my arm and I then turned and staggered over the small retaining wall again and made my way towards the alleyway I had come out of. Someone then grabbed me and carried me down into the first house in Joseph's Place. Sometime later I was taken out and placed in an ambulance and taken to Altnagelvin Hospital.

At no time that day was I armed with a weapon or a nail bomb.

* * * * * * * * * * * *

Daniel McGowan
MAINTENANCE SERVICEMAN, AGED 37

On Sunday, 30 January 1972, I left my brother-in-law's house at St Columb's Street and walked down behind the rear of the houses at Joseph's Place in the direction of the Rossville Flats. I had proceeded about 20 yards along the rear of these houses when I heard what I thought was either a rubber bullet or gas gun being fired. I proceeded on and was about 15 yards from the northern end of the houses at Joseph's Place when I heard a large volley of shots. I got to the end of the houses and went out into the forecourt facing the row of shops at Joseph Place. I looked down to my left in the direction of Rossville Street and I noticed a young man lying on the ground near the telephone kiosk at the gable wall of the flats on Rossville Street. I also noticed a young girl who was in a hysterical state just outside the chemist's shop at the western end of the row of shops. I also noticed two soldiers on their knees in firing positions at Glenfada Park. Then I noticed a man whom I now know as Patrick Campbell staggering in a drunken fashion about 20 yards from me just above the butcher's shop at Joseph Place. He shouted to me, 'I'm shot, son, I'm shot.' I ran over and caught him by the arm and helped him along towards the rear of the houses on Joseph's Place. Just as I had pushed him round the corner of the rear of the houses my right leg folded underneath me and I realised then that I was shot. I went unconscious for a very short while. When I came to, I dragged myself round the corner of the houses and proceeded along for about 15 yards. While I was doing so I heard another burst of gunfire but I can't say where it came from. Two men came and dragged me along by the arms and put me into a car at St Columb's Wells. I was eventually taken home and subsequently taken to Altnagelvin Hospital in an ambulance. At no time during the period I have described was I armed with a gun, a nail bomb, a stone or any other implement.

* * * * * * * * * * * *

Patrick (Barman) Duffy
Storeman in Gas Company, aged 51

I was a steward in the parade and when the parade came to William Street, it halted and after a few seconds I saw water being sprayed on the photographers. I then went to some waste ground (above O'Donnell's chemist shop) as CS gas was being fired into the crowd. I tried to help some people who had been affected by the gas — one young girl and a boy. I then proceeded to the Rossville Street Flats where I noticed a boy with a badly gashed face. Fr Daly then arrived on the scene and asked me to check the back of the shops for suspicious characters. On the way back, I contacted a car to take the boy to the hospital. When the car left, I was standing at the doorway to the flats at the William Street end. A crowd of people then rushed around the corner and headed for the stairs. Two Saracens then came around the corner into the square behind the flats. These Saracens were travelling very fast and they stopped dead at the corner. I saw a boy who was actually struck by one of the Saracens and his body somersaulted a few times. My view was then blocked by another Saracen which arrived. Two soldiers jumped out of the back and rushed at me in the doorway. I appealed to the soldiers not to fire gas or rubber bullets as the stairs were packed with women and children. One of the soldiers kicked me in the pelvis and as I did not drop to the ground, he fired a rubber bullet from close range at me. This bullet struck me in the left thigh. The soldier then pointed the rifle at my head and was going to shoot me when William McIntyre tackled the soldier and pushed him out of the way. The other soldier then hit a woman with the butt of his rifle. These soldiers then left the premises and I could hear shots outside, but I could not see anything as we were sneaking up the stairs. On arrival at the third floor, the soldiers fired at us every time we moved. We did not move for about five minutes. We then sneaked up slowly to the sixth floor and I looked out through the gaps in the windows — bullets were coming from all directions — we came under fire every time we moved our heads. I noticed a crowd running in the direction of the Bogside coming from William Street. I saw Fr Daly running with the crowd and I saw a boy falling to the ground directly behind Fr Daly. The latter turned around and went back to the boy who had fallen and a few other boys turned back amid rapid fire from the soldiers, to help the boy. Fr Daly was giving the boy the last rites. Fr Daly was waving a white flag for about 5–10 minutes to try and get the boy away. The soldiers were still shooting in his direction. I then saw a pile of boys lying on the ground and the soldiers were still shooting. We then made our way to the top floor and went into a house in which there were forty people altogether. I waited there until the army dispersed and then I sneaked out and went home.

* * * * * * * * * * * * *

Bridget McGuigan

I am the wife of Bernard McGuigan who was killed. On 30 January 1972 he left home to join the Civil Rights march. He was wearing a navy anorak, and a blue grey suit and brown shoes and grey socks. He never owned a scarf or wore one and if one was found near him it could not have belonged to him.* He also had a piece of orange towelling which I had soaked in vinegar in case he was caught by CS gas. My husband has never possessed weapons and indeed abhors violence and as Treasurer of the Blighs Lane Tenants Association, he was endeavouring to obtain a hut or a hall for the use of boys so that they could be kept off the streets and away from stone throwing.

I know that on 30 January he had no weapons and he had no intention of attacking the soldiers.

I have a brother-in-law who is at present serving in the RAF and both my father and father-in-law fought in the British forces in the 1914–18 war.

---

* According to Lord Widgery, the scarf was found to have 'a heavy deposit of lead, the distribution and density of which was consistent with the scarf having been used to wrap a revolver which had been fired several times'. Widgery concluded: 'The paraffin test . . . constitutes grounds for suspicion that he had been in close proximity to someone who had fired' (paragraph 74).

Epilogue

In April 1992, shortly after the remarkable series of events surrounding the twentieth anniversary of the massacre of Bloody Sunday, a small group of people — mainly relatives of some of the victims of Bloody Sunday — met in the Bogside and established a campaign which, in the next five years, would place the outstanding issue of justice for their deceased relatives, and for many people in Derry and Ireland, firmly on the local, national and British/Irish agendas.

The ensuing campaign has taken many forms — from protesting against 'royal' visits, to forcing John Major to respond (albeit negatively) to the just demand for a re-investigation into the killings and cover-up. For their trouble Bloody Sunday Justice Campaigners have been harangued by BBC reporters for 'dragging up the past' and have had their office smashed up by the RUC.

Our campaign was established because of the unfinished business of Bloody Sunday. It's a matter of the whos, whys and hows and the fact that for too long, families shattered by the impact of losing a loved one on Bloody Sunday have not been able to put their lives back together, because of the absence of justice. It is clear that neither the dead nor the living can rest easily while the injustice remains.

Vengeance and retribution are not part of the remit of this Campaign. We would like to forgive. However, when the perpetrator refuses to express some kind of remorse and more often than not treats us with disdain, the matter of forgiving and forgetting is severely compounded.

Within the pages of Don Mullan's book you will have found no justice or equality of treatment — but you will have found a lot of truth.

Truth and time are on our side.

Bloody Sunday Justice Campaign
10 December 1996

Appendix 1

Confidential Downing Street Minutes, dated 1 February 1972

10, Downing Street,
Whitehall.

1 February 1972

The Lord Chief Justice last evening accepted the Government's invitation to conduct a Tribunal of Inquiry into the events in Londonderry on 30 January. He came round, with the Lord Chancellor, to see the Prime Minister at 7.20 p.m. yesterday evening.

The Prime Minister, expressing the Government's gratitude to the Lord Chief Justice, said that this was not the sort of subject into which Tribunals of Inquiry had been asked to inquire on previous occasions; nor perhaps was it the sort of subject that those who designed the 1921 Act originally had in mind. It followed that the recommendations on procedure made by Lord Salmon might not necessarily be relevant in this case. There were a number of points to which he thought it right to draw the Lord Chief Justice's attention:

(a) This was clearly a matter which should be dealt with while the events were fresh in people's minds.

(b) Great emphasis had been placed, during the discussion in the House of Commons that afternoon, on the importance of a speedy outcome to the Inquiry.

(c) The Inquiry would be operating in a military situation, with Troops coming and going and required for operational duties; this underlined the importance of speed.

(d) All the pressures were for a public Inquiry. It was, however, necessary to bear in mind the possible risk to members of the armed forces, and even the others, who give evidence to the Tribunal. There was a risk that, if the Inquiry was not held in public, some would condemn it as invalidated on the ground that they had been unable to see and hear what took place. It would be necessary to consider whether and how witnesses could be protected and whether and how access to the Tribunal's proceedings could be limited.

(e) It had to be remembered that we were in Northern Ireland fighting not only a military war but a propaganda war.

The Lord Chief Justice said that he saw the exercise as a fact-finding exercise. The Tribunal would be asked to inquire into what happened, not into motives. It would help if the Inquiry could be restricted to what actually happened in those few minutes when men were shot and killed; this would enable the Tribunal to confine evidence to eye witnesses. The Lord Chancellor agreed that this should enable the Tribunal to deal with the main question, whether the Troops shot indiscriminately into a crowd or deliberately at particular targets in self-defence.

The following procedural points were discussed:

(i) The Prime Minister asked whether the Lord Chief Justice wished to have two other people sitting with him, as had been customary in recent Tribunals of Inquiry. The Lord Chief Justice said that he saw no advantage in this case in having a Tribunal of three, and would prefer to do it on his own.

(ii) The Prime Minister said that, in order to prevent any attempt to invalidate the Tribunal on the ground that law and order was not a Westminster responsibility, it was proposed that the Tribunal should be appointed under resolutions passed both at Westminster and at Stormont. The Lord Chief Justice made no objection to this.

(iii) The Prime Minister said that it would have to be decided where the Tribunal should sit. It probably ought to be somewhere near Londonderry; but the Guildhall, which was the obvious place, might be thought to be on the wrong side of the River Foyle.

One possibility would be to find a suitable meeting place a little distance away from Londonderry. The Lord Chief Justice said that he thought that the Tribunal would have to be held in Londonderry, so that people were not inhibited from giving evidence to it.

(iv) The Prime Minister said that it was for question whether the Attorney General should appear as counsel for the Tribunal. The Lord Chancellor doubted whether the Attorney General should appear as counsel for the Tribunal, though he might need to appear as counsel for the Army. The Lord Chief Justice said that he did not want to take the Attorney General from his other work and he thought that a competent Queen's Counsel could undertake the duties of counsel for the Tribunal in this case. The role of counsel for the Tribunal might well be less important in this instance than in some previous Tribunals. It was agreed that the Northern Ireland Attorney General should not be invited to serve as counsel for the Tribunal.

(v) The Prime Minister said that in the case of previous Tribunals the Treasury solicitor had gathered depositions and other evidence in advance so that the Tribunal were able to know in advance the evidence they would be hearing. This made for a long and cumbersome procedure. It was not clear whether some of the witnesses who might otherwise give evidence would be prepared to comply with such a procedure. But the procedure was of course for the Lord Chief Justice to decide. The Lord Chancellor suggested that the Treasury Solicitor and the Cabinet Office should provide the secretariat for the Tribunal, and that the Treasury Solicitor would need to brief counsel for the Army. The Lord Chief Justice said that it did not seem to him to be the sort of Inquiry in which preliminary statements and depositions would be called for.

(vi) The Lord Chief Justice said that one difficulty would be to find who would be prepared to speak and give evidence on the 'other side' of the case from the Army. He hoped that it would in the event be possible for there to be some coordination of the presentation of the case on that side, so as to make the handling of the Inquiry manageable.

(vii) The Lord Chief Justice said that he would need to think further about whether the Inquiry should be held in public or in private. The Lord Chancellor said that the essential thing was to safeguard witnesses. As the Prime Minister had said, there were various ways in which this might be done. The Lord Chief Justice would need to bear in mind that the I.R.A. would certainly be wishing to take vengeance for the 13 men who had been killed, and might be interested in trying to identify at the Tribunal soldiers who were involved in the shootings. Perhaps the right course would be for the Lord Chief Justice to wait, and see what the Army proposed in this regard; they would no doubt put forward requests by counsel at the preliminary meeting of the Tribunal to consider procedure.

(viii) It was suggested that the 'other side' would have to be given the opportunity to make representations to the Tribunal about procedure. This would involve some sort of public announcement as soon as possible after the passage of the resolutions setting up the Tribunal, inviting representations to be made to the Tribunal, either in writing or possibly at the preliminary meeting.

(ix) The Lord Chief Justice said that on the assumption that the resolutions were passed by 2 February, his aim would be to have a preliminary meeting in Londonderry as soon as possible in the following week. This would give time for a public announcement, and for the administrative and security arrangements for the Tribunal to be organised. Presumably it would be for the authorities to make the administrative and security arrangements, and for the Treasury Solicitor to organise a public announcement.

(x) It was agreed that further consideration would have to be given to the question where the Lord Chief Justice would stay while the Tribunal was sitting. One possibility, which attracted the Lord Chief Justice, was that he should stay with the Governor of Northern Ireland and should be flown to Londonderry by helicopter for the sessions of the Tribunal.

The Prime Minister said that terms of reference for the Tribunal were now being drafted. He was hoping to be able to announce the Inquiry and its terms of reference, in a statement after Questions on

Tuesday 1 February, so that the Motion could be taken in the House of Commons later in the day. Arrangements would be made for a similar Motion to be taken in Stormont.

I am sending copies of this letter to John Graham, David Owen, Robert Andrew, Leonard Davies, Tony Hetherington and Burke Trend.

G.L. Angel, Esq.,
Home Office.

APPENDIX 2

Memorandum from Widgery Secretary
Referring to Civilian Eyewitness
Statements, dated 10 March 1972

MEMORANDUM

STATEMENTS COLLECTED BY THE NCCL

1. Much publicity has been given during the Tribunal — and indeed before it opened — to the 700 or so statements collected by the National Council for Civil Liberties. A very large number of these are in fact of no use. It is likely however that had these statements been received at an earlier stage the Treasury Solicitor would have thought it worthwhile to take statements with a view to the writers giving evidence. The LCJ did not see any of the 700 statements until 9 March. Mr Stocker, Mr Hall and myself all discussed the matter with him at different times on that date. I said that if I had been advising a Minister, I would have strongly urged the desirability of taking evidence from at least a few of these potential witnesses, since it was clear that if this was not done there would subsequently be heavy criticism. The LCJ said that he fully understood this point, but did not see how he could avoid such criticism in any case. He considered that the statements, which must surely have been ready for some little time, had been submitted at this late stage to cause him the maximum embarrassment. He was satisfied that there was no real halfway course between not calling any of these witnesses and calling a very large number of them, which he was not prepared to do at this stage. From what he had seen of the statements, only 15 of which Mr Stocker had thought it worthwhile to draw to his

attention, he did not think that the people who wrote them could bring any new element to the proceedings of the Tribunal. I enquired whether the LCJ intended to make a public statement about the 700 statements. He said that he did not, but agreed that he should deal with the matter in his report. He was quite prepared to say in the report that the Tribunal had taken note of all the statements, on the basis that they had all been inspected by Counsel for the Tribunal or by Treasury Solicitor's officers. Indeed, in the last resort he was prepared to read them all himself, though Mr Stoker assured him that this was not necessary.

2. For the purposes of the report we need to be quite sure about the timetable as follows:-

Date of receipt of statements in the Treasury Solicitor's Office in London: 3 March, 1972.

Date of receipt of statements by the Treasury Solicitor's representatives in Coleraine: 4 March, 1972.

Date of reference to Mr Stoker: 8 March, 1972.

Date of reference to LCJ: 9 March, 1972.

We should in due course ensure that a reply is sent to the telegram sent to Mr Stocker by the International League of the Rights of Man, New York, about the 700 statements.

This question was further discussed with the LCJ on 10 March. Mr Hall said that there were four statements he would like to have seen given in evidence, bearing on the deaths of:-

Gilmour   Doherty   McKinney (G)

In particular, two statements in relation to Gilmour were inconsistent with the evidence given by Miss Richmond, and were probably much more reliable than her evidence. These two statements were consistent with the forensic evidence, whereas Miss Richmond's evidence was not. The LCJ's view remained unchanged.

It is important that the LCJ's report should not include references to the deaths of these four men which could be criticised as being contradicted by evidence which was available to the Tribunal but not considered by it. If the Chief refers for example to Miss Richmond's evidence he will need also to refer to having seen statements which present another and possibly more reliable account of the same events.

STATEMENTS OF THE WOUNDED

3. It would also be appropriate to include in the report a passage indicating that, for obvious reasons, the wounded had not been invited to give evidence in the Tribunal, but that the statements which some of them had made had been carefully considered.

W J Smith
10 March, 1972.

APPENDIX 3

Note on Results of Post-Mortem Examinations

On Bloody Sunday, William Nash, Michael McDaid and John Young were shot at the rubble barricade adjacent to Rossville Street High Flats.

The trajectory line of each bullet was strikingly similar in all three cases. The trajectory line in each case, being from the front to the back and from above to below, had an angle of approximately 45 degrees.

There is a clear eyewitness account concerning William Nash, stating that he was crossing the rubble barricade, going towards Free Derry Corner, when he was shot and fell backwards.

From the post-mortem evidence that exists it is clear from this statement that this man could not have been shot by soldiers in Rossville Street, who were behind him. Equally, if he were upright or almost upright he could not have been shot from ground level.

The conclusion to be drawn from the forensic evidence, allied to the eyewitness account, suggests the likelihood that William Nash was killed by a bullet fired from the vicinity of the Derry Walls.

There is also the possibility that Michael McDaid and John Young may have been shot from a similar firing position.

Raymond McClean LRCP & SI. LM
6 November 1996

APPENDIX 4

Details of Clothing Worn by Deceased on Bloody Sunday

Jackie Duddy: Dark striped jacket, red shirt, blue jeans, black boots.

Patrick Doherty: Black and grey coat, black leather jacket, blue sweater, brown trousers, brown boots.

Bernard McGuigan: Blue nylon anorak, blue suit jacket, blue and purple waistcoat, white shirt, blue and red tie, blue suit trousers, brown shoes.

Hugh Gilmore: Brown anorak, multi-coloured sweater, yellow shirt, blue jeans, black shoes.

Kevin McElhinney: Brown suit jacket, brown and green pullover, pink shirt, brown suit trousers, brown boots.

Michael Kelly: Light blue jacket, mustard pullover, light blue trousers, brown tie.

William Nash: Brown jacket, brown waistcoat, yellow patterned shirt, yellow and brown tie, brown trousers, leather boots.

Michael McDaid: Green checked sports jacket, blue shirt, blue and orange tie, grey trousers.

John Young: Blue anorak, round-neck sweater with gold and white bands at arms and waist, black and white checked shirt, green trousers, brown suede shoes.

Jim Wray: Brown corduroy jacket, dark grey polo-neck sweater and green polo-neck sweater, white shirt, denim jeans, brown boots.

Gerard McKinney: Brown overcoat, brown suit, beige fairisle pullover, white shirt, brown and beige striped tie.

William McKinney: Grey car-coat, black blazer, maroon v-neck pullover, blue shirt and tie, charcoal grey trousers, black shoes, black-rimmed glasses, carrying an 8 mm movie camera.

Gerard Donaghy: Blue denim jacket, blue sweater, blue shirt, blue denim trousers, black boots.

APPENDIX 5

The Scene of Bloody Sunday

The following map was produced to assist *Sunday Times* readers in following the Widgery Tribunal of Inquiry. It is generally accurate with a few exceptions. The following should be noted:

William Street
The circled A indicates the initial confrontation between marchers and the army at the barricade. Back along William Street (near bottom of map) two circles indicate where Damien Donaghy and John Johnston were shot at 3.55 p.m. The arrows indicate the advancing 1 Para towards the Rossville Street barricade and the Rossville Flats car park at 4.10 p.m.

Rossville Street Car Park
Jackie Duddy (killed); Margaret Deery, Michael Bridge, Michael Bradley, Patrick McDaid (wounded). Alana Burke was struck by one armoured vehicle and seriously injured.

Rossville Flats Forecourt-Joseph Place
Paddy Doherty, Bernard McGuigan (killed); Daniel McGowan and Patrick Campbell (wounded).

Rossville Street Barricade
Hugh Gilmore, Kevin McElhinney, John Young, William Nash, Michael McDaid and Michael Kelly (killed); Alexander Nash (wounded).

Glenfada Park Courtyard
Jim Wray (killed); Paddy O'Donnell, Daniel Gillespie, Joseph Mahon, Michael Quinn and Joseph Friel (wounded).

Glenfada Park Alleyway-Abbey Park
Gerard Donaghy, Gerard McKinney and William McKinney (killed).

The Derry Walls
The Sunday Times 'Insight' team did not examine the role of the British Army on the Derry Walls. While the Walls do appear on the top right corner, the map does not include the derelict houses just beside the Walker Monument, from where army snipers were also operating.

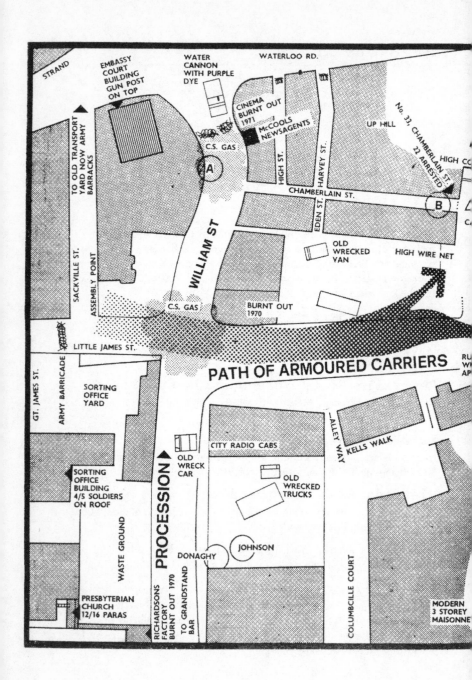

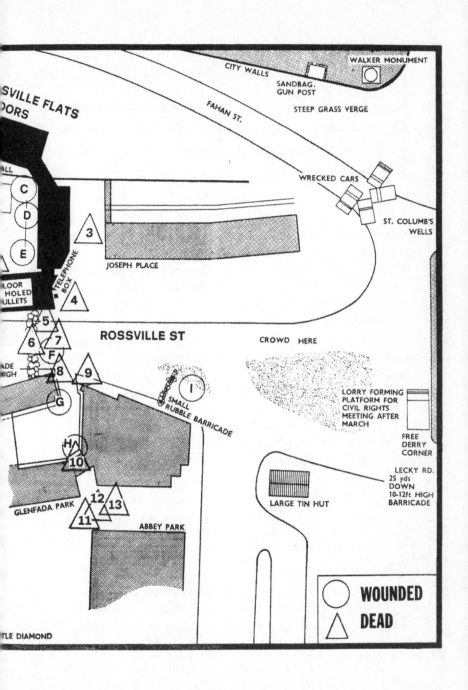

Messages from Army and Police Radio
Transcripts and from the Log Book of
the Headquarters of the 8th Infantry
Brigade

Many eyewitnesses testified to gunfire coming from British Army
positions in the vicinity of the Derry Walls on Bloody Sunday. Lord
Widgery chose to ignore this body of evidence, accounting for only
the 108 bullets that 1 Para allegedly fired. The following transcripts
not only confirm army fire from the Walls on Bloody Sunday, but
also record 'hits'.

At 4.15 p.m. the following communication was sent:

Army: *Zero this is 90 Alpha sit. (situation) rep. (report) at 1615
on William Street. Seven pigs of call sign Hotel 12 call sign
65 in the area of Rossville Street in the Rossville flats.
Rossville and William street are relatively quiet. We just
had two shot at one of our patrols on the city wall 1614
over.*

HQ: *Zero out. . . . (page 25)*

Army: *Hello Zero this is 54 Alpha. Reference two shots returned at
gunman near Bogside Inn, man seen to fall at 1620 hours.
One further shot was fired from that area of the Bogside
Inn towards our Busker patrol on the wall, over.*

HQ: *Zero roger. (page 26)*

HQ: *. . . 54 this is Zero reference your report of a man seen to
fall near the Bogside Inn, why was this man fired at, over.*

Army: *54 Alpha this man was fired at because he fired four shots
at us, over.*

HQ: Zero out. . . . *(page 27)*

Army: Hello Zero this is 54 Alpha we have had two further shots
fired at our call sign Quebec 21 at the junction of Bishop
street — Long Tower. Two shots returned, details later, over
. . . . *(page 31)*

Army: . . . We just had three shots at OP Kino on the city walls,
wrong two shots fired. Three shots have been returned by
Quebec call sign, over.

HQ: Zero roger. . . . *(page 32)*

Army: Zero this is 54 Alpha, reference the reports from call sign
90 Alpha of the shootings. Call sign Quebec 23 has had one
low velocity shot fired at him from Fahan Street, hit one of
our soldiers in flak jacket. We don't believe his is a casualty.
One round was returned, no hit. Subsequent to that call
sign Quebec 21 had one round fired at it and two shots
were returned. No casualties on either side, over.

HQ: Roger, Zero. *(page 32)*

The following messages were radioed by the police sometime
between 4.15 and 4.30 p.m.:

Police: Delta 7 to November. Shots were fired at the army on the
wall from the area of the flats. Fire was returned and one
person was seen to fall. We have nothing further over:

Novem.: Roger...

A few minutes later, the following message was sent:

Police: Delta 7 to November. The man fired at by the army was
seen to fall in the vicinity of the Bogside Inn and not the
flats as indicated by you, over:

Novem.: Roger. . . .

It is worth noting that November hadn't indicated anything. Both
messages had been relayed by Delta 7.

The Log Sheet from the HQ of the 8th Infantry Brigade, detailing
the activities and reports from several regiments on 30 January
1972, again confirms army gunfire from the vicinity of the Derry
Walls.

At 6.20 p.m. serial number 241 records the following details from
I Royal Anglians, headed Shotreps:

Timing between 1615 and 1640

1. *Gunman GR [Grid Reference] 43061657 fired 2 rds at Roaring
   Meg. C/S 21 (Long Tower   St fired 2 X 7.62 back. Gunman
   fell and was dragged back into Meenan Sq.*

2. *C/21 (Long Tower St) fired 5 X 7.62 at gunman seen GR 42571625.
   Seen to fall — dragged away.*

3. *1 X 7.62 at gunman GR 48011629 by C/S 23 (Barrack St) —
   stepped into alleyway.*

4. *3 LV [low velocity] fired at C/V 23 (Barrack St). I shot his soldiers
   flak jacket — no cas. . . . 8 X 7.62 returned at gunman GR
   43021632. Not known if hit.*

There are variances between the radio transcripts and the log sheet.
The radio transcripts claim only one gunman hit. The log sheet
claims two. The radio transcripts report one low-velocity shot fired
at Quebec 23 from Fahan Street, hitting a soldier's flak jacket, with
one round returned. The log sheet claims three low-velocity shots
fired with eight rounds returned.

The log sheet establishes the location of Quebec 23 as Barrack
Street. The low-velocity shot which hit the soldier's flak jacket at this
location was, according to the radio transcripts, fired from Fahan
Street.

We have often heard of the magic bullet involved in the assassination of President John F. Kennedy. It is interesting to consider that,
from Fahan Street, this bullet would have had to negotiate several
obstacles — including corners, embankments and a couple of streets
— before reaching a flak jacket in Barrack Street.

The soldier hit never gave evidence and neither were his dam-
aged flak jacket nor the bullet ever produced as evidence. Why?

APPENDIX 7

The Statement of Soldier 027

In the wake of the first publication of *Eyewitness Bloody Sunday* in Ireland in January 1997, statements from two members of the British Army have come to light. These statements, from 'Soldier 027' and 'A British Officer,' are devastating to the official British version of events in that they corroborate the civilian eyewitness testimonies collected in this book.

Soldier 027's testimony was certainly a most extraordinary and unexpected document. It was written in the mid-1970s by a former member of the Paras Anti-Tank Platoon, which had been intimately involved in the Derry murders. Extracts from the document were first published by journalist Tom McGurk in the Irish newspaper *The Sunday Business Post* on 16 March 1997.

Soldier 027's Statement to the Widgery Inquiry

Soldier 027's statement is disturbing in a number of crucial areas:

- He states that in advance of Bloody Sunday, troops within the regiment were hyped up by an officer who informed them '... we want some kills tomorrow.'

- He states that he saw civilians, amongst them women and children, fleeing in terror. He saw no civilians carrying guns or throwing bombs. Concerning his comrades who were firing into the crowd he recalls thinking, '... do they know something I don't know? What are they firing at?'

- He states that he received on his radio a cease-fire order from Major Loden which he relayed to the soldiers in his platoon. The serious wounding and murdering of civilians in and from Glenfada Park took place after the cease-fire order had been communicated. He describes civilians in Glenfada Park standing with their hands in the air when shot.

- The cease-fire order which Soldier 027 received is nowhere to be found in the Porter tapes, lending weight to the belief that the crucial operational orders were being passed on a secure radio link. Recordings and transcripts from the secure link, if they exist, would help to establish the full truth about the tragic consequences of the day.

- He states that soldiers in his platoon were using non-issue rounds, some of which were dum-dum bullets, outlawed under the Geneva Convention.

- He states that Crown lawyers tore up the statement he had prepared for the Widgery Tribunal and presented him with a statement they had written which deliberately blurred the clarity and detail of what Soldier 027's recently published statements say he witnessed. (Extracts from the statement that Soldier 027 claims was written for him by Crown lawyers also appear in this chapter.)

The implications of what Soldier 027 claims to have occurred, both during the Para operation on Bloody Sunday and the interference of the Crown lawyers, are of the most serious and disturbing nature, to say the least. They confirm our long-held suspicions that the Widgery Tribunal of Inquiry, presided over by the Lord Chief Justice of England (with the full sanction of the British government at the time), was an orchestrated official cover-up.

Irish Taoiseach John Bruton, responding to press questions about the revelations, expressed deep disquiet concerning the allegation that evidence had been interfered with. He said that this new information would form an extremely important part of the dossier of new evidence about Bloody Sunday which the Irish government would present to the British government.

The Fianna Fáil leader, Bertie Ahern, went further. Responding to the revelations contained in Soldier 027's testimony, he said the British authorities 'need to acknowledge Bloody Sunday for what it was, an inexcusable act of State terrorism that was subsequently covered up and spawned many other evil acts.'

The following is an edited – for reasons of length – extract of Soldier 027's account of the events leading up to and during Bloody Sunday on 30 January 1972.

One night in January 1972, I was sitting with the rest of my "muck-ers" of the Anti-Tank Platoon in the Barrack when Lieutenant 119 came in and informed us that we were due for an operation in Londonderry the following day. He said that the heart of Derry had been bombed out, several hundred soldiers had been hospitalised and that not one arrest had been made. We knew that the Creggan estate was an IRA fortress, conning-towers, machine guns and barbed wire as well as landmines guarding its approaches. The people of the Creggan had not paid rent and had hijacked all their food for several years. This was the symbol which led to the name 'no go area'.

As I looked at my friends I could see that after all the abuse and nights without sleep, frustration and tensions this is what they had been waiting for. We were all in high spirits and when our Lieutenant 119 said, 'Lets teach these buggers a lesson – we want some kills tomorrow,' to the mentality of the blokes to whom he was speaking this was tantamount to an order – i.e., an exoneration of all responsibility.

The account goes on to describe the trip to Derry until finally Soldier 027 and his Parachute Support Company were positioned in a churchyard on the edge of the city centre. When the riot happened at the William Street barricades they could hear the noise and smell the CS gas.

Adrenaline was running. There was excitement in the air. I know I speak for the majority when I say that the common feeling amongst us was, please let us be called in – we'll go nuts if we miss a chance like this. In retrospect I can see what followed was only a natural conclusion to the foundations and dictates of fate laid down over the previous months. A thing no self-respecting Paratrooper would be seen dead using is CS gas, but now, to our utter consternation, we could see rising into the crisp winter sky great clouds of CS being carried in our direction. Before I could get my gas mask on I caught a couple of breaths which filled me with nausea and sickness. My eyes streamed with water, I was not alone with this, and as the gas had been thrown by the crowd we were raring to get at them.

Then I heard Major Loden's voice crackle on the radio: "Machine guns and anti-tanks, mount up and move in.' Coughing and spluttering, filled with all the emotions conceivable, we moved down to the army barricade at Rossville Street (I should mention that while we were in the churchyard, four or five yards away from me I saw a pall of dust and chips of concrete fly from the ground. It didn't occur to me until minutes later that we were under fire). The scene that confronted us at Rossville Street was wooden and barbed wire barricades moved back to allow us through. Army vehicles of all descriptions behind which were huddled large groups of crap hats. [In 'Para language' crap hats are members of all other non-Paratroop regiments.]

Can't handle it, eh? is the best way I can describe our feelings on seeing these blokes who couldn't manage the rudiments of soldering, i.e., spreading out. We were about to show them how. With visions of gross [sic] on a wave of excitement to the point of shouting, we swept past them and on in to Rossville Street. In front and to the left was Rossville flats; to our right a complex of low flats and walkways; in between the two was an enormously animated crowd with a frontage of about 150 yards, a low barricade rising in front of them. We swerved to a halt, still wearing our gas masks, which we quickly pulled off as we leapt out.

There were only two platoons involved in the main conflict. One, on the left hand side of the street, advanced leapfrog fashion to the base of Rossville flats. I was in the other which skirmished through broken bottles and bricks down the right-hand side of the road. As we moved along the wall towards the crowd I noticed several strikes in the roadway beside us. ['Strikes' means shots fired at them.]

I was with the leading group of half a dozen as we reached a small garden on the corner of Kells Walk. At this point, approximately a hundred yards short of the crowd, Lance Corporal F went into the kneeling position and fired at the centre of the crowd from behind a low wall some two feet high which ran around the garden. Soldier G immediately jumped down beside him and also opened fire. Just beyond the wall on the pavement Soldier J also commenced firing. Looking at the centre of the barricades I saw two bodies fall. I raised my rifle and aimed, but on tracking across the people in front of me could see women and children, although the majority were men, all wildly shouting, but could see no one with a weapon, so I lowered my rifle. I can best describe my feelings as amazed, although this is very inadequate. I remember thinking, looking at my friends who had now grown to half a dozen in a line side-by-side, do they know something I don't know? What are they firing at?

Opposite us I could see [other soldiers] helmeted and black-faced in a standing position, pumping off rounds at quite a rapid rate. In the initial 30 seconds I would say that a hundred rounds were fired at the crowd. A thing which struck me was the time which elapsed from the commencement of firing to the time when the people in the crowd began to realise what was happening. Several people had dropped, bodies were being dragged away, men were lying on their faces crawling along the pavement in front of Rossville flats in an effort to get away. After an eternity of timeless moments and sights, Major Loden's voice came on the radio and ordered a cease-fire. I knew the blokes were getting in while the going was good, as people with gleeful expressions were running up from the rear and elbowing their way through to get into the firing line. I shouted the order, "cease-fire", and ran along the line tapping them on their shoulders.

Soldiers E, H, G and Lance Corporal F and myself then leapt the wall, turned right and ran down Kells Walk into Glenfada Park, a small triangular car park within the complex of flats. A group of some 40 civilians was there running in an effort to get away. Soldier H fired from the hip at a range of 20 yards. The bullet passed through one man and into another and they both fell, one dead and one wounded. He moved forward and fired again, killing the wounded man. They sprawled together half on the pavement and half in the gutter. Soldier E shot another man at the entrance of the Park who also fell on the pavement. A fourth man was killed by either Soldier G or Lance Corporal F. I must point out that this whole incident in Glenfada Park occurred in fleeting seconds and I can no longer recall the order of fire or who fell first but I do remember that when we first appeared – darkened faces, sweat and aggressions, brandishing rifles – the crowd stopped immediately in their tracks, turned to face us and raised their hands. This is the way they were standing when they were shot.

Men and women whimpering and crying and trembling with fear with their hands on their heads, we frog-marched them at a jog-

trot to the rear, which was an open area 150 yards behind us. A Catholic priest ran across to the bodies shouting about giving the last rites – he was clubbed down with rifle butts. A hysterical woman, short, fat, about 50 years old, dressed in black, was crying uncontrollably about one of her sons being shot. She too was beaten and I recall soldiers kicking her when she was on the ground. In an instant the car park was empty. I stood there alone and watched as four men entered dressed in donkey jackets and flat caps. I raised my rifle and aimed at them. They picked up the two bodies that had fallen together and started to carry them out of the car park. I hesitated and didn't fire. The fear which comes from being alone, and silence, all of a sudden filled me and I moved back down Kells Wall expecting to be shot at any second.

Caught up in the intensives [sic] *of the moment without a thought of yesterday or tomorrow, I probably naively (as I think now) was filled with an overwhelming desire that the truth should be known. I didn't want to drop my friends into trouble and hadn't thought anything along those lines. It was more a feeling that an incident had occurred and that I had seen the bodies removed. I remember thinking – illogically, as it turned out – that no one would ever know about it. As a result, when I reached the area where the prisoners were spread-eagled against the walls, I grabbed one of a large group of pressmen who was standing there and said as accurately as I can remember, 'There are a lot of bodies down there – you've got to come and see them.' From the time of the shooting in Glenfada Park to this action on my part it was probably no more than two minutes, however, as I was dragging my pressman off, a plain-clothes character approached us, informed me that he was an officer and asked me what I was doing. This brought me to my senses; remembering I had a black face and there was still a lot of commotion going on, I broke off and rejoined my Platoon.*

When we finally got into the 'pig' [army slang for APC, armoured personnel carrier] *everyone including myself was laughing and joking on an intense wave of excitement as we worked out how many rounds we had fired. Several of the blokes had fired their own personal supply of dum-dums.* [This is the first ever admission that illegally held non-army-issued bullets were fired on the day. This was never admitted at the Widgery Tribunal.]

Soldier J, for one, fired 10 dum-dums into the crowd but as he has still had his official quota he got away with saying that he never fired a shot in the subsequent investigation. This happened with several people in my vehicle. Soldier H fired 22 rounds but was stupid enough to boast about it within the sergeant's hearing before he could spread them out, i.e., add a few to each of our tallies. We coasted round the area and there was none of the usual abuse which follows an Army action. They really didn't know what had hit them. We parked for a moment behind Rossville flats and a civilian got in, a PR man, and came out with the profound statement 'Yous will need some public relations work around here after this.' We all laughed, feeling very pleased with ourselves.

In preparation for the Widgery Inquiry the members of the parachute regiment were confined to Palace Barracks, their HQ in Holywood, County Down. In preparation for the inquiry there they underwent extensive interrogation.

When the Widgery Tribunal got underway, this was a personal affront and the common feeling amongst us was, Who the hell's side is the British government on? In our eyes we were being tried by our own leaders, a sop to IRA aggression, the people we were at war with … On arrival in Coleraine by helicopter [the Widgery Tribunal was moved out of Derry City and instead took place in Coleraine] *we flew along the river which runs through that town and sat down between some trees outside the court house where the Tribunal was in progress. Disguised and escorted, I was led through a mass of waiting pressmen and reporters, and shown into some offices within the building. Here there were a number of soldiers from my platoon, all disguised as I was, and we spent some time poring over arid photographs along with* SIB [Special Investigation Bureau] *trying to establish which shots had been fired by whom and from where. What a farce. We were grinning at each other and drawing haphazardly all over the place, with a result that the authorities finished up with a series of photographs of sophisticated looking spiders' webs, which bore no relation to fact.*

I was then interviewed in an office by two Crown lawyers on Lord Widgery's team … I rattled off everything I had seen and had done. The only thing I omitted were the names and the manner in which people had been shot. Apart from that I told the truth which I wanted to convey.

Then to my utter surprise one of these gentlemen said; 'Dear me, Private 027, you make it sound as though shots were fired at the crowd, we can't have that, can we?' And then he proceeded to tear up my statement. He left the room and returned 10 minutes later with another statement which bore no relation to the fact and [I] was told with a smile that this was the statement I would use when going on the stand.

What a situation! The Lord Chief Justice of Great Britain, the symbol of all moral standings and justice, having his minions suppress and twist evidence. With or without his knowledge, who can tell? I was amazed! ...

The following are extracts from the Widgery Statement that Soldier 027 claims was written for him:

I then heard a shout from our rear to 'cease-fire'. I cannot say who gave the original order because it was repeated by those near me....

I followed a group of soldiers, E, F, G and H, round the corner of the building and into Glenfada Park. I was a short distance behind them and as they went out of my view round the corner I heard several SLR shots. I cannot say who fired and neither can I say what targets they engaged. ... Then I saw a male civilian in his early twenties wearing blue clothing and with long hair lighting something in his hand. I then heard someone say drop it but I do not know who said that or whether it was directed at the youth holding the petrol bomb. As he attempted to throw the bomb, E knelt and fired at the youth at an estimated range of 20 yards....

As the park emptied I saw three male bodies lying at the far end of the park. They appeared to be dead. I subsequently saw these bodies being removed through the exit by male persons dressed in donkey jackets and flat caps ....

Soldier 027's Statement to the Saville Inquiry

Soldier 027 gave a 35-page statement to the Saville Inquiry, which he signed on 7 June 2000. In total the statement has 192 numbered paragraphs. In paragraph 185 he acknowledges authorship of the statement which formed the basis of *The Sunday Business Post* article published in March 1997: 'That article contained extracts from the statement I had written in 1975.'

Soldier 027 states that during his time in the Army he 'carried a field note pad and made a note of [his] thoughts and of events from time to time. I also made some notes on other loose bits of paper' (paragraph 169). He states that they were the notes of a nineteen-year-old and are not at all as he sees things now. When he left the Army in 1974 he had 'two or three clumps of such paperwork', containing notes that were both descriptive and reflective, 'made within hours or, at the latest, days of the event in question...' (paragraph 170). His collection also included a diary.

Soldier 027 says that in 1975, during a visit to New York, he had a chance meeting with an American freelance journalist who was interested in the conflict in Northern Ireland (paragraph 171). During a conversation that lasted a few hours, he says he must have told the journalist of material he had collected from his time in Northern Ireland. He continues, 'After I returned home, without being selective or really looking through it first, I sent this material to him in New York (paragraph 172). Amongst the material he sent was, he states, 'an account in statement form of my memory of Bloody Sunday.' In paragraph 174 he states: 'It seems ridiculous, looking at the sensitive nature of the document, that I would have let it out of my hands in that way, but I do not think that I was conscious of its sensitive nature at the time.' It was, he states, 'a quarter of a century later,' when next he saw the statement (paragraph 176).

In paragraph 177 Soldier 027 comments on this document. Understandably, after over twenty-five years, his memory is not as fresh as when the statement was written in 1975. He says: '... I have no reason to think the account incorrect, but I do not have the clarity of thought at present to confirm those details which may have been influenced subsequently by having read Don Mullan's book and read and seen other material ...' (paragraph 177.10). He continues: 'The statement ... refers to individuals in the crowd in Glenfada Park being shot having raised their hands ... that is not something that I have a clear memory of at this stage' (paragraph 177.11).

Regarding the use of dum-dum bullets he states: '... there is reference to the firing of dum-dum bullets. I could not have known that at the time ... All that I can say at this stage is that I do remember dum-dum bullets being passed around our vehicle before we went into the Rossville Street area ... but I do not know who the dum-dums belonged to...' (paragraph 177.15).

With regard to his Widgery statement he says: ' ... it states that the lawyer who interviewed me in Coleraine "proceeded to tear up my statement". I cannot remember him actually tearing it up and maybe that was just a figure of speech to denote the manner in which it was being taken away' (paragraph 177.16). However, elsewhere he says, regarding the lawyer: 'My understanding now it that the lawyer was from the Treasury Solicitor's office ... I was aware at that time that he was part of the Tribunal and was one of Lord Widgery's employees' (paragraph 160). 'The lawyer was there to take a statement from me ...' (paragraph 161). 'When I went into the office, my idea was to tell the truth, trying as far as possible to indicate what had occurred, but with omissions, to avoid dropping people directly in it' (paragraph 162). 'I began to give the lawyer my recollections ...' (paragraph 163). 'At the point when I described the shooting from the small wall by Kells Walk towards the centre of the crowd behind the Rubble Barricade, the lawyer stood up and expressed surprise and said something like "We can't have that, can we Private? That makes it sound as if shots were being fired into the crowd," or something very similar. I was very surprised ... I thought that I had already watered down what I was saying and I was being told that even that was unacceptable ... I wondered what was acceptable if this wasn't? ...' (paragraph 164). 'The man then took the statement and left the room. When he returned some time later ... a written or typed statement was given or shown to me. What was written did not accord with what I had told him earlier ...' (paragraph 165). 'After the statement was signed by me and I left the room, I remember seeing one or two of the other soldiers going in to give their evidence to the Inquiry. I fully expected to do the same myself and had no reason to think otherwise. However, I was not called to give evidence and that was the end of my involvement. I do not recall being given any reason for why I was not called' (paragraph 167).

Soldier 027 concludes his statement as follows:

'Unspeakable acts took place on Bloody Sunday. There was no justification for a single shot that I saw fired ... even if there were incoming strikes as we debussed (which I cannot remember now), it was still no excuse for the shooting that I saw occur' (paragraph 190).

'My view is that the events that day within my own platoon were triggered by two individuals [Lance Corporal F and Soldier G] with a game plan and when they saw that they could bring it into action, they did so and others joined in. There was no command to prevent or stop this happening. Having said that, I believe there is little to be gained by certain soldiers on the ground, those pulling the triggers, being held up as scapegoats for what happened that day. The attributes and mentality of a battalion like 1 Para and the way in which it operated were known. The responsibility for its actions lies with those who selected and directed an outfit like that. It is noticeable that no one in authority has taken responsibility for orchestrating the situation. Instead, we have the unsightly spectacle of some officers busily pointing the fingers at each other' (paragraph 191).

'What is really at stake is bigger than pursuing individuals and private retribution. The whole incident served as a catalyst and spawned an escalation in violence, with the ensuing death and misery of thousands of people and the blight of many more lives. It may be that some other catalyst would have arisen in any event, but that is just speculation. Bloody Sunday was such a catalyst. If it can be acknowledged that errors and mistakes were made at all levels and that the gratuitous stupidity of individuals was to blame, hopefully something positive will emerge that will contribute to bringing a little light into what was a bleak and dark chapter in the history of the province. Perhaps, years ago, the appropriate people were too entrenched in their own ideas for this to be possible; I would like to think that the position may now be different. I believe now that there will be a positive effect if something close to the truth of what actually happened that day does surface' (paragraph 192).

Since Soldier 027 must give oral evidence before the tribunal, his statement has not yet been tested or challenged by Counsel for the Inquiry, the Bloody Sunday families and the army.

APPENDIX 8

The Statement of a British Army Officer

On 4 March 1997, I gave a public lecture on Bloody Sunday at White Rock College, Belfast. The lecture had been extensively advertised in the local press. Upon my arrival the Principal of the College gave me a letter which had been posted March 1. The letter was from a Mr Paddy McGarvey, the founder-director of an organisation called the Irish Parliament Trust, founded in 1986. The letter simply stated: 'I need to meet you, which may be of some benefit to you and the relatives.'

When I contacted McGarvey he informed me he had been appointed an official observer to the British Irish Inter-Parliamentary Body in 1996. This is a joint body of British MPs and Irish TDs who meet regularly to discuss matters of mutual interest concerning Northern Ireland. McGarvey informed me that while attending the 1996 Autumn Plenary Session of the British Irish Inter-Parliamentary Body, he was approached by a man who said he had been an officer of field rank in the British Army in the early 1970s, which involved tours of duty in Northern Ireland. The man told McGarvey he wished to talk to him about the events and the cause of Bloody Sunday in Derry.

I encouraged McGarvey to maintain contact with the ex-officer and I gave him a copy of *Eyewitness Bloody Sunday* which he sent to him. Subsequently, McGarvey travelled to England in mid-May 1997 and 'after two days of discussion' at the home of the ex-officer, he took a statement from him, the full text of which appears in this chapter.

The document confirms our growing belief that the role of General Robert Ford, the GOC of British Land Forces in Northern Ireland in 1972, needs further examination. Ford was in Derry on Bloody Sunday. His presence on the day and his role have never been satisfactorily explained. It is clear from the ex-officer's statement that disquiet exists within British Army senior circles concerning the way Lord Widgery attempts to exonerate Ford, leaving Brigadier MacLellan to carry the burden of responsibility. MacLellan was in the official operations room situated within Ebrington Barracks, Derry. He was de facto the officer in charge of the Army on the ground that day. It is clear from listening to the Porter tapes that MacLellan is confused as developments progress.

Implicit in our research is the growing suspicion that there was, on Bloody Sunday, an operational plan with a plan. The relationship between General Ford and Lieutenant-Colonel Dereck Wilford, the Commander 1 Para, needs further study. Increasingly, I am of the opinion that while Ebrington Barracks was the official operations room on Bloody Sunday, the Derry Walls was the actual operations centre from where another plan may have been coldly over-riding the orders of Brigadier MacLellan. The statement of McGarvey's ex-officer makes some startling and disturbing claims, including that General Robert Ford was present on the Derry Walls.

Statement:

Following the publication of the Widgery Tribunal Report dated April 1972, I became aware that my fellow officers were as puzzled about its findings as were members of the public. It was felt that the Army's version of what had occurred had not come through correctly, even though senior witnesses had told the truth to the very best of their beliefs.

I now learn from the views of an unnamed ex-2nd [sic] Paratrooper, published in Irish newspapers, that the statements made by him and other soldiers in readiness for the Tribunal were taken from them in Coleraine by Treasury solicitors assisting Lord Widgery, and returned to them with alterations. Whether the events I am about to recount were described in those original statements and then expunged by the Government solicitors taking statements in London and Coleraine, I have no way of knowing. My information is based on a briefing on Bloody Sunday.

The blame for what happened lies entirely at the door of the GOC Northern Ireland, Major-General Robert Ford. He made himself directly involved in Londonderry that day, contrary to the operation order and contrary to the explanation as to his conduct given by Widgery. The Tribunal's finding that his presence was only that of an observer was inaccurate.

As Widgery also reports, General Ford, on 25th January, had placed the Commander of 8 Infantry Brigade in charge of the operation, and ordered him to prepare a detailed, written plan. The brigade commander was Brigadier A.P.W. MacLellan, MBE, assisted by Lieutenant-Colonel (then Brigade Major) M.C.M. Steele, both of whom controlled the situation from the operations room in Ebrington Barracks.

They were not on the streets of Derry at any relevant time, but General Ford was, in civilian clothes, and interfering by giving direct orders to individual officers and troops.

The Operations Order initiated by Brigadier MacLellan had been approved by Headquarters N. Ireland and was distributed to all those taking part, yet in turning up at the barricade – really like a bad penny – and without the knowledge of the brigadier, he caused the chaos that resulted in the tragedy of 13 dead and 13 wounded, as indeed the Widgery Report said he would have done, had he interfered.

Other than the Widgery note that he gave command to HQ 8 Brigade, there is no further mention of General Ford's evidence. Instead, there is the following exculpation of his behaviour in Paragraph 23 on Page 8:

Another unjustified criticism of General Ford was persisted in throughout the tribunal hearing. It was said that when heavy firing began and it became apparent that the operation had taken an unexpected course, the General made no attempt to discover the cause of the shooting, but instead washed his hands of the affair and walked away ... This criticism is based on a failure to understand the structure of command in the army. The officer commanding the operation was the Commander, 8 Brigade, who was in his Operations Room and was the only senior officer who had any general picture of what was going on. General Ford was present on the streets of Londonderry as an observer only. Although he had a wireless equipment in his vehicle he was not accompanied by a wireless operator when on foot ... When the serious shooting began, the General was on foot in the neighbourhood of Chamberlain Street and had no means of knowing what was going on. Nothing would have been more likely to create chaos than for him to assume command or even to interfere with radio traffic by asking for information ... Instead, he did the only possible thing by going at once to an observation post from which he could observe the scene for himself.

I see from Mr Mullan's book that the then Official IRA admit shooting first, and at troops who were moving forward as 'snatch squads,' and I leave it to others to comment on such wild irresponsibility of firing at troops so close to their own civilians.

Who authorised retaliatory fire against the IRA? The Ops Room demanded to know – the answer came back – the GOC. Until that point the Operations Room did not know of General Ford's presence in Derry. The observation post that General Ford later went to was on the walls of the City where he repeated the encouragement to fire at individuals that he had previously given to the barricade. (I believe he wanted to teach the rioters a lesson). I should say here that the introduction of élite troops into a fraught situation in which the ordinary resident units are already in place is an invitation to trouble unless their action is tightly controlled. The Paras are inclined to the view, 'Out of the way, you lot. We're here and we know how to deal with it.'

The GOC's interfering conduct broke that control. He was in civilian clothes, in a vehicle equipped with communications, accompanied by at least two uniformed soldiers, a driver and a radio operator, so he could hear what was happening. He made himself known to officers at the barricade, unnerving of itself for all of them and I am told he stood beside individual Gunner soldiers on the walls and directed their fire with exhortations to hit indicated targets.

The rather laboured account in Widgery of his 'observer-only' role begs the question that he could hardly take command – causing chaos, says Widgery – when he himself had just caused it. Widgery's published excuse that General Ford could not possibly know what was happening ignores the point that he had no business there, and the Brigadier MacLellan had no knowledge of him being there until the shooting started. Initially an observer, he got involved and thereby removed control of the operation from the brigade commander.

The Widgery Report mentions that a Company Sergeant Major was demanding of his soldiers 'What are you doing? Who are you firing at?' – the questions posed too late.

I am advised that what I am saying is hearsay, as I was not on duty in Derry that day. I assure you it is the truth because it is told against the British Army's otherwise excellent record in Northern Ireland. The account is not Mess gossip either, but a de-briefing from a more senior ranking officer who was there and in a position to know exactly what happened. It was all so very sad.

The political direction of the army has been to be strictly neutral at all times between the Catholics and the Protestants. Under no circumstances were we allowed to take sides, with a sort of motto: 'Live Horse and you'll Get Grass' – and we'd all be out of there by 1975. Bloody Sunday ripped all that apart.

End of statement.

APPENDIX 9

The Breglio Report

Extract from 'Bloody Sunday' The Breglio
Report, *by Robert J. Breglio, published
by Bloody Sunday Justice Campaign, New
York, 14 March 1997.*

Having met with Don Mullan in Staten Island on
23 November 1996, and after examining various autopsy and medical reports, I consented to travel to Derry in Northern Ireland to
conduct an independent ballistics investigation and evaluation of
the chain of events that occurred relative to the day known as
Bloody Sunday.

(1)
The Shooting Dead of William Nash (19),
Michael McDaid (20) and John Young (17).

On Sunday, January 26th, 1997, I visited the area of the Derry Walls
and walked along the wall looking down at the area of Glenfada Park
and Rossville Street to make a determination of the probability of
shooting positions that could concentrate on the area of Glenfada
Park.

After examining the autopsy and medical reports of William Nash,
John Young and Michael McDaid and noting the similarities and
consistencies of the angle of the trajectories of the fatal wounds sustained by these three young men, I will further conclude that in my
professional opinion the projectiles that struck William Nash, John
Young, and Michael McDaid originated from an area up in the vicinity of Derry's Walls and were fired by a high powered weapon using
telescopic sights.

I also note that Channel Four News (UK), on the 17 January 1997, posed the same questions to another ballistics expert, Dr Hugh Thomas, Consultant Surgeon, Prince Charles Hospital, Merthyr Tydfil, Wales.

Alex Thompson of Channel Four News showed Dr Thomas ... diagrams ... giving details of the entry and exit wounds, together with trajectory details concerning the killings of William Nash, Michael McDaid and John Young. He asked Dr Thomas the following question: 'Could they (Nash, McDaid and Young) possibly have been hit by soldiers at ground level?' Dr Thomas replied:

> *No they couldn't have! This shot could only have come from a higher level. It would be almost impossible for those three men in the few seconds available to them to bend down to exactly the same angle and face exactly the same way and be shot in exactly the same fashion. It would be extraordinary and almost unheard of. So, I would say definitely not.*
>
> *It's likely to be a marksman, an exceptionally good marksman, firing towards, obviously, and in actual fact, firing quite fast at the three suspects who were clumped in the same area. You would only need literally a fraction of a second to align the next individual and complete the job.*

APPENDIX 10

General Ford Memo

The true role of General Robert Ford before, during and after Bloody Sunday is yet to be fully evaluated. It is to be hoped that the Saville Inquiry will help clarify the extent to which Ford shaped events on the day and why he personally journeyed to Derry on 30 January 1972 to monitor developments.

It is clear from reading the radio logs from the day that the man in charge of army operations on Bloody Sunday, Brigadier Patrick MacLellan, appeared to be confused as events unfolded and wasn't, as he thought, fully in charge. A question still to be answered is whether or not Ford and the Commander of 1 Para, Colonel Derek Wilford, had a particular understanding of how army operations on the day were to unfold — an understanding not shared by Brigadier MacLellan.

The release of General Ford's memo, entitled 'The Situation in Londonderry as at 7th January 1972', by the Saville Inquiry assists in bringing perspective to the strategic thinking of this very senior British Army officer. Clearly he had identified the 'Derry Young Hooligans' as a prime target who needed to be taught a lesson. Clearly he had considered the possibility of inflicting fatalities amongst those considered ringleaders. He had developed his thinking to the point of having specially adapted sniper weapons sent to the city for this very purpose.

General Ford also noted that the military authorities had to consider the possibility of a Northern Ireland Civil Rights Association (NICRA) march from the Creggan Estate to Guildhall Square taking place on Sunday 16 January 1972. He stated that it was possible that there would be some type of a battle. Ford stated this exactly two weeks before the Bloody Sunday march. This information was also passed onto 1 Kings Own Border regiment and 1 Para.

General Ford's memo does not definitively answer, as many suspect, whether Bloody Sunday was premeditated and politically motivated. Nonetheless, it brings into sharper focus that very possibility, the consequences of which still reverberate to this very day.

If you are interested in viewing General Ford's memo in its entirety you can find it on the official website of the Saville Inquiry at **www.bloody-sunday-inquiry.org.uk**.

AFTERWORD

The Hidden Tension that is Already Alive

A BBC journalist, whom I met in Derry during 1997, described *Eyewitness Bloody Sunday* as the book that reopened the Bloody Sunday case. When it was released in Ireland on 13 January 1997, neither I nor the families of those who died on Bloody Sunday foresaw its far-reaching impact. Veteran Irish Civil Rights activist and renowned journalist Eamon McCann described reaction to the book as phenomenal. On the twenty-fifth anniversary of Bloody Sunday, Bishop Edward Daly, a witness to the events and whose testimony appears in the book, said publicly that the contribution that *Eyewitness Bloody Sunday* had made could not be exaggerated.

Research for the book formed the basis of a major Channel Four News Bloody Sunday Special on 17 January 1997, which stunned the British establishment into silence. In the months that followed, that silence was perhaps the most poignant response to the powerful truth that these eyewitness statements have always contained.

I am increasingly of the opinion that Lord Chief Justice Widgery's failure to give proper consideration to the hundreds of testimonies presented to him by the Northern Ireland Civil Rights Association was not a result of pure racist arrogance. On the contrary, I believe that it was primarily because Lord Chief Justice Widgery and his legal advisers could see precisely the powerful consistency of truth that the testimonies contained. Such evidence, if fully aired at his Tribunal, would have made their concoction of deceit impossible to sustain.

Speaking in New York on 14 March 1997, John Kelly, brother of murdered Michael Kelly and chairperson of the Bloody Sunday Justice Campaign, succinctly placed the eyewitness statements in their proper historical context when he said:

> *Today . . . is our first step in placing Bloody Sunday on the international human rights agenda. It is appropriate that we should do*

so in New York, since it was here, twenty-five years ago, that the British government, through the British Information Services, issued to the world media a web of lies and misinformation . . . It is now our turn to tell our story and thankfully, at long last, the world seems ready to listen.

Four Powerful Ingredients

As the twenty-fifth anniversary of Bloody Sunday approached, the following four powerful ingredients fused, making it possible to tell the full story of Bloody Sunday:

- The publication of *Eyewitness Bloody Sunday*
- The subsequent Channel Four News reports
- The Porter Tapes — intercepted sound recordings of British Army and RUC communications
- The Walsh Report, which analysed the original statements of implicated soldiers

The publication of *Eyewitness Bloody Sunday*, as well as finally giving a voice to the civilian demonstrators who witnessed the events of that day, exposed facts that support the hypothesis that snipers, in the vicinity of the old Derry Walls, may have shot dead three of the victims on the day.

The second ingredient was an independent investigation carried out by the Channel Four News team, who rigorously investigated the assertions contained within *Eyewitness Bloody Sunday*. Channel Four News subsequently broadcast several Bloody Sunday Special Reports, which profoundly weakened the official version of events.

The decision by a local amateur radio enthusiast, Jimmy Porter, to publicise the actual sound recordings of the army and police radio messages, which he had intercepted on the day, was the third factor that helped lead to further exposure of the full story of Bloody Sunday. These messages add considerable strength to the belief that paratroopers at ground level were not the only military killers on the day.

Finally, there was the analysis of statements, given by implicated soldiers to the Military Police in the immediate aftermath of Bloody Sunday, which had recently been deposited in the Public Records Office. Professor Dermot Walsh of Limerick University Law Department was asked by the Bloody Sunday Trust to analyse and assess them. His investigations concluded that statements were changed up to four times in advance of the Widgery Tribunal — apparently in order to choreograph the official version of events of Sunday, 30 January 1972.

All of the above factors created a heightened awareness, which resulted in 40,000 people participating in the twenty-fifth anniversary Bloody Sunday Commemoration March — the largest commemorative gathering ever.

Mounting Political Pressure

Political pressure began to mount. Labour MP Jeremy Corbyn and SDLP Leader John Hume both placed Early Day Motions in the House of Commons calling for a new independent inquiry. Seventy-two Members of the Westminster Parliament signed the motions. During a House of Commons debate on 30 January 1997, the then Secretary of State for Northern Ireland, Sir Patrick Mayhew, wondered why I had not given the new evidence on Bloody Sunday to 'the appropriate authorities' — the appropriate authorities being the Royal Ulster Constabulary, who are themselves implicated in the cover-up.

On 14 February 1997, a meeting which had been arranged by John Hume was held between the relatives of the Bloody Sunday victims and Sir Patrick Mayhew. During the meeting at Stormont Castle, the Secretary of State was presented with a complete dossier of all of the 'new' evidence available at that time. He promised that he would review the material thoughtfully and thoroughly before coming to a decision.

The following day Sir Patrick infuriated the entire nationalist population on the island of Ireland when, in response to a question about an official apology for Bloody Sunday, he said, 'An apology is for criminal wrongdoing and there is nothing in the Widgery Tribunal Report to suggest that.' Furthermore, the Secretary of State said that an apology would be unjust to those who took part in the tragic events — in other words, those members of the Parachute Regiment and other regiments who murdered neighbours, friends and loved ones of the people of Derry on Bloody Sunday.

Meeting with the Irish government

Sir Patrick Mayhew's comments were received with incredulity, which in turn developed into a discernible undercurrent of nationalist anger. In response, the Bloody Sunday Justice Campaign publicly called for a meeting with the then Taoiseach, Mr John Bruton. On Thursday, 19 February 1997, a delegation of fourteen victims' family members, a representative of the Bloody Sunday wounded, Madden & Finucane Solicitors, Jane Winter of British Irish Rights Watch and I met with the Taoiseach at Government Buildings in Dublin. The Taoiseach was joined by his coalition partners, Minister for Foreign Affairs Mr Dick Spring TD and Minister of Social Welfare, Mr Proinnsias de Rossa. The Taoiseach informed the delegation that the government had decided to prepare its own assessment of all the new material for presentation to the British government. He informed the delegation that the British government had indicated it would welcome this assessment and that Sir Patrick Mayhew's comments did not detract from their earlier expressed willingness to look at all so-called 'new' evidence.

The families also met with opposition leaders, including the current Taoiseach, Bertie Ahern, and left Dublin in the knowledge that for the first time in their long and lonely campaign they had cross-party support throughout the whole of Dáil Éireann — it was a historic turning point in the Bloody Sunday Justice Campaign. The families were, on that occasion, also welcomed to the residence of the then US Ambassador Jean Kennedy Smith, who said she would keep the US State Department fully informed of all future developments in the case.

Leakage in Official Bloody Sunday Position

Leakage in respect of the official British position on Bloody Sunday began to gain momentum. On 16 March 1997, journalist Tom McGurk of *The Sunday Business Post* published extracts from a document written by a former member of the 1st Battalion of the Parachute Regiment (1 Para) who was a participant in the Paras' operation on Bloody Sunday (see Appendix 7). The author of the document was identified by McGurk as Soldier A. He is, in fact, Soldier 027 in the Bloody Sunday Inquiry. This soldier was a witness to the chilling executions in Glenfada Park where he saw unarmed civilians shot with their hands in the air or while lying wounded on the ground.

A further development was a statement received from a former British Officer who served in Northern Ireland in 1972 (see Appendix 8). That statement is inaccurate when it suggests that I stated the IRA had opened fire first on the British Army. However, the most important element of the officer's statement relates to the activities of General Robert Ford, the British Army commander of Land Forces in Northern Ireland. The officer's statement lends weight to the growing suspicion that, on Bloody Sunday, there may have been a plan within a plan. The statement appears to confirm the distinct possibility that, while Brigadier MacLellan theoretically had overall responsibility for the military operation on the day, such responsibility may have been superseded by General Ford and possibly also by Lieutenant Colonel Derek Wilford, the commander of 1 Para, via a secure radio link. Furthermore, the statement also reinforces my own personal suspicion that while the official Operations Room was situated within Ebrington Barracks, Derry, the actual operations were directed from the Derry Walls by General Ford using the aforementioned secure radio link. This may not be the case, but it is reasonable to say that it deserves fuller investigation.

A further weakening blow to the results of the Widgery Tribunal occurred in mid-March when Mr David Capper, a highly respected and senior BBC journalist, revealed for the first time that Lord Widgery had misrepresented his Tribunal testimony concerning the timing of a shot that Mr Capper had heard fired at the army. Lord Widgery gave the impression that the shot was fired just prior to the paratroopers' advance. The shot that Mr Capper heard occurred up to two hours beforehand.

International Support

Pressure soon began to mount from several international sources. In a letter sent to the British Prime Minister, John Major, co-signed by six international human rights bodies, Amnesty International asserted its support for the growing demands for the new independent inquiry into Bloody Sunday.

On St Patrick's Day 1997, the Chairperson of the Bloody Sunday

Justice Campaign, John Kelly, and I, were invited to the White House reception in honour of the Taoiseach, Mr Bruton, and Mrs Bruton. On the following day, we were invited to address Washington's National Press Club. On that same afternoon our delegation, which included Kay Duddy, sister of murdered Jack Duddy, and Mickey McKinney, brother of murdered William McKinney, attended Capitol Hill, where we met Congressmen Richard Neale, Peter King, James Walshe, Thomas Manton and Ben Gilman. The Congressmen pledged their support for the Bloody Sunday campaign and presented the delegation with a letter that had been sent to John Major, which called for the establishment of a new independent inquiry.

Irish Government's Assessment of New Material

Steady progress continued with the Irish government's assessment of all 'new' evidence and material relating to Bloody Sunday. The Taoiseach, Mr Bruton, gave permission for me to read in detail the penultimate draft of the government's dossier, which was to be presented to the British government when finalised. On 28 May 1997, the Taoiseach presented the victims' families with a detailed briefing on the Irish government's dossier. The families again met with the leaders of the other Dáil Éireann political parties, together with the US Ambassador, Jean Kennedy Smith. On that same afternoon, representatives of the Bloody Sunday victims' families and the wounded accompanied the author to Áras an Uachtaráin, where a copy of *Eyewitness Bloody Sunday* was presented to the then President of Ireland, Mrs Mary Robinson.

On 24 June 1997, the Irish government's dossier on Bloody Sunday was presented to the new British Prime Minister, Mr Tony Blair, through the Anglo-Irish secretariat at Stormont Castle. In a letter to Mr Blair that accompanied the dossier, the Taoiseach, Mr Bruton, said:

> In the light of the Assessment, the victims of Bloody Sunday were a unique group in that the injustice of their fate — at the hands of those whose duty it was to respect as well as uphold the rule of law — was compounded by a second injustice arising directly from the Widgery Report.

At a meeting on 2 July 1997, the new Taoiseach, Mr Bertie Ahern, met with a Bloody Sunday delegation. He fully endorsed the comprehensive assessment of the new material and evidence undertaken by the previous Irish government and added that it was his intention to follow this up 'with vigour and determination'.

The following day, I accompanied this delegation to London, where its members handed a petition in to 10 Downing Street. This document, which was signed by 40,000 people, demanded the repudiation of the Widgery Tribunal Report and the establishment of a new independent inquiry. Afterwards, the delegation sat down to a working lunch with the new Labour Secretary of State for Northern Ireland, Dr Mo Mowlam. During this meeting Dr Mowlam said she expected to make an announcement on the British government's response to all 'new' evidence within months.

The final, and undoubtedly most symbolic, part of the delegation's London visit was at the *Memorial Stone to Innocent Victims* at Westminster Abbey (unveiled by Queen Elizabeth 11 on 10 October 1996). Here the delegation laid a wreath in memory of the fourteen innocent Derry men who marched 'in the mistaken belief that they had the right to Peaceful Protest' and were killed by Her Majesty's troops.

Twenty-Sixth Anniversary of Bloody Sunday

As the twenty-sixth anniversary of Bloody Sunday approached, diplomatic pressure mounted. The Irish government informed the British government that it planned to publish the contents of its Bloody Sunday Assessment. On 23 January 1998, the Taoiseach, Mr Ahern, honoured a commitment he had made the previous year and visited Derry to lay a wreath at the Bloody Sunday memorial in the Bogside. He met with the Bloody Sunday families and wounded on that occasion and informed them that the British Prime Minister had requested a delay in the publication of the Irish government's Assessment to allow Mr Blair time to read it personally. The Taoiseach said that, during a telephone conversation, the British Prime Minister questioned whether a new inquiry would only open up old wounds. 'No', the Taoiseach replied emphatically, 'because these are wounds that have never closed.'

As the countdown to Bloody Sunday's twenty-sixth anniversary began, expectations of an announcement increased, and, at around 6.00 p.m. on 28 January 1998, the telephone in John Kelly's home rang. 'It's Mo, John,' the voice informed him, 'I'm calling to let you know that the Prime Minister is going to make an announcement about Bloody Sunday in the House of Commons tomorrow.'

It was my great privilege to gather with the families and wounded in the Ráth Mór Centre, Creggan, at 3.00 p.m. on Thursday, 29 January 1998, to listen to Mr Blair's announcement. He praised the dignity of the families during their long campaign and then announced that he had decided to set up a new Bloody Sunday Tribunal of Inquiry. Lord Mark Saville of Newdigate was named as Chairman of the Tribunal, and he was to be joined by two other judges who would be drawn from the British Commonwealth. The terms of reference of the new Inquiry are as follows:

> [to inquire into] the events of Sunday, 30 January 1972, which led to loss of life in connection with the procession in Londonderry on that day, taking account of any new information relevant to events on that day.

Following the announcement, the families and wounded gathered in Derry's Guildhall for a press conference at which they issued a cautious welcome to the Prime Minister's announcement. One journalist privately expressed surprise at the apparent lack of euphoria on the part of the families. Perhaps he was comparing Mr Blair's announcement to establish a new Bloody Sunday Inquiry with the jubilation that accompanied the release of the Birmingham Six or the Guildford Four. All cases were undoubtedly miscarriages of justice of immeasurable magnitude. However, in the Birmingham and Guildford cases, ten innocent people were given their freedom after decades of wrongful imprisonment. The case of the Bloody Sunday families and wounded was quite different. They had merely been given the prospect of a new inquiry, having been forced to endure the ignominy of a long and lonely campaign for truth and justice. Prime Minister Blair's historic announcement had simply turned back the clock to approximately 4.30 p.m. on Sunday, 30 January 1972, when the Paras' guns were silenced at last and the people of Derry began to count their dead. The Bloody Sunday families and wounded now faced the trauma of a new inquiry and the reliving of the awful horrors of that life-shattering day. While there was certainly a sense of their struggle having crossed a line of historical dimensions, the families realised that this was merely the beginning of a long, sad and arduous journey. Euphoria was an emotion that was a universe away.

The Irish government published its Bloody Sunday Assessment on the same day that Mr Blair announced the setting up of the new Inquiry.

The Saville Inquiry

On Friday, 3 April 1998, Lord Mark Saville of Newdigate arrived in Derry, accompanied by Sir Edward Somers of New Zealand and Mr Justice William Hoyt of Canada, to make an opening statement regarding their Inquiry. At 10.00 a.m. precisely, the three men entered the main hall of Derry's Guildhall as the great clock chimed above. Lord Saville said that the Bloody Sunday Inquiry intended to carry out its duty 'with fairness, thoroughness and impartiality'.

With the support of the Bloody Sunday families and wounded, I joined the legal team of Madden & Finucane, Solicitors, in the triple role of adviser, assistant and press secretary, for six months.

Initial engagement with the Inquiry caused concern and disquiet amongst the victims' families, the wounded and their legal team. For example, the Inquiry attempted to limit their legal representation to one senior counsel and two junior counsel, which almost mirrored a highly contentious ruling by Lord Chief Justice Widgery in 1972. It was only after a concerted effort by the families and their legal team — which culminated in a preliminary public hearing in Derry on 20 and 21 July 1998 — that the Saville Inquiry agreed a total representation of five senior and five junior counsel. This was considered by the representatives of the Bloody Sunday families and wounded to be the minimum legal team necessary to present and conduct their case adequately at the new Inquiry. Since that ruling, representation has increased, with four families exercising their legal and moral right to engage their own separate legal teams.

A further disturbing development occurred in July 1999 when the British Court of Appeal overruled the Saville Inquiry's decision not to grant blanket anonymity to the soldiers who participated in the events of Bloody Sunday. Soldiers argued that the new inquiry would put their lives at risk if they were named in public. Saville, while ruling against blanket anonymity, offered a 'special reasons application' for anyone who believed they had a case to make – this was to facilitate soldiers, on an individual basis, to apply to the Inquiry for anonymity by demonstrating they had special and specific reasons to fear for their safety. However, the Inquiry's ruling was challenged and the British Court of Appeal overruled their judgement on the basis that the right to life of the soldiers was paramount.

Lawyer Peter Madden responded to the decision by saying: 'The road has ended as far as anonymity is concerned because the tribunal is not going to appeal against it. The fairness of an English judiciary is now in direct conflict with an international tribunal's standard of fairness.'

Despite this, it was not to be the last time that the British justice system was to interfere with the independence of the Bloody Sunday Tribunal of Inquiry.

Formal Opening of Bloody Sunday Inquiry

On Monday, 27 March 2000, the Bloody Sunday Tribunal of Inquiry formally opened.

The previous evening a candlelight procession quietly made its way from Free Derry Corner to Derry's Guildhall. There was poignant symbolism in seeing veteran Civil Rights campaigner Eamon McCann step onto the platform lorry to address the gathering outside the Guildhall. It was to prevent him, Bernadette Devlin, Ivan Cooper and other Civil Rights leaders from reaching this very spot that the Paras were deployed in Derry on 30 January 1972.

There was a sense of the unstoppable progression of history. Just as King Canute failed to halt the encroachment of the tide, neither too could the might nor brutality of a government-sanctioned British Army regiment halt the march of a risen people. We had arrived and the walls of Jericho were crumbling in the face of families who had never given up on defending the innocence of their loved ones.

McCann spoke with riveting eloquence and passion:

Everything is in place to lay out the truth, to lay out what happened on January 30, 1972. All that remains to be discovered is whether the will exists to seek out the truth and to lay it out for the world to see. We will watch to discover whether the truth is at last to be made available.

Conor Duddy, a nephew of murdered Jack Duddy, then read a statement on behalf of the families.

We say again that all those killed and injured on Bloody Sunday were innocent. We restate our determination to establish the truth of what happened in our town on that day, and to achieve justice . . . We do so mindful of the vast suffering endured by so many others over the years of conflict . . . We see Bloody Sunday in Derry in the context of the history of our own country and also in the context of the suffering of peoples around the world whose rights have been denied, and lives snatched away, by the forces of oppressive power.

The victims of Bloody Sunday are listed in a litany, which includes the innocent dead of My Lai in Vietnam, of Sharpeville in South Africa, of Dili in East Timor. In asking for justice for the dead and injured of Bloody Sunday, we add our voices to all those that cry out against tyranny in our world.

The following morning I had the privilege of walking with the families and wounded from the location of Barrier 14 on William Street, where the Bloody Sunday march was halted, and again processing with quiet dignity to the Guildhall.

Inside, the ornate chamber had been transformed into a virtual-reality courtroom with dozens of high-tech terminals and scores of lawyers facing three elevated chairs occupied by Lord Saville, Sir Edward Somers and Mr Justice William Hoyt. Nothing before in British or Irish legal history has been conducted in this way. The spoken word is instantly translated into text on the terminals. The O.J. Simpson murder trial in America was our first glimpse of this technology. Each evening the full transcript of the proceedings are placed on the Inquiry's Internet site: http://www.bloody-sunday-inquiry.org.uk. A video link to a nearby cinema is available for the public, particularly on occasions when the Guildhall will be unable to accommodate local interest.

At 10.30 a.m., Lord Saville uttered a few opening remarks and invited Counsel for the Tribunal, Christopher Clarke, QC, to take the floor — and history began. Almost immediately, Saville's approach as a commercial lawyer became apparent. Lord Widgery conducted his 1972 Inquiry into Bloody Sunday like a high-speed steamroller, issuing his crushing report ten weeks after the event. Saville's Inquiry will take at least three years. The Widgery Tribunal sat for twenty days in total. The opening statement by Counsel for the Saville Tribunal lasted forty-two days!

This Tribunal will be exhaustive, systematic and very expensive. It will cost at least STG£100 million, perhaps even double that amount. It is the scandalous legacy and responsibility of Edward Heath and the former Lord Chief Justice of England, Lord Widgery. British soldiers, including members of the 1st Battalion of the Parachute Regiment, murdered fourteen unarmed civilians on Bloody Sunday. Lord Widgery murdered the truth.

Britain's Historic Role in Ireland

There was no implicit criticism of the now discredited Lord Widgery. But immediately Saville's Tribunal did what Widgery had failed to do, by setting Bloody Sunday in a political and historic context with particular reference to the introduction of Internment without Trial in August 1971.

Secret documents, military memos and memoirs, letters exchanged between the Officer Commanding, General Tuzo, and Unionist Premier Brian Faulker, were woven into a fascinating tapestry. All of a sudden it became clear that this costly exercise was not just about the stated objective of discovering the truth of Bloody Sunday. This Inquiry will also be, by extension, a public evaluation of Britain's historic role in Ireland and how its policy, in the wake of the just demands of the early Northern Ireland Civil Rights Movement, became so militarised. At its core will be a re-evaluation of the relationship between Britain and Ulster Unionism and how that relationship ultimately led to thirty years of political conflict and the embarrassment of this Tribunal of Inquiry before the international community.

Ministry of Defence

There are many, however, within the British Establishment who deeply resent the Inquiry and it appears that, while the Ministry of

Defence is co-operating, it is doing so grudgingly.

On the second week of the Inquiry, for example, Christopher Clarke, QC, sharply criticised the Ministry of Defence for its failure to secure weapons used on Bloody Sunday, even after the Inquiry had requested it to do so. Clarke said that their disappearance was 'a matter of very considerable concern' to the Inquiry. The Inquiry was informed that two weapons were destroyed after it had asked the Ministry of Defence to preserve them and that a bar be placed on their movement from storage.

During their opening statements to the Inquiry, lawyers representing the Bloody Sunday families consistently criticised the Ministry of Defence's failure to have a permanent legal team in attendance. The disappearance of the rifles, and the failure of the Ministry of Defence to have a permanent presence, unmasks an attitude of arrogance and resentment towards the Inquiry.

In advance of the opening of the Inquiry *The Daily Mail* and *The Daily Telegraph* ran a campaign in support of the Bloody Sunday Paras that culminated in the embarrassing sight of their commander on the day, Colonel Derek Wilford, dragging sackloads of petitions to the door of 10 Downing Street.

Martin McGuinness

The second week of the Inquiry pointed up the potential for spin and the kind of dirty tricks that will be employed to muddy the waters. It appeared that the only method available for the British Ministry of Defence to salvage some perverse dignity was by sowing a whole new myth — by attempting to shift blame for Bloody Sunday onto Sinn Féin Education Minister, Martin McGuinness, MP, MLA.

Counsel for the Tribunal informed the Inquiry that intelligence documents stated that an informer codenamed 'Infliction' told an intelligence handler around April 1984 that Martin McGuinness had admitted to him that 'he had personally fired the shot from Rossville Flats in the Bogside that had precipitated the Bloody Sunday episodes'.

Another classified document, allegedly produced in May 1984, refers to an 'in confidence' conversation with another senior member of the Provisional IRA codenamed 'Observer B', who said that

McGuinness personally fired the shot. A note attached to this document stated, however, that 'although we have no collateral for the above reports there is intelligence that McGuinness was actively involved in PIRA attacks in the city shortly after Bloody Sunday'.

McGuinness described the allegations as a 'pathetic fabrication'. He continued: 'If this is the best that the British military can do they are going to have a miserable time in Derry's Guildhall for the next two years. This is an attempt by the British military to divert attention away from the fact that the Paras killed fourteen innocent civilians on that day.'

In an interview I conducted with Mr McGuinness following the allegations, he stated: 'If this information was in the possession of the military since 1984, why wasn't I arrested or questioned?' Representatives of the Bloody Sunday families also spoke to me and expressed anger at the way Counsel for the Tribunal handled this 'evidence': 'Up until now, we have been impressed by the way the Tribunal has dealt with evidence which was well founded,' said Tony Doherty, whose father Patrick was one of the fourteen killed on Bloody Sunday. 'But the introduction of "evidence" that appears to be concocted begins to smell of Widgery.'

One of the wounded, Michael Bridge, telephoned me to express disquiet and deep annoyance. 'The Paratrooper who tried to kill me has been granted anonymity and immunity in this Inquiry. Yet, here we have the Inquiry's Counsel naming people on the basis of hearsay and innuendo. It is unjust and unfair. How does he expect to gain the confidence of the families and, more importantly, the public?'

Public Interest Immunity Certificates

In early December 2000 the British Home Secretary, Jack Straw, and Defence Secretary Geoffrey Hoon entered the scene in a disturbing way. Both Ministers applied for Public Interest Immunity Certificates (PIIC) in relation to the alleged operatives 'Infliction' and 'Observer B'.

It would appear that the British Military Establishment does not want lawyers for the Bloody Sunday families and wounded to have full access to the submissions of these alleged agents. Why? We can only presume that the fears cited by the British cabinet ministers that full disclosure would harm the British security services is but a smokescreen and part of an emerging agenda aimed at sowing seeds of doubt in the wider public mind.

Martin McGuinness's solicitor, Barra McCrory, applying for a legal team to represent the Minster at the Inquiry stated:

> It is becoming clear as each day goes by that there is, perhaps, an unspoken suggestion that the Irish Republican Army and activities of IRA people on [Bloody Sunday] led to this incident and that there was no fault on the part of the soldiers . . . As it is being suggested of Mr McGuinness that he was not only in a position of responsibility with that organisation, and would have had control of those people on that day, but that he was the person who started the whole thing by firing the first shot . . . this elevates his importance to this tribunal onto a par with the importance of the soldiers.

All of this leads one to conclude that the aim of the British Ministry of Defence is to entice Martin McGuinness onto the Inquiry stand for an open season and to broaden the agenda beyond the confines of Bloody Sunday. Whatever his personal political views, McGuinness has a responsibility to the Bloody Sunday families and wounded not to fall into this trap. The Ministry of Defence's game is to attempt to lessen the impact of its army's barbarity on the day and its major contribution to the escalation of the thirty-year conflict. The Ministry intends doing this by trying to introduce a litany of IRA atrocities and ultimately, on the basis of very dubious intelligence 'evidence', attempt to paint Martin McGuinness as the source of all evil and the real cause of Bloody Sunday. It seems absurd, but that appears to be the picture emerging.

On Wednesday, 3 May 2001, Martin McGuinness revealed publicly that he had made a statement to the Saville Inquiry admitting that he was the Provisional IRA's second-in-command in Derry at the time of Bloody Sunday. He also stated that it was his intention to testify before the Inquiry. 'I will tell them there were no [Provisional] IRA units on the march, no [Provisional] IRA weapons in the area and no [Provisional] IRA shots fired at the army,' he said.

At the time of writing, Lord Saville and his colleagues have yet to issue their judgement on whether or not to grant the PII Certificates for the alleged agents. Whatever the ruling, their decision is likely to be judicially reviewed. It is widely expected that should Saville and his colleagues refuse to grant the certificates, the British Judiciary will, once again, overrule their decision on the grounds of the alleged agents' right to life.

People on the streets of Derry are watching developments with a certain incredulity and suspect the emergence of a murky plot, the closing scene of which is an attempt to wreck the Inquiry. Lord Saville may be forced to conclude that the Inquiry cannot continue since he does not have the legal authority necessary. At the time of writing, a ruling on the Public Interest Immunity Certificates has yet to be made by the Inquiry.

Secret Burials

Prior to the Christmas recess of 2001 the Bloody Sunday Inquiry had sat for 179 days and heard the testimonies of almost 460 civilian witnesses. It is interesting to observe from the public gallery the tactic employed by Counsel representing the soldiers. The testimony of each civilian witness is trawled through for any sign of inconsistency or contradiction that might be exploited as a means of rationalising the almost impossible task of justifying the ferocity of the Paras' attack on a civilian demonstration.

By such trawling, Counsel for the Army has attempted to suggest that where civilian eyewitnesses give slightly different coordinates regarding where they recall seeing the dead and wounded of Bloody Sunday fall, this accounts for actual hits of gunmen and bombers who mysteriously disappeared after the so-called 'fire fight' on that terrible afternoon. They have accepted that the 27 'known' people killed and wounded that day were innocent of wrongdoing and, very significantly, have not attempted to justify their shooting. However, Counsel for the Army has attempted to suggest that over 30 bodies of dead and injured are unaccounted for. Unsustainable attempts have been made to suggest that perhaps up to 34 bodies may have been spirited away for secret medical treatment or burial in unmarked graves. When Michael Topolski, QC, acting for the family of Paddy Doherty (a father of six shot dead on Bloody Sunday) asked Dr Edward Daly on 6 February 2001 what he thought of the suggestion of secret burials, the retired Bishop of Derry told the Tribunal, 'It is offensive nonsense'.

Venue for Paratroopers' Testimony

Another important ruling made in August 2001 by Lord Saville and his colleagues, Mr Justice Hoyt and Mr Justice Toohey (an Australian who has replaced Sir Edward Somers) was overruled at the Divisional Court, London, on Friday, 16 November 2001. The Tribunal had ruled that the soldiers are required 'to give their oral evidence at the Guildhall [Derry], which in our view is where the Inquiry should be conducted'. The Divisional Court, however, ruled that Derry was too dangerous for the Paras to return to. While the Court's ruling was not a surprise, it was the second time that the British Judiciary interfered with the independence of the Saville Inquiry.

Even the discredited Lord Widgery and former Prime Minister Edward Heath saw the importance of holding the original Bloody Sunday Inquiry in Derry. During their meeting at 10 Downing Street the day after the massacre (see Appendix 1), both agreed that while Derry's Guildhall was 'on the wrong side of the river', their legal charade should, nonetheless, sit 'a little distance from Londonderry' — hence the choice of Coleraine for the original Tribunal venue.

The Bloody Sunday families and wounded were understandably furious at this development and welcomed the decision by the Saville Inquiry to counter-appeal this latest ruling.

The Saville Inquiry has been portrayed by influential elements of the Tory Press as a virtual 'witch hunt' against the Paras. As we have seen, prior to the opening of the Inquiry, we had the spectacle of the Bloody Sunday Paras commander, Colonel Derek Wilford, dragging sacks of protest mail, generated by *The Daily Telegraph* and *The Daily Mail*, to the door of 10 Downing Street. Judging by this response, it can be expected that the Bloody Sunday families may have to run the gauntlet of Para supporters and their families as they come and go to a venue based in England. Such a scenario is unacceptable and a violation of the families' basic human rights.

The Paras, naturally, have argued that their lives would be in danger if they returned to Derry to give evidence to the Saville Inquiry. In response to the Divisional Court's ruling, Derry solicitors Desmond J. Doherty, McCartney & Casey and MacDermott & McGurk issued a joint press release on behalf of their clients stating: 'Despite the fact that their loved ones were murdered and injured by the British Army they do not want any harm to come to any soldier who travels to Derry to testify before Lord Saville's Inquiry.'

Indeed, it can be argued that those Paras who wish to tell the truth might be in greater danger from their own former colleagues than they are from dissident Irish republicans. The Saville Inquiry has already placed one former Para, Soldier 027, on a witness protection scheme because of his testimony with regard to the shooting of unarmed civilians. He is not being protected from dissident Irish republicans but from his own.

The former RUC, not a sympathetic force to the cause of Irish nationalism, provided Lord Saville with a security assessment which stated that adequate security could be provided for the Paras should they come to give evidence at the Guildhall. Furthermore, throughout the 1980s, potentially more dangerous legal proceedings were held in Derry and throughout Northern Ireland — involving Supergrass informers — yet the security forces were able to adequately police them.

John Kelly, whose brother Michael was killed on Bloody Sunday, said: 'We feel we are in a no-win situation. This is the second decision that has gone in favour of the soldiers. They already have the cloak of anonymity to conceal them. What are they afraid of? There is only one answer. They fear the truth and cannot, therefore, look the people of Derry in the eye.'

The Bloody Sunday families point out that witnesses who might be described as detrimental to their viewpoint have given their evidence and have not been harassed or interfered with. 'Tribunal staff and lawyers representing the Army are occasionally recognised walking through the centre of Derry and have never been abused or intimidated.' Kelly also pointed out that on the day before the Divisional Court's ruling in favour of the Paras, Queen Elizabeth II and the Duke of Edinburgh were in Derry and there were no incidents. 'The Paras will not be touched,' says Kelly, 'because the families and the city wants to put Bloody Sunday behind us. We want the full truth to be ventilated, but it must be done in Derry, the scene of the crime.'

The press release issued by the Derry solicitors, quoted above, concluded: 'Our clients feel that the language of this morning's judgement is the language of colonialism and ignorance.'

They have a point. One of the judges who overruled Saville was the Honourable Mr Justice Jeremy Mirth Sullivan. Sullivan has been Attorney General to the Prince of Wales, HRH Prince Charles, since 1994. Charles, amongst his many royal accolades, holds the rank of Colonel-in-Chief of the Parachute Regiment. One can understand the perception of the families and wounded created by the fact that one of the judges who dealt with the case in London has such a close association with the Paras' Command-in-Chief.

Solicitors Madden & Finucane, who represent the majority of the Bloody Sunday families and wounded, also issued a press statement, saying:

> Our clients, whilst extremely disappointed, are not surprised given the succession of favourable rulings from the English Courts in favour of the Paras. The willingness of English Courts to interfere in the decision-making of this distinguished international tribunal is without parallel in modern history.

On Wednesday, 19 December 2001, the Bloody Sunday Tribunal's Appeal was, not surprisingly, dismissed by the Court of Appeal (Civil Division), London. The judgement, handed down by Master of the Rolls, Lord Phillips, stated: '... we intend to remit this matter to the Tribunal with a direction that the soldier witnesses' evidence should not be taken in Londonderry'. The ruling of the Court of Appeal upheld the previous ruling by Lord Justice Rose and Mr Justice Sullivan on 16 November 2001, citing, once again, Article 2 of the Human Rights Convention: 'Everyone's right to life shall be protected by law.'

The judgement recognised that: 'The majority in Londonderry, and that majority includes the families of those who were killed or injured on Bloody Sunday, wish the Inquiry well and are anxious that it should continue to be peacefully held in Londonderry.' However, the Court of Appeal cited the dangers posed by dissident Republican elements 'who are not prepared to observe the cease-fire, but are anxious to disrupt the peace process', as its primary reason for ruling against Derry. 'In particular,' the judgement stated, 'the Republican group that describes itself as the Continuity IRA is not observing the cease-fire. These elements pose a threat to the Inquiry and those who are or will be taking part in it, and in particular the soldier witnesses.'

The judgement referred to the transcript of a meeting involving Lord Saville and security personnel, held on 18 June 2001, during which threat assessment was discussed and, in particular, the security of the Guildhall. The judgement states: 'We propose to refer to the passages in the redacted transcript that are of particular relevance.' An opinion offered to Lord Saville at that meeting by 'military participants' and which was relied upon by the Court of Appeal, echoed those of Prime Minister Heath in his meeting with Lord Widgery at 10 Downing Street, on 31 January 1972, concerning the location of the Guildhall (see Appendix 1). The judgement states:

> 46. *Early on in the meeting Lord Saville discussed the vulnerability of the Guildhall as a venue with one of the military participants. The latter said that even with the best sort of co-ordination and planning there would be a significant vulnerability either to the witnesses, but more probably to those seeking to safeguard the witnesses. 'When you plan a military operation you plan it on the basis that you always try to choose the ground that you are going to operate on ... In this case we would be operating on the ground that the terrorist believes is his.'*

Simply stated, the Court of Appeal was persuaded that the Guildhall was '... thought to be on the wrong side of the River Foyle.

This decision was made, it should be noted, in the context of a highly disciplined Provisional IRA ceasefire and the beginning of PIRA decommissioning. It must and should be noted that recent activities of dissident Republicans in the city have provided comfort to the Bloody Sunday Paras and gifted their legal representatives with persuasive arguments as to why Derry's Guildhall posed a risk to their clients. However, it should also be noted that those same dissident Republicans know that any attack on the Bloody Sunday Tribunal (which includes participating military witnesses) would have far-reaching consequences for their already depleted support base following the Omagh Bomb attack on 15 August 1998. Lord Saville and his colleagues, in reaching their assessment that the Guildhall was both safe and the appropriate place for military witnesses to testify, would have done so with acquired local knowledge, developed since they first came to Derry on 3 April 1998.

It is my opinion that dissident Republicans would not dare to pose a threat to military witnesses attending this Inquiry. Their reluctance to do so would not be for fear of having to penetrate military protection but principally because the epic struggle of the Bloody Sunday families in achieving this historic Tribunal has, in a very real sense, elevated it, within Irish nationalism and republicanism, to a near sacrosanct position. That is not to say that the Tribunal is considered to be beyond fair criticism, but that it is considered beyond physical abuse.

The latest judgement, while ruling against Derry's Guildhall, left the decision as to 'where and how [soldiers] evidence should be taken' to Lord Saville and his colleagues for further consideration.

On 21 December 2001, Solicitor to the Bloody Sunday Inquiry, WJ Tate sent a letter to all interested parties stating:

> I refer to the direction of the Court of Appeal that the soldiers' evidence should not be taken in Londonderry. In the light of that the tribunal is currently minded to continue to sit in Londonderry during the duration of that evidence hearing it by means of a video conference link from some place in Great Britain that is yet to be decided and to which it is intended the public will have access.

Tate asked any of the parties who had objections to this course to put them in writing to the Tribunal since it "is currently not minded to have any oral hearing to consider this issue."

One thing is certain: the families and wounded wish — and believes it their human right — to see the people in the flesh who propelled their lives into an unresolved thirty-year-long nightmare. To deprive them of their right to be physically present when soldiers are giving evidence, would be an appalling abuse.

Sadly, the interference of the English Judicial system with this historic international tribunal serves only to undermine public confidence in its ability to achieve its stated objective of establishing the truth about Bloody Sunday with 'fairness, thoroughness and impartiality'.

On Tuesday, 15 May 2001, Bernadette Devlin McAliskey testified before the Inquiry. In 1972, aged twenty-two, she was Member of Parliament for Mid-Ulster. On Bloody Sunday she was speaking at Free Derry Corner when the Paratroopers made their advance into Derry's Bogside. At the end of her testimony Mrs McAliskey expressed her personal doubts about the ability of Lord Saville's

Inquiry to achieve Truth and Justice. 'This [Inquiry] should be held somewhere else, where the accused is not running the party,' she told a packed Guildhall. She suggested that the proper forum was the International Court of Justice at the Hague. 'No Inquiry established, funded and controlled by such a powerful, vindictive, ruthless and experienced perpetrator of terror as the British State can reasonably be expected to bring in an honourable verdict of "Guilty as Charged" against that State,' she concluded.

The summer 2002 recess of the Tribunal arrived with growing disillusionment and a sense that Bernadette McAliskey's prediction may, sadly, yet be proven correct.

The Tribunal is now set to move to London's 'Methody Hall', close to the Palace of Westminster, sometime during late 2002. After yet another epic fight the families and the wounded won their right to attend the hearings in the British capital at the expense of the British Exchequer. The Tribunal has agreed to pay for travel and accommodation for two members of each family, including the wounded, each week that the hearings are held in London. Family units, however, will be denied the right to be present when the killers of their loved ones are testifying. So too will Derry's public, many of whom were traumatised by the events of Bloody Sunday and who will have to watch proceedings at Derry's Guildhall via a video satellite. It is shameful that the English judiciary has humiliated the Bloody Sunday Tribunal and undermined its independence. This is a judiciary that, once again, has interfered with the victims' basic human rights.

Lawyers for the families see the inevitability of decisions favourable to the British military having their origin in what one Derry solicitor described as 'the very first virus' — that of granting the military the right to anonymity.

Attorney Desmond Doherty, who represents the family of Bernard McGuigan, commented:

> With the backup of the Court of Appeal and with the strength of Article Two of the Human Rights Convention, the issue of venue, like anonymity, could go no further. While it was galling for the families of those murdered to witness the soldiers responsible for their killing rely on a Human Rights article, in practical terms the issue of venue was lost because of it.

The Box of Mendacity

Predictably, as one attorney described it, 'the next move by the military to discredit, disrupt and destroy the Inquiry, and undermine the public element of it was on the issue of screening.' It was a move to prevent the families of those murdered on Bloody Sunday, and the wounded, from physically seeing those responsible for the events and their cover-up.

It began in early 2002 when a small number of former Royal Ulster Constabulary (RUC), applied for the right to give their testimony before the Tribunal from behind screens. The Tribunal upheld their application. However, lawyers for the families challenged this decision but the High Court in Belfast ruled in favour of the police. Applications for screening rights reached farcical proportions when a well-known RUC officer, Brian McVicker, who had been a leading investigator into the 1998 Omagh Bombing case, applied for screening. His application was upheld by the Inquiry and he eventually gave his evidence from what has become popularly known in Derry as 'The Box of Shame' and 'The Box of Mendacity'.

'With nauseous predictability,' says solicitor Desmond Doherty; 'this was the drip feed which lead to a flood of applications from military personnel who were involved in Bloody Sunday.' Soldier 'B' (involved in the wounding of Damien Donaghy and John Johnston) and soldier 'J' (a member of the Paras Anti-Tank Platoon) were immediately granted screening rights on the grounds of 'national security'. Since 'national security' was cited, no one, except the Tribunal members know what the grounds are. There is, according to Doherty, 'no way of legally challenging this decision and it has led to a lot of speculation as to who and what 'B' and 'J' are today.'

An application for screening rights by soldier 'H', the man who fired 22 unaccounted shots (including two bullets more than he had been legally issued with), is still waiting for approval, along with applications from other soldiers. Another applicant was soldier 027 who has already been granted 'protection' and financial support by the Tribunal. Some people believe that the 'protection' is from former Para colleagues, not Republican paramilitaries. On 27 June 2002 the Tribunal wrote to lawyers for the families and wounded as follows:

A matter has arisen concerning soldier 027. It is impossible to give

244 EYEWITNESS BLOODY SUNDAY

> *details of this matter, for reasons of his security, but we have con-*
> *cluded that in consequence of it, we must grant soldier 027's appli-*
> *cation for screening, which we accordingly do.*

The issue of Public Interest Immunity Certificates (PIIC), referred to above, is still pending. PIIC's can be issued in respect of documents as well as alleged 'agents'. There has been considerable redaction of documents because of PIIC. One alleged agent, 'Infliction', who claims Martin McGuinness admitted to firing the first shot on Bloody Sunday, has been re-named 'Invention' by the Derry public, since the MoD are determined to keep him from having to face questioning by lawyers for the families. PIIC are, according to Desmond Doherty, 'yet another virus affecting the health of the Tribunal and the necessary oxygen of public respect'.

Senior politicians, such as former Prime Minister Edward Heath, who conspired to keep the Tribunal out of Derry in 1972, and civil servants who worked with Lord Widgery on the original Bloody Sunday Inquiry, have also applied for the right to give their evidence in London, not Derry. It is expected their application will be upheld. Some have applied on the grounds of age and health, yet many of the civilian witnesses who have already testified before the Tribunal, were equally advanced. One witness, Mr. Pearse Doherty, the father of attorney Desmond Doherty, was eighty-one-years old and had survived nine heart attacks. 'I would,' he says, 'have travelled to London or beyond if that was the right place for me to speak my truth about Bloody Sunday.'

Meltdown?

At the time of writing despondency and depression is discernible amongst the families and their lawyers. One solicitor commented:

> *It may not be the personal fault of Lord Saville, but it is a symptom*
> *of the virus which was put into the system from the start. The despon-*
> *dency which is occurring is exactly what the British military estab-*
> *lishment want.*

The solicitor believes that their tactic has, as their aim and hope, the complete collapse of confidence in the Inquiry by the Bloody Sunday families, forcing them to walk away. 'What they don't understand,' says the solicitor, 'is the absolute resolve of the families and wounded, and Irish people in general, in dealing with human rights issues. They will persevere to the end in pursuit of the truth about Bloody Sunday.'

With the public nature of the Inquiry being continually eroded, elements of the British media are also sniping at it, concerning escalating costs. Some of these elements are not surprising but a recent leader in the liberal UK broadsheet, *The Guardian*, took the families by surprise. On 8 July 2002, it stated:

> *Lord Saville's inquiry into the events of Bloody Sunday has been sitting since 1998. So far, it has had 224 sitting days, has heard from some 550 witnesses and its costs are climbing towards the £100m mark.*
>
> *It has not, however, yet heard form a single British soldier who participated in the events of January 30, 1972, in Derry, nor from any member of the Provisional IRA who was there on the day other than Martin McGuinness. When he adjourned the inquiry for its summer recess last week, Lord Saville estimated that a further 18 months of hearings will be required for him to get through the more than 200 witnesses who still remain, possibly including Sir Edward Heath. This means that the Saville report will not be published before 2004 at the very earliest...*
>
> *It is easy to call for an inquiry. It is much less easy, as Saville is showing, for an inquiry to do its job properly, never mind to achieve either the emotional or political closure that it is claimed such probes will bring. Inquiries are regularly presented as opportunities for truth and reconciliation. In Northern Ireland they are arenas for myth and confrontation. In such an unreconciled society, and in the light of the Saville experience, fresh calls for further inquiries should be treated with caution and scepticism.*

Sadly, the leader writer failed to acknowledge the dignity and cautious goodwill with which the Bloody Sunday families and wounded openly engaged with the Saville Inquiry. It is they who have earned the right to be sceptical given their experience of the British judicial system, dating back to 30 January 1972. It is they who have witnessed, firsthand, the cynicism with which conservative and military elements of the British establishment have resentfully engaged and sought to frustrate or corrupt the work of two Public Inquiries into Bloody Sunday. It would have been helpful if the leader writer had specifically spelled out precisely why the Saville inquiry is not able 'to do its job properly'.

Operation Apollo

Perhaps the cynicism and resentment towards the Saville Inquiry is best illustrated by the attitude evidenced in an email sent by a Major Alisdair Johnston on 6 September 1999, to a colleague, Major Peter McCutcheon. It concerned the Inquiry's enquiries about missing Bloody Sunday weapons which it had ordered to be handed over for independent forensic examination.

He wrote:

> Peter
>
> Here's a good one for a Monday Morning. The Bloody Sunday enquiry are after records (if any) of what happened to the Bloody Sunday weapons! Can you please make contact with Mark Bailey of Cen Sec – he will, I imagine, be the action officer on this one.
>
> On Tuesday, the Battle of Hastings enquiry will want to find the longbow which put Harold's eye out..........!

Despite the Inquiry's order, rifles with crucial forensic evidence disappeared or were destroyed. This led to an investigation, ordered by the Inquiry, headed up by the West Mercia Constabulary, code-named 'Operation Apollo'.

Their conclusion of their investigation stated:

> The enquiry team is wholly satisfied that no criminal offences have been committed in relation to this matter. There was no conspiracy to destroy weapons or conceal evidence from the Tribunal.
>
> What occurred was a combination of mistakes, human error and negligence.

The West Mercia Constabulary is the Ministry of Defence's own police! Their logo declares:

TOGETHER – WORKING FOR SAFETY AND JUSTICE

When I read Johnston's comments about 'the Battle of Hastings enquiry will want to find the longbow which put Harold's eye out.........!' I could not fail to think of the weapon used to execute Bernard (Barney) McGuigan, an unarmed forty-one-year-old father of six who, despite grave dangers, waved a white handkerchief as he slowly made his way towards a wounded and dying civilian, Patrick Doherty. A paratrooper, most likely soldier 'F', took him in his sights from Glenfada Park and fired at his head. The bullet, quite possibly a *dum dum*, entered just below his left ear and exited at the tip of his right eye, leaving a massive wound from which blood ran like an open tap.

The following day I remember finding a heavily bloodstained blue and white Civil Rights banner that had been used to cover the horrific sight of this gentle and humane soul, callously slain while showing 'no greater love' towards a wounded neighbour. A brick sat in the middle of the bloodstained banner upon which had been placed an open 'Bow Peep' matchbox. In the matchbox had been placed a human eyelid and eyelashes. I was fifteen. I will never forget it.

I can't help thinking that Johnston may have been aware that the Ministry of Defence were in possession of Barney McGuigan's murder weapon. Is this what he meant by 'the Battle of Hastings enquiry will want to find the longbow which put Harold's eye out..........!'?

It is understood that one of the rifles that had gone 'missing' was, in fact, the rifle of soldier 'F', who is the paratrooper widely believed to have murdered Barney McGuigan, and others.

We will never know, for who would expect the Ministry of Defence's very own police to find its military personnel guilty of a 'criminal offence'?

Bloody Sunday's Sundance and Berlin's Golden Bear

In 1972 the people of Derry were in their political infancy. Unlike the British Government and its spin doctors, we did not understand the power of the first soundbite. The Bloody Sunday corpses had barely gone cold when the lies began to circulate the globe. Those of us who had witnessed the brutality could hardly believe our ears when we learned that the innocent and unarmed dead had suddenly been transformed into gunmen and nail bombers. We had fled in terror as the Paras' onslaught cut down 27 civil rights demonstrators, 13 of whom died that day. Now we were hearing that as the Paras had entered the Bogside they had come under a fusillade of bombs and bullets and had returned fire at armed insurgents, a number of whom, so the story went, were on the British Army's wanted list.

The Bloody Sunday families were traumatized and numbed. How do ordinary people fight back at a political monolith with such far-reaching power and influence? How does one deal with a devious establishment capable of pretending concern by setting up a Tribunal of Inquiry while, at the same time, planning at 10 Downing Street, the day after the massacre, the murder of truth?

When Lord Chief Justice Widgery issued his whitewashed report the families knew they had been conned and thus began an epic struggle which is now the wonder of the world. Widgery and Prime Minister Heath completely underestimated the determination of the Bloody Sunday families and wounded to one day see justice done. They failed miserably to understand the power of the truth to both haunt and heal.

Thankfully, despite the brutality of our colonial history, Irish people learned that there are many British people who are fair-minded and fearless in defence of truth and justice. In 1998 I met two of them: Mark Redhead and Paul Greengrass. They were filmmakers who wished to make a film about Bloody Sunday and invited me to join them as a co-producer. For three years I worked closely with these two men and I can honestly say they are two of the most honorable human beings I have ever encountered. They are men of integrity for whom political compassion is a motivating force.

The process of making 'Bloody Sunday' was by no means easy. By any standards the scale of what we attempted to achieve, with a budget of less than $5 million, was ambitious beyond belief. However, it became clear, right from the start, that both actors and productions staff saw the making of 'Bloody Sunday' as a labour of love and were prepared to work long hours and endure appalling weather conditions to see it made. My abiding memory on set will always be the general atmosphere of cooperation and goodwill. Of course, there were times when nerves were frayed and tired minds became irritable. But every day on set saw renewed commitment to completing the task.

It was an extraordinary mixture that Redhead and Greengrass brought together. It had the potential of becoming a potent cocktail of bitter disputes and angry words. Who could have thought that former British soldiers (some of which had been Paras) could meet and mix with actors and extras from Derry (some who had relatives murdered on Bloody Sunday) in an atmosphere of mutual respect, with a shared determination to tell the truth of that terrible day?

The result is a dramatization that is as close to the actual terror and trauma of the day as those of us who experienced it can remember.

We brought the film to Derry on January 6, 2002, with no small measure of apprehension and unease. The people of Derry, particularly the families and wounded, were always going to be the most critical audience since many had been there when the cold brutality of the actual drama was experienced. As the private screening for the families and wounded rolled, I sat beside Ivan Cooper, brilliantly played by actor James Nesbitt, through whose eyes we see much of the civilian perspective. It was, indeed, humbling when the families rose and gave the film a standing ovation at the end. This was repeated at two further screenings in Derry's magnificent 'Millennium Forum' with one respected journalist describing the movie as 'a pain-filled masterpiece'.

Nine days later we attended our first screening at the world renowned Sundance Film Festival, started by Robert Redford some 20 years ago to help showcase low-budget movies. The Sundance audience, dedicated and discerning moviegoers, are renowned for their ability to kill or give life to a movie. All five screenings had been sold out weeks before we arrived so it was clear the subject matter of the film was eagerly awaited. Tristan Whalley of Portman Film, responsible for selling the movie internationally, nervously told me that three things were important as we went to the first screening in the Egyptian Theater, Park City, Utah. It was important, he said, that the audience stays till the end, that they applaud at its conclusion and that most stay for the question and answers session following the screening. We got all three!

We left Sundance before its conclusion, happy in the knowledge that we had been showcased, but never expecting to win a top award. I traveled alone to New York and shortly after touch down my mobile phone rang with Paul Greengrass excitedly hoping I was still in Utah. Word was reaching us that we had won a prize.

Unfortunately none of us were there to collect the prestigious 'Audience Award' in the Festival's World Cinema Section. The Sundance audience had voted us 'Best Film'.

Two weeks later we were in Berlin, attending one of the world's most renowned Film Festivals. We were amazed to be greeted at our Press Conference by over a hundred journalists who were quite obviously deeply moved by the film. Two thousand people turned up at the magnificent Sony Centre Complex for our first screening. Again we were greeted with loud applause at the end of the film.

There was much stiff competition in Berlin which seemed out of our league. Ron Howard's *A Beautiful Mind* (hotly tipped for several Oscars); Costa-Gavras' *Amen*; Francois Ozon's *8 Femmes*; Lasse Hallstrom's *The Shipping News*; Richard Eyre's *Iris* to name only some of the films featured. They included Hollywood stars such as Judi Dench, Kevin Spacey, Julianne Moore, Russell Crowe and Kate Winslet.

On Saturday, 16 February, 2002, I was out walking with my son Carl when my mobile phone rang. It was Tristan Whalley of Portman Film to tell me he had just received word we had won the Festival's top prize: 'The Golden Bear Award' for best film. We also won the festival's 'Ecumenical Award'.

Since then the film has won awards in Portugal and Australia. Demand in Italy was such that from four original cinemas, over 60 copies where showing simultaneously nationwide throughout May and June 2002.

This edition of *Eyewitness Bloody Sunday* is published to coincide with the release of the film in the Americas during the Autumn of 2002.

It seemed magic dust had somehow been sprinkled around our film. And then I remembered the Bloody Sunday dead and their loved ones in whose memory we had all worked with such integrity. This was their film. This was their day. The spirit of truth was let loose in the world. The lies, so callously dissiminated thirty years ago by the British Information Services had, at long last, met their match. Paramount Classics bought the rights to distribute our film in Canada, USA, all of Central and South America, Australia, New Zealand, South Africa and Japan. Individual distributors bought the rights for France, Germany, Belgium, Spain, Italy, Luxembourg,

Greece, Turkey and Portugal. Others followed.

And what was most special was the realization that this was an Irish and British co-production. And therein lay its great strength and international appeal. It couldn't be so easily dismissed as Irish propaganda. In Paul Greengrass and Mark Redhead, former Lord Chief Justice Widgery and Prime Minister Heath had met their match! I am proud to call these two Englishmen my friends.

Speaking at a Human Rights Symposium at University College Galway, during February 2002, law lecturer, Angela Hegarty, reflected on the contribution of *Bloody Sunday* and another television film, *Sunday*, to the search for truth. She said:

> As the Inquiry continues to sit, two new films dramatising the events of Bloody Sunday have been made. 'BLOODY SUNDAY', directed by Paul Greengrass and made by Granada TV for British commercial television and 'SUNDAY' written by Jimmy McGovern for Britain's Channel 4 TV were broadcast to coincide with the 30th Anniversary of Bloody Sunday. The production of the two films has driven the debate about what happened on Bloody Sunday back onto the mainstream agenda in Britain in a way that the Inquiry's proceedings, reported intermittently in the British media, has not. Arguably these two films – and the poems, songs and plays about the events – have had a far greater impact upon public consciousness than the Inquiry's proceedings. Notwithstanding that they are prompted by the inquiry, they may contribute more to public understanding of the notions of truth and human rights than the legal processes they shadow.

Conclusion

Lord Saville and his colleagues have accepted an unenviable task. Time will tell if they can be the healers of historical wounds. It is no easy task, especially with the world watching their every move.

In my Introduction it is stated that the resolution of this great injustice could form part of the healing process in the Northern Irish conflict. However, to do so it is necessary for all sides in the unresolved issues to accept full responsibility for their actions. Bloody Sunday was a terrible act, carried out by military personnel whose behaviour (and not only on Bloody Sunday) against a civilian population has yet to be fully investigated.

With the establishment of the new Bloody Sunday Inquiry, the British government has the opportunity to put the record straight on great wrongs of historic proportions upon the island of Ireland. Lord Saville of Newdigate, Chairman of the new Inquiry, and his co-panellists, Mr Justice Hoyt and Mr Justice Toohey, are faced with an enormous responsibility. As we have seen, the Inquiry cannot presume to have the confidence of the families who have lost loved ones, the Bloody Sunday wounded or, indeed, the wider nationalist community in general. The findings of Lord Chief Justice Widgery's Tribunal cast a long shadow of suspicion in many people's minds, and engagement with the new Inquiry will always be in the knowledge that its predecessor caused great distress and hurt through the same powers they now possess. Saville, Hoyt and Toohey may yet contribute to the healing process so necessary between the peoples of Ireland and their British neighbours, if they apply themselves to the fair and impartial unravelling of the truth, which was promised in their opening statement. In order for them to do this, however, there must be no further erosion of their independence by the British judicial system.

At the time of writing, the vast majority of citizens upon the island of Ireland have voted overwhelmingly in favour of the 1998 Good Friday Agreement and, despite setbacks and difficulties, political institutions are functioning and IRA decommissioning has begun. This is an unprecedented opportunity that all our political leaders must seize with hope, courage and imagination. The just and truthful resolution of Bloody Sunday must also be part of that opportunity. In the words of Dr Martin Luther King, Junior:

> We merely bring to the surface the hidden tension that is already alive. We bring it out in the open, where it can be seen and dealt with. Like a boil that can never be cured so long as it is covered up but must be opened with all its ugliness to the natural medicines of air and light, injustice must be exposed with all the tension its exposure creates, to the light of human conscience and the air of national opinion, before it can be cured . . .'

Don Mullan
Dublin, 12 August 2002

INDEX OF EYEWITNESSES

* Denotes those statements prepared separately for the Widgery Tribunal of Inquiry.

PICTURE ACKNOWLEDGMENTS

Section 1

Pages 1, 2, 6 and 7, Courtesy of R. White

Pages 3 and 8, Courtesy of Colman Doyle

Pages 4 and 5, by kind permission of the families of the victims

Section 2

Page 1, courtesy of the *Irish Press*

Page 2, (top) courtesy of Colman Doyle; (bottom) courtesy of Fulvio Grimaldi

Pages 3 and 5, courtesy of Gilles Peress/Magnum Photos Ltd

Page 4, (top) courtesy of Lawrence Doherty/Derry Journal;
(bottom) courtesy of Gilles Peress/Magnum Photos Ltd

Page 6, (top) courtesy of the J. Morris/*Daily Mail*;
(bottom) courtesy of Colman Doyle

Page 7, (top) courtesy of Fulvio Grimaldi; (bottom) courtesy of Colman Doyle

Page 8, Courtesy of Hugh Gallagher

Appendix 5

Map © John Butterworth/*The Sunday Times*,
London 6th February 1972

INDEX

Names of dead and wounded are in bold